Buddhism and the Coronavirus
The Buddha's Teaching on Suffering

The Sussex Library of Religious Beliefs & Practices

This series is intended for students of religion, social sciences and history, and for the interested layperson. It is concerned with the beliefs and practices of religions in their social, cultural and historical setting. These books will be of particular interest to Religious Studies teachers and students at universities, colleges, and high schools. Inspection copies available on request.

The Ancient Egyptians   Rosalie David

The Bhagavad Gita: A text and commentary for students   Jeaneane Fowler

Buddhism   Merv Fowler

Buddhism and the Coronavirus: The Buddha's Teaching on Suffering   Jeaneane Fowler

Causality: Macrocosmic and Microcosmic Theories of Cause and Effect in Belief Systems   Jeaneane Fowler

Chinese Religions   Jeaneane Fowler and Merv Fowler

Christian Theology: The Spiritual Tradition   John Glyndwr Harris

Gnosticism   John Glyndwr Harris

Hinduism   Jeaneane Fowler (published 1997, compact 192-page edition)

Hinduism: Beliefs & Practices: Major Deities and Social Structures (expanded edition)

Hinduism: Beliefs & Practices: Religious History and Philosophy (expanded edition)

Hindu Goddesses   Lynn Foulston

Humanism   Jeaneane Fowler

Islam   David Norcliffe

The Jews   Alan Unterman

The Protestant Reformation: Tradition and Practice
Madeleine Gray

Sikhism   W. Owen Cole and Piara Singh Sambhi

T'ai Chi Ch'üan   Jeaneane Fowler and Shifu Keith Ewers

Zen Buddhism   Merv Fowler

Zoroastrianism   Peter Clark

Of related interest

Chanting in the Hillsides: Nichiren Daishonin Buddhism in Wales and the Borders   Jeaneane Fowler and Merv Fowler

An Introduction to the Philosophy and Religion of Taoism: Pathways to Immortality   Jeaneane Fowler

Perspectives of Reality: An Introduction to the Philosophy of Hinduism   Jeaneane Fowler

World Religions: An Introduction for Students   Jeaneane Fowler, Merv Fowler, David Norcliffe, Nora Hill and Diane Watkins

This book is dedicated to the outstanding, compassionate, and loving carers at The Cedars at St Anne's Nursing Home in Chepstow, South Wales.

With deepest thanks for all they have done and continue to do each day for those who come into their care.

Wendy Ballard	Gillian Lawrence
Mariana Ungureanu	Lisa Greenwood
Saloti Meli	Bethan Ayre
Helen Burton	Maria Davies
Maria Tribol	Anna Vigurs
Alison Baldwin	Katrina Morris

Buddhism and the Coronavirus
The Buddha's Teaching on Suffering

JEANEANE FOWLER

Brighton • Chicago • Toronto

Copyright © Jeaneane Fowler, 2021.

The right of Jeaneane Fowler to be identified as Author of this work has been asserted in accordance with the Copyright, Designs and Patents Act 1988.

2 4 6 8 10 9 7 5 3 1

First published in 2021 in Great Britain by
SUSSEX ACADEMIC PRESS
PO Box 139
Eastbourne BN24 9BP

Distributed in North America by
SUSSEX ACADEMIC PRESS
Independent Publishers Group
814 N. Franklin Street
Chicago, IL 60610

All rights reserved. Except for the quotation of short passages for the purposes of criticism and review, no part of this publication may be reproduced, stored in a retrieval system, or transmitted, in any form or by any means, electronic, mechanical, photocopying, recording or otherwise, without the prior permission of the publisher.

British Library Cataloguing in Publication Data
A CIP catalogue record for this book is available from the British Library.

Library of Congress Cataloging-in-Publication Data
To be applied for.

Paperback ISBN 978-1-78976-068-2

Typeset and designed by Sussex Academic Press, Brighton & Eastbourne.
Printed by TJ Books Limited, Padstow, Cornwall, on acid-free paper.

Contents

Preface and Acknowledgements   ix

Introduction   1

1 The Buddha   6
Life and death of the Buddha   6
The Buddha's *Dhamma*   12

2 Viruses: Friends and Enemies   15
The virosphere   15
The origins of viruses   18
Bacteria   25
Characteristics of viruses   26
Symbiosis of virus and host   35
Viral enemies and their causes   38
Coronaviruses   51
SARS   51
MERS   53
Covid-19: a new virus   54
Characteristics of Covid   55
The source and causes of Covid-19   57
The immune system   59
Measures for protection and prevention   64
The new normal   65

3 The Noble Truth of Suffering   67
The Four Noble Truths   67
Desire and aversion   77
Mind and body   80
The Five Aggregates   82
Change and transience   85

4 The Second Noble Truth of the Cause of Suffering   87
Craving, *tanha*   87
Impermanence, *annica*   94

The three evils/poisons	98
Greed	98
Hatred	100
Delusion/stupidity	101
No-self, *anatta*	105

5 The Third Noble Truth of the Cessation of Suffering 112
Nibbana	112
Dependent Origination	114
Kamma	124
Death	129
Rebirth	132

6 The Fourth Noble Truth: The Noble Eightfold Path 140
The Noble Eightfold Path	141
Right view/understanding	144
Right thought/intention	146
Moral and ethical conduct	149
Right speech	150
Right action	154
Right livelihood	161
Right effort	163

7 The Noble Eightfold Path: Mindfulness and Concentration 166
Mind and body	166
Meditation/mindfulness	169
The calm mind	172
Concentration, *samadhi*	179
Meditation: The medical evidence	183
Insight meditation, *vipassana*	187

8 The *Brahma-vihara*: Love, Compassion, Sympathetic Joy, Equanimity 191
Metta: Love, loving-kindness	193
Karuna: Compassion	198
Mudita: Sympathetic joy	202
Upekkha: Equanimity	203
Human folly	205

Epilogue 210

Notes   Further Reading   Index   221–248

Preface and Acknowledgements

As I sit here writing these words towards the end of October 2020, Wales, where I live, has just been notified that the whole nation will have to go into a second lockdown at the end of the current week. That lockdown will be for a minimum of two weeks, reflecting the case in so many parts of the United Kingdom. The stark fact is that Covid-19 never went away and as we approach the end of autumn and enter wintertime in the northern hemisphere, all the criteria the virus needs to multiply will be met. We will all move indoors, move closer to each other, and give the virus what it needs to pass on its millions of virus particles. The appetite for further lockdowns in the UK is dissipating as the weeks go by, irrespective of the consequences for many of those who may contract this virus, in particular those individuals in vulnerable groups. We have been relatively safe here in Monmouthshire in the southeast corner of Wales but that is no longer the case as the virus is reaching out to spread even here. We will have to deal with Covid-19 for many months to come and it is hoped that, as a consequence, humanity globally will take time to face the fact of pandemics of this nature and those that are sure to come our way in the future. And the cause of such pandemics, as I seek to show in this book, is humanity itself.

I was invited by Sussex Academic Press on 2 April 2020 to write this book. It was the day after my mother's burial with just four close family members at the graveside, given lockdown restrictions. I needed reflective time to ponder on so many questions about life, on the ways in which we live it, and on the strange and weird times into which we were quickly projected. The book has provided answers for me and hope it will do so also for those who read it. I am therefore very grateful for the opportunity to explore this topic and would like to thank the team at Sussex Academic Press for the suggestion, the scope to write the book in whatever way I wished, and the continued support while I worked. As the virus was subsiding in the summer months, I had a feeling that it would rise again very soon; and it did.

While not a practising Buddhist, I have taught Buddhism at undergraduate and postgraduate levels at the University of Wales, Newport, for many years. Because the teachings of early Buddhism transcend religion and reach out into more humanistic realms, its thought structures are not alien concepts rigidified to a certain ancient age, but are eternally relevant to what it is to be human. It is not necessary to be a Buddhist to understand the fluid reality of the Universe, or the shadowy nature of the self. And while suffering may seem a morbid foundation for Buddhist teachings, the Buddha's message is full of optimism. There are answers that Buddhism gives to why we suffer.

With prolonged lockdown there have been no libraries available for me to acquire valuable inter-library texts, but I have been fortunate to have help and support from my neighbour and friend, consultant anaesthetist, Dr Diane Watson. Diane provided me with a number of medical sources that made my work so much easier and I am very grateful. We all know how invaluable the care has been at the frontline of the National Health Service here in the UK and around the world and I want to highlight one particular area of that care because I came to understand it so well. Staff in care homes worked against all odds to provide care for residents – residents who could no longer have visits from their families. The staff were very often left unprotected without efficient personal protective equipment for far too long. I was very fortunate that my mother died just before we were denied being able to visit her, and before she had to endure the traumas of the pandemic. I have dedicated this book to the carers at The Cedars at St Anne's Nursing Home in Chepstow because I had first-hand experience of the incredible love and care that the twelve staff gave to my mother. That care was clearly evident in so many care home contexts throughout the whole of the UK and it was a privilege for my husband and me to witness such outstanding altruism.

This book has a message for humanity. Few, I think, will have made the connection between the Covid-19 virus and the unkindness of humanity to our planet, but the connection is absolutely clear. Unless humanity *globally* changes its practices and ways of life, coronaviruses and other infections will remain with us. I hope this book will make people think and find ways to overcome the incessant harm we create to our home on Earth.

Wentwood View
Autumn 2020

Love that lies like a soft but firm hand on the ailing beings, ever unchanged in its sympathy, without wavering, unconcerned with any response it meets. *Love* that is comforting coolness to those who burn with the fire of suffering and passion; that is life-spending warmth to those abandoned in the cold desert of loneliness; to those who are shivering in the frost of a loveless world; to those whose hearts have become as if empty and dry by the repeated calls for help, by deepest despair.

*Nyanaponika Maha Thera
on the Metta Sutta*

When we face some tragic situation, it reveals the deeper human values of compassion. Usually people don't think about these deeper human values, but when they see their human brothers and sisters suffering the response comes automatically.

Dalai Lama

Love without desire to possess, knowing well that in the ultimate sense there is no possession and no possessor – this is the highest love.

Metta Sutta

Looking into life, we notice its changeful nature continually moving between contrasts. We notice rise and fall, success and failure, loss and gain; we meet honour and blame and we feel how our heart responds to all that with happiness and sorrow, delight and despair, disappointment and satisfaction, hope and fear. These waves of emotion carry us up, and fling us down; and no sooner do we find some rest, than we are in the power of a new wave again. How can we expect to get a footing on the crest of the waves? How shall we erect the building of our life in the midst of this ever restless ocean of existence, if not on the Island of Equanimity.

Nyaponika Maha Thera

The Buddha, the Compassionate Teacher, is no more, but he has left a legacy, the sublime *Dhamma*. The *Dhamma* is not an invention, but a discovery. It is an eternal law; it is everywhere with each man and woman, Buddhist or not Buddhist, Eastern or Western. The *Dhamma* has no labels, it knows no limit of time, space or race. It is for all time.

Thera Piyadassi

The search for a spiritual path is born out of suffering. It does not start with lights and ecstasy, but with the hard tacks of pain, disappointment, and confusion. However, for suffering to give birth to a genuine spiritual search, it must amount to more than something passively received from without. It has to trigger an inner realization, a perception which digs beneath the facile complacency of our usual encounter with the world to glimpse the insecurity perpetually gaping underfoot. When this insight dawns, even if only momentarily, it can precipitate a profound personal crisis. It overturns accustomed goals and values, mocks our routine preoccupations, leaves old enjoyments stubbornly unsatisfying.

Bhikkhu Bodhi

We humans like to think that we're special, but to a killer virus we are just the same as a bat or a baboon. A virus such as AIDS that once hid in the bloodstream of a jungle beast can swiftly explode into an unconquerable pandemic, killing millions around the world. When a human eats or is bitten by a disease-carrying creature, a virus like SARS, Ebola, or Zika gains a foothold. Our own selfish behaviour raises the risk at every turn. The Brazilian farmer who burns a forest to make way for cattle invites disease closer. And all of us who greedily warm the planet through our consumption of fossil fuels make it easier for disease-carrying creatures like mosquitoes to thrive.

Jonathan Quick

While the human race battles itself, fighting over ever more crowded turf and scarcer resources, the advantage moves to the microbes' court. They are our predators and they will be victorious if we, Homo sapiens, do not learn how to live in a rational global village that affords the microbes few opportunities. It's either that or we brace ourselves for the coming plague.

Laurie Garrett

So many people have died, so many families are in mourning, so many communities have been left scarred by disease. We have been shocked by the power of a virus to throw our societies into chaos, to deprive us of our lives and liberties, and to destroy economies. COVID-19 invites us, calls on us, requires us to rethink who we are and what we value.

Richard Horton

Somewhere out there a dangerous virus is boiling up in the bloodstream of a bird, bat, monkey, or pig, preparing to jump to a human being. It's hard to comprehend the scope of such a threat, for it has the potential to wipe out millions of us, including my family and yours, over a matter of weeks or months. The risk makes the threat posed by ISIS (Islamic State in Iraq and Syria), a ground war, a massive climate event, or even the dropping of a nuclear bomb on a major city pale by comparison.

Jonathan Quick

Do we really want to live in harmony with nature? Are we truly the people we think we are? These are simple yet extremely challenging questions. If we answer yes to either or both, which not only is politically correct but also ethically and ecologically correct, we are compelled to move forward with grace, humility, respect, compassion, and love. We will need to replace "mindlessness" with "mindfulness" about our interactions with animals and the Earth. Nothing will be lost and much will be gained. We can never be too generous or too kind.

Jane Goodall and Marc Bekoff

Some of life's greatest lessons are learned at the worst times and from the worst mistakes.

Gianluca Vialli

Introduction

Buddhism – in particular early Buddhism – and the coronavirus are separated by over two millennia of time – a vast amount of time by any standard. Melding the two together might seem an impossible task but the fact that Buddhism is practised so widely today is suggestive that there is a certain measure of timelessness in its message. The Buddhism that I shall be dealing with in this book is early Buddhism, that contemporaneously practised by Theravada Buddhism as the more conservative strand of the many branches of Buddhism. Early Buddhism reaches right back to the time of the Buddha in roughly 400 BCE and is engaged with the first teachings of Buddhism and the words of the Buddha himself, as much as they can be transmitted accurately through the long passage of time. The Buddha's early teaching centred on *Four Noble Truths*, the truths of suffering, its arising, its cessation, and the pathway for its cessation, and it is these four Truths that will provide the content for all of the Buddhism throughout this book. While we need to ask just how early Buddhism would answer the difficult questions posed by the present pandemic of the coronavirus there has always been little will in conservative Buddhism to update, adjust and develop the original teachings of the Buddha. But such adjustment, I believe, is not necessary for there are aspects of the early teaching from which we can learn a good deal to help us on our pathway through these difficult times and through life as a whole.

Buddhism in any of its many manifestations is a way of life and in early Buddhism the Buddha was very much concerned with the nature of personality and how it can be can be changed to incorporate a higher level of well-being. I think many will approach this book with the thought in mind: What can I gain from Buddhism, what can it do for me? While there is no way in which Buddhism has all the answers to every problem in life, there are many aspects of early Buddhism that point to great truths about the nature of the self, about the true reality of the Universe and about how we can adjust our actions of thought, word and deed to lead happier existences. The Buddha begins with a premise that all life is suffering and suggests a cure for it. He was very much like a physician, identifying a problem, isolating its cause, showing that it can be overcome, and providing the means for its end.

These were not philosophical answers but pragmatic ones. If you are struck with a poisonous arrow, you do not want to listen to theories about from where the arrow came, what type of bow shot it, from where the poison came, it is the cure that is exigent. The Buddha's teachings are for active practical use with a good deal of effort, not for passive theoretical analysis, and I am asking the reader here to approach the Buddhism in this book in the same way. The teachings of the Buddha overlap significantly because the Buddha revealed the truth as he saw it from different directions. A theory such as Dependent Origination, for example, will be found underpinning his teaching on the self, on impermanence, on *karma*, and so on: so it is as if the same thing is being said again and again but from different perspectives and starting points. For those searching for answers, they are certainly there in early Buddhism, and those answers begin with the individual, the conditioned individual tossed around on the waves of life, one minute on a crest and the next in a trough. Self-examination to discover exactly who and what we are is no less an important aim for each of us today as it was at the time of the Buddha. But whatever the answers that emerge, they are not commandments, prohibitions, rules and regulations: they are presented by the Buddha as guidance, guidance for a different pathway in life and possibilities for new ethical footsteps.

All of us in the contemporary world are living with the threat of Covid-19, the new or mutated coronavirus that has meant isolation, illness, death, separation from loved ones, economic hardship, and massive uncertainty for the future. When the President of the United States of America survived Covid-19 he said: "Don't be afraid of Covid, don't let it dominate your life!" That is hardly good advice for those desperately ill from it or for those who could contract the illness in the future if they drop their protective guards. This is a virus that should not be underestimated, and since it is likely more of the same will follow, we must learn from it. My purpose in writing this book is to show in what ways we need to learn and need to adapt to avoid further pandemics in the future. Most important, if everyone understood the nature of viruses and the ways in which they affect humans, maybe human behaviour would change. And yet, no government information or documentary takes this route, leaving us in ignorance of our own roles in creating suffering from viruses. So part of my purpose in writing this book is to address that issue. While the text is academically presented, I have not overburdened the reader with endless endnotes. Nor have I kept out of the book subjective experience on my part where it is relevant. This weird, critical and stressful time is not one that demands cold, analytical, academic treatment but, where possible concerning the content, a little warmth and humour here and there.

To be absolutely fair to both aspects of this text – early Buddhism and the coronavirus – it will be necessary in some places to treat each in a discrete way. That said, there are a considerable number of points in both aspects that complement each other admirably. But to do justice to both topics it would not be credible to force the content to meld together in an artificial way because this is impossible. Chapter 1 is one such discrete area; a short chapter that introduces the reader to the Buddha, his life, death, and teaching or *Dhamma*. There are aspects of the Buddha's life here that are foundational to his search for truth, namely his view of suffering, and the search for a cure to suffering.

Chapter 2 is a much longer chapter that deals with viruses in considerable depth. This is an important chapter for the understanding of the causes of pandemics or, in the Buddha's view, the causes of suffering brought by the present pandemic. I believe we need to understand the worlds of viruses, the complexity of the virosphere and how viruses originated. Since they predate humans by millions of years, perhaps billions of years, we need to understand the nature of them and the means we provide for them to transmit and infect. This chapter presents viruses as friends as much as enemies, but takes time to demonstrate how past and present virus epidemics and pandemics are the result of adverse human interaction in the ecosystems of the world, and humanity's shocking invasion into the world of creatures. The coronaviruses are also explored in this chapter along with Covid-19, its characteristics, and the source of its outbreak.

Chapter 3 moves back to early Buddhism to examine the first of the Buddha's Noble Truths, the nature of suffering, and here the two aspects of early Buddhism and the coronavirus meld particularly well. There is a good deal in this chapter that incorporates the Buddhist nature of the self and its search for happiness, its desire for happiness and aversion for unhappiness. And the chapter begins the process of deconstructing the self into impermanent, conditioned components – the Buddha's *Five Aggregates* – that will feature again and again in later chapters.

The second Noble Truth of the cause of suffering is the subject of Chapter 4. This chapter moves the desire for happiness in Chapter 3 to a stronger level, the level of *craving*, and introduces the concept of *volition* behind all our thoughts, words and actions as causative to much of our suffering in life. Again, it will deconstruct the sense of *me* that results in suffering, but examine, too, how that *me* was lessened in these stressful times by those who adopted more altruistic thoughts and practices with examples of selfless beauty of soul in characters such as Captain Tom – now a global celebrity. But a crucial and fundamental teaching of Buddhism is the *impermanence* of all phenomena in the Universe and the impermanence of you and me. That is a discrete Buddhist topic in this chapter. Three evils/poisons are introduced in this chapter: they are greed/desire, hatred/aversion, and delusion/stupidity and they will feature repeatedly in later chapters. They supply remarkably relevant headings under which the greed and stupidity of governments have added to the suffering engendered by the coronavirus; but the greed of us as individuals and our inability to look beyond ourselves to see the reasons why this virus has reached pandemic levels is also an important part of this chapter. Buddhism has three basic facts concerning existence: suffering, which will feature throughout this book; impermanence, which is met earlier in this chapter; and the theory of *no-self*, important enough to require some discrete analysis in this chapter.

The third of the Four Noble Truths focuses on a cure for suffering and is the subject matter of Chapter 5. The ultimate cure is *nibbana* (Sanskrit *nirvana*), though the Buddha recognized that it would be a very distant aim for many. For those of us who are ordinary mortals, the Buddha set about deconstructing the self from another direction, not from the Five Aggregates that feature in Chapter 3, but from a theory known as *Dependent Origination*, a theory that says everything that is depends on other causes – a combination of multiple ones – for its existence, and that includes the self. I could not treat early Buddhism without including the Buddhist theories of *karma*, or *kamma* in the Pali of early Buddhism. This, too, features in Chapter 5 along with death as a very relevant area of concern for all of us today in the face of Covid-19. However, Buddhism has a belief in rebirth, and it would not have been a true portrayal of Buddhism to omit it, so I have placed that here in the context of this chapter.

The last of the Four Noble Truths is the famous *Noble Eightfold Path* that provides the content for Chapter 6. More than any previous chapter, this one melds the two sides of this book into one. The Noble Eightfold Path speaks at once to the individual but also to wider communities, to governments and nations. Consider, for example, right speech as one of the eight, and the ways in which presidents and politicians have misled their nations. In no other time has restraining from false speech been needed: the Buddha could well have rephrased the tenet as "refraining from false news"! But if this book has an overriding message it is of the incessant harm humanity is doing to the planet and its non-human inhabitants. Here is the cause of viruses invading humans from animals. The call of the Buddha to right action as one of the Eightfold Path includes abstaining from taking life, and that aspect certainly combines the Buddha's words of the past with the exigencies of the present in which we, as humans are slowly killing our planet. As a lover of nature and of animals and all creatures, I found the research here hard going and will leave the reader to glean from the internet more sad information if he or she has the courage to do so: I didn't. Then, there is right livelihood, a precept that really raises questions on the ways in which we are prepared to earn our living in today's world. Two important areas of the Noble Eightfold Path I reserved for the penultimate chapter, Chapter 7. These are mindfulness and concentration, the meditative practices that calm the mind and focus thoughts in a concentrated way. Many of us would not reach the higher stages of meditation but there are simpler steps for calming the mind so that suffering is lessened. I have taken pains in this chapter to give the medical evidence that shows how meditation affects the brain in such a way that there are beneficial results for the mind and body. For those who might be tempted to engage in the higher levels of concentration I have outlined these too.

The final chapter is concerned with the *Brahma-vihara*, four mind states that are loving-kindness; compassion; sympathetic joy; equanimity. These are the highly positive states of being for the best of humanity and the best of Buddhists. I think we would all have been moved many times by the incidents we have witnessed of immense kindness and love that has been displayed by so many individuals during these unprecedented days, weeks, and months of isolation, suffering, and for so many, death. But I do not end on a happy note for the message of this book is the rather stark one that humanity has upset the balance of nature so much that we ourselves have caused this present pandemic and its concomitant suffering. Covid-19 is on the rise again now in the late autumn of 2020. The link between the pandemic and its cause in our harm of the planet and, most definitely, in the dangerous animal factories and markets where animals are herded together in bad conditions, invites viruses to cross into humans. We need to fear viruses: they have been here far longer than us. But the natural world has to fear us, for we have become the virus of the planet. The tenets of early Buddhism are relevant to our contemporary times. The effects of Covid-19, on the other hand, are very fluid and are continually changing in daily manifestations in the world. And the world, too, is constantly responding in many different ways to the pandemic. I am aware that facts will change between completion of the book and its final form. So in order to bring information up to date, I shall include an *Epilogue* with the aim, as much as possible, of engaging with current changes before the book goes to press.

1

The Buddha

Buddhism is not a single pathway and in the centuries of its spread it has encountered other cultures and adapted to indigenous ideas making it diverse and fluid. While no one doctrine informs the present expressions of Buddhism, the root of all Buddhism lies in the life and teachings of *the* historical Buddha, Siddhatta Gotama, a man born in India into the Sakka tribe in the fifth century BCE. Siddhatta was his personal name and Gotama his family name.

Life and death of the Buddha

Traditionally, the death of the Buddha is said to have occurred in 486 BCE but a more accurate date is now thought to be about 400 BCE or slightly later, and since he lived for eighty years his suggested life is beginning to find a good deal of consensus as 480–400 BCE rather than the earlier dates of 566–486 BCE, but sources will vary. The accounts of his life, written centuries after his death, are surrounded by hagiographic legends and myths, but we should be wary of eschewing such details: Rupert Gethin is to the point when he says that "many of the details of his early life given in the oldest sources remain evocative of some memory of events from a distant time. If we persist in distinguishing and holding apart myth and history, we are in danger of missing the story's own sense of truth."[1] The Buddha may have been a wandering *samana*, a spiritual "striver", living and thinking separately from the established Hindu societal constraints either independently or as part of a larger group much as the Jains. His life would have been similar to the *samnyasin* or "renouncer" of the fourth of the Hindu four stages of life.

The best account of the life of the Buddha, the *Buddhacarita*, "The acts of the Buddha", was not written down until the first century work of the Indian poet Ashvaghosha.[2] It was written mainly in Sanskrit, though texts of early Buddhism were composed in Pali and since I am concentrating on early Buddhism and the time of the Buddha himself, it is the Pali that I shall be using throughout. According to accounts of his life, Siddhatta was born into opulent circumstances as the son of a wealthy tribal king of the Sakka clan. In hagiographic legend, miracles accompanied the conception and birth of Siddhatta and the characteristic marks on the Buddha's body – wheel marks on his feet, webbed fingers and toes, a soft mark between his eyes, long earlobes – are still to be seen on his iconography today. According to Ashvaghosha's tale, a sage, Asita, came to visit the young baby and told his father that Siddhatta would become a sage, a wandering man who would give up worldly life. Much as today when offspring decide to "do their own thing" and go off alone travelling the world, his parents were alarmed at the idea of Siddhatta becoming a wanderer. Those of the day went from place to place, half naked, never knowing from where their next meal would come, and never settling. Thus, Siddhatta's father decided his son should never leave his opulent home and made certain that his son's life was filled with everything he could wish for. Siddhatta had a wonderful life, the kind of life that so many would relish today – an abundance of money, no shortage of food, and every possible luxury. He married, bore a son, and only knew of life outside the palace from those within its confines. But, as with so many rich individuals past and present, something was missing, something that invaded his subconscious, though not something he understood. He felt, so the *Buddhacarita* tells us, like an elephant locked up inside a house. His opulent life resulted in a myopic view of reality as a comfortable surface happiness that would be lasting: but something was deeply missing.

Siddhatta eventually persuaded his father to permit him to view the world outside his opulent and exquisite palace home. His father craftily made certain that nothing should shock his son into a change of heart about his life by removing all old and sick people, beggars, and the mentally sick, from the immediate surroundings. The trickery, however, did not work and it is here that the foundation of the Buddha's understanding of life began. Whether illusion or reality, while being driven in his chariot, Siddhatta saw an old man. In shock, he asked his charioteer the meaning of what he saw and realized for the first time in his life, "like a bull when a lightning-flash crashes down near him"[3] that the fate of all was to become old. The shock was massive: it was his first glimpse of suffering: "So that is how old age destroys indiscriminately the memory, beauty, and strength of all! And yet with such a sight before it the world goes on quite unperturbed."[4] Siddhatta had his first experience of suffering in the form of old age, and he feared deeply the fact that he, too, and all whom he knew, would become old one day.

On a second excursion from his luxurious home, Siddhatta saw a man with a diseased body. Again, the shock was deeply, deeply disturbing. But what was even more disturbing was the sight of people taking no notice. He said: "This then is the calamity of disease, which afflicts people! The world sees it yet does not lose its confident ways. Greatly lacking in insight it remains gay under the constant threat of disease."[5] On a third excursion from his home, Siddhatta saw a corpse and realized for the first time the reality of death for all creatures. He said: "This is the end that has been fixed for all, and yet the world forgets its fears and takes no heed! The hearts of men are surely hardened to fears for they feel quite at ease while travelling along the road to the next life."[6]

Here I want to pause for a moment to consider the pandemic of Covid-19 in our present existence. How far do we shield our minds from the harsh realities of old age, sickness and death in our normal lives? The experience of the present pandemic has pulled us up with something of a shock. Like the Buddha, we have to face old age, sickness and death with a new vision – not as events that we mostly put to the backs of our minds unless we are intimately involved, but the very real possibilities of our own fragility, and whether young or old, that this disease, this virus, can render us chronically sick or lead to our deaths. What the Buddha came to realize was that these three aspects – old age, sickness and death – were endemic to living and were at the very heart of the nature of suffering. Normally, we are entrenched in our own desires – the need to succeed, the need to have this or that, the need to avoid this or that – now we have to address suffering in the face of Covid-19. We have to stare in the face of suffering and alter our normal view of life. We are suddenly faced with suffering that is beyond our understanding, beyond anyone's experience, as if reality is delivering a mighty shock, letting us know that we are not invincible, that there is no distinction as to who will live and who will die. Perhaps this will enable the reader to contemplate something of the shocking realization about life and death that Siddhatta experienced.

But to return to Siddhatta, these experiences of old age, sickness and death resulted in his viewing his opulent life as devoid of any meaning. He found the impermanence of all things particularly disturbing and could not understand why, in the light of such a condition people acted as if nothing were wrong. To those in his luxurious palace he said "how strong and powerful must be your own mind that in the fleeting pleasures of the senses you find no substance! You cling to sense-objects among the most frightful dangers, even though you cannot help seeing all creation on the way to death. By contrast I become frightened and greatly alarmed when I reflect on the dangers of old age, death, and disease."[7] On a visit to the countryside, he was radically saddened by what he saw – the land littered with the tiny creatures that had been killed from the work of the plough, the ploughmen who "suffered from wind, sun, and dust, and how the oxen were worn down by the labour of drawing".[8] For a while he sat alone in deep concentration until his mind became stable and detached from any desire for sense objects. In this state, the beginnings of his *Dhamma* were laid down and he knew what his destiny should be: "Pitiful, indeed, that these people who themselves are helpless and doomed to undergo illness, old age, and destruction, should, in the ignorant blindness of their self-intoxication, show so little respect for others who are likewise victims of old age, disease, and death! But now that I have discerned this supreme Dharma,[9] it would be unworthy and unbecoming if I, who am so constituted, should show no respect for others whose constitution is essentially the same as mine."[10] At that point, Siddhatta saw a mendicant, a wandering recluse in search of salvation, who explained that he had no home, no possessions and no desires. From that moment on, Siddhatta knew he wished to follow the same path.

After returning to the palace, Siddhatta made plans to steal away in the night. He left to begin a life that was the total opposite of luxury, a life of extreme asceticism; his mission, to find the answers to the suffering endemic in all life. He embarked on a religious, spiritual life believing that this would provide salvation from suffering. It was a total denial of sense satisfaction, a starving of the body, strict fasting, self-torture, and almost perpetual meditation. He wanted liberation, enlightenment, and an awakening that would bring answers to why suffering is endemic to all life. But after six years, he came to realize that inward calm cannot be obtained when the body is weak, so he abandoned his austerities, ate, rested, and built up his physical strength. Neither an opulent life with minimum cares nor a life of ascetic denial solved the problem of human suffering and its causes, so he sat down beneath an *asvatta* or *pipal* tree – the *bodhi* tree as it came to be known – and meditated deeply: it was there that he found the answers to his search and awakened to the truth of life. He said:

> I wandered without respite
>   A journey of many births,
> Seeking the house-builder.
>   Painful is birth again and again.
> House-builder, I have seen you:
>   You shall not build a house again.

> All your rafters are broken:
> > Your ridge-pole is destroyed.
> The mind, freed from conditioned things,
> > Has reached the end of cravings.[11]

At this point Siddhatta "awakened" and became the Buddha, "the enlightened one", and his words in the previous passage indicate that he had come to an end of the cycles of births and deaths, the "house builder" as he put it. He was a "thus gone" or "thus come", a *Tathagata*, as other Buddhas in former aeons, and completely awakened to the nature of reality. That reality, as we shall see below, was a total understanding of the causes of suffering in all life. The Buddha saw things as they really were; the true characteristics of phenomena.

After his enlightenment, the Buddha became teacher to a small group of five mendicant ascetics, ones he had known before his enlightenment. Here were the first followers and a small community that expanded in the years to come. Those who also became enlightened as a result of the Buddha's teaching were known as *arahats*. The Buddha himself was referred to as such. *Arahats* were liberated from the cycle of rebirth, *samsara*, the repeated birth and death that enslaved a being for aeons: they were able to teach others what they themselves had discovered, spreading the teaching of the Buddha far and wide. There were some who felt the need to make a distinction between the Buddha, who had awakened quite by himself, and the *arahats*, who had needed his guidance and teaching, so the temptation to see the Buddha as superior to *arahats* was evident from a very early period. Nevertheless, the Buddha was a human being and not divine. This early period of Buddhism was informed by what are known as the *Three Jewels*. First was the Buddha himself; second was the *Dhamma* (Skt. *Dharma*), the teaching of the Buddha and the Truth to which he became enlightened; third was the community of originally monks and later, nuns, the *Sangha*, which grew up around the Buddha.[12] To become a monk or nun, it was necessary to state three times that one took refuge in the Buddha, the *Dhamma* and the *Sangha*.

During his lifetime, the Buddha gave no indication that someone should succeed him after his death. Instead, he said that the *Dhamma*, his teaching, should be the guide for the monks.
Perhaps it was partly the absence of any successor that facilitated the projection of the nature of the Buddha as greater than any god or mortal. Additionally, the Buddha identified himself as the body of *Dhamma*, the *Dhamma-kaya*, *Dhamma* itself, so in following the

Dhamma, a being became the *Dhamma* and, hence, the Buddha. This point was an important one in the later development of Mahayana Buddhism. The Buddha refused to comment on what would be his post-mortem experience. In the *Potthapada Sutta* he said: "I have not declared that the Tathagata neither exists nor does not exist after death, and that all else is false." His reason, as he stated in the following verse, was "that is not conducive to the purpose, not conducive to the Dhamma, not the way to embark on the holy life".[13] The conservative view of the Buddha was one that saw him as beyond the world and without any influence on the lives of humankind: his *Dhamma* preserved his nature. Yet, before he died the Buddha gave instructions that after his death relics of his body should be placed in *thupas* with the statement that whoever undertook devotional acts at such *thupas* would reap benefits. Such words did much to promote devotional Buddhism from the earliest times, not only connected with the growth in the number of *thupas*, but also in devotion centred on trees grown from cuttings and seeds of the *bodhi* tree; devotional praxis such as circumambulation of sacred places; offerings; images of the Buddha; and hagiographic biographies of his life developed as time passed.

Throughout Buddhism the term *Middle Way* became very important as a means for articulating what Buddhism is. In early Buddhism, it referred to the Middle Way between opulent indulgence, such as that in the Buddha's early life, and the asceticism that followed it. But there was also a Middle Way between the view that the Buddha, or any being, continued to exist forever after death – *eternalism* – or did not exist at all post-death – *annihilationism*. But whatever the Middle Way between these two extremes was, it was not articulated by the Buddha. Conservative early Buddhism was left with the *Dhamma*, the key to the causes of suffering, and an explanation of existence. The *Dhamma* was ultimate Truth and, as such, was eternal. The Buddha awakened to it and discovered it deep within himself but he did not *create* it or *cause* it: the *Dhamma* simply *is* for all time and beyond time. So the monks and nuns were left with the Buddha's *Dhamma* that was teachings about such Truth. They were also left with the memories of what the Buddha said, and such teachings were recited regularly by the monastic disciples. Then, too, there were rules of conduct for the monastic living of the monks and nuns. Later came commentarial explanations about the Buddha's teachings. These three aspects came to be known as the *Three Baskets (Ti-Pitaka)*, the *Vinaya-Pitaka*, which contained rules for monastic living; the *Sutta-Pitaka*, believed to be the words of the Buddha;[14] and the extensive discussions of the *Suttas* in the *Abhidhamma-Pitaka*. These three "Baskets" became the established canon of Buddhist scripture preserved in Pali by the conservative Buddhism of the Theravada school in Sri Lanka, Thailand, Cambodia and Burma to the present day. The canon of the surviving school of Buddhism known as Theravada is perhaps the closest we can get to the actual words of the Buddha.[15]

The Buddha's *Dhamma*

In his deep meditation under the *bodhi* tree, as Siddhatta Gotama became the Buddha, he awakened to a unique understanding of the nature of all reality. Underpinning his whole view of reality and everything in it, including the self, was that everything is *conditioned*. So profound was this truth that the Buddha, ever a pragmatist, maintained a "noble silence" about ultimate questions as inimical to the path of enlightenment. Importantly, while the Buddha was born into the Hindu religion with its belief in an indescribable Absolute that could take many forms, in one blow, the Buddha dispelled all such theories. He rejected a permanent self, an *atman*; he rejected a First Cause from whom the substance of the Universe was created or from which the cosmos was emanated; no "Being" brought forth all things, nor was there a "Not-Being" as the beginning of all. For the Buddha there was no God at all. No one and no thing helped him to become enlightened to the real nature of things: he did it *by himself*, by alterations in his own state of mind. What the Buddha taught instead was his fundamental teaching in the *Dhamma*.

The *Dhamma* is both the teaching of the Buddha and an impersonal, eternal Truth about reality. So close are these two aspects that whoever sees *Dhamma* sees the Buddha. The *Dhammapada* says: "The Dhamma-drinker sleeps happily with clear mind. The wise man always delights in the Dhamma taught by the Noble Ones."[16] In the *Majjhima-Nikaya* the Buddha said of the *Dhamma*: "This doctrine to which I have attained is profound, recondite, and difficult of comprehension, good, excellent, and not to be reached by mere reasoning, subtile, and intelligible only to the wise."[17] The wisdom of the *Dhamma* Edward Conze termed "the crown of all Buddhist endeavour".[18] *Dhamma* means law, what is right, what is Truth and in the Buddha's use of it, it was indicative of the eternal Truths that made up the cosmos. Because it was inherent in the cosmos rather than being extraneous to it *Dhamma* was fundamental to all things and always there irrespective of a Buddha. Thus, the *Dhamma* of the Buddha was not a manual of praxis; it was far deeper than that. And yet, the Buddha always advocated practice as the necessary method for acquiring wisdom, compassion, morality and equanimity. The *Dhamma* was causality, reality, the natural law of the cosmos, the central tenet and heart of Buddhism, and I must iterate that the Buddha eschewed any idea of a force outside nature and the cosmos – no First Cause, God, Ground of all being or ultimate Source. The Buddha even likened the *Dhamma* to a raft one uses to cross a river; when the further shore, enlightenment, is reached, it has to be abandoned.

The lack of a divine creator in Buddhism is crucial to the understanding of the Buddha's message. Creation in Buddhism was never a point in time: rather it is a continual process of evolution, changing sustainment, and eventual involution after which the whole process begins again. In fact, the Buddha had a remarkably futuristic view of multiple universes in which a new universe could arise anywhere in the cosmos in processes that take place over aeons, billions of years – a projection of the human mind into timeless eternity. And what is noteworthy here is pointed out well by Peter Harvey when he writes that without any agent or creator, Buddhism has no theological problem of evil and suffering, so it inevitably avoids "the problem of how an all-powerful, all-knowing, all-loving God could create a world in which evil and suffering exist."[19] I want to take Harvey's point further by pointing out that a God of this nature would have had to create viruses as well as humans simply because, as we shall see in Chapter 2, viruses were around long, long before any human, primate or animal, and were quite probably there when the very first cellular life began. Those who wish to take a theistic stance to creation of the Universe or of our planet cannot really avoid assigning the creation of viruses to whatever divine being or agent they posit as creator.

The reality to which the Buddha awoke at his enlightenment was that life is unsatisfactory and suffering (*dukkha*), that there is no real self, and that all compounded things are impermanent. These are the three characteristics or "marks" of Buddhism that were articulated at the second sermon of the Buddha to a very small group of monks shortly after his enlightenment. In this, his early teaching, the Buddha de-substantiated the whole of the phenomenal world.

I shall take up these characteristics of existence in Chapter 3 when I examine suffering as the first of them. The idea of all life as suffering stemmed from the Buddha's pre-enlightened experiences and the fact that he had not entertained any idea of suffering prior to his excursions from his palatial home. The theme of suffering, so essential to his *Dhamma*, enters all the major theories of early Buddhism – the three marks, the *Four Noble Truths*, *Dependent Origination* and beliefs about *karma* and rebirth. These are aspects I shall take up in later chapters, but now we must embark on the roots of our present-day suffering in Covid-19 by understanding first, the nature of viruses and how they create suffering or assist us in avoiding it.

2

Viruses

Friends and Enemies

My intention in this chapter is to examine viruses as a discrete topic. It is my belief that we can only understand the nature of the present pandemic if we get to grips with the very nature of viruses and, critically, the causes of their emergence in human beings and of the suffering their infections entail. Understanding how far humanity itself must accept responsibility for its own suffering is a key issue that will be raised again and again throughout this book. This chapter has to start responding to that issue by an in-depth study of what we today regard as our enemy. Why is it here? What have we done to deserve it? And if we are ever free from it, how can we ensure we will be free from future such pandemics?

The virosphere

Viruses outnumber the total of all life forms, whether creature or microbe. They form the *virosphere*, a massive biomass of enormous complexity and diversity with millions of different kinds of viruses. Every single cell in existence is likely to be infected by a large number of viruses.[1] They are thoroughly ubiquitous and found in every depth of the Earth, below Antarctic ice a mile down in newly discovered lakes, and even in the staggeringly hot hydrothermal vents deep in the ocean. Wherever there is life, there are viruses. If you swim in the ocean and swallow a mouthful of water, you will have swallowed two hundred million viruses, and there are more viruses in a litre of coastal seawater than there are people on Earth. We eat billions of them daily and breathe in billions with every breath. Our own genetic profile carries alongside it the genomes of viruses and there are more of them in and on just one of us than all the inhabitants of the world. The diversity of all these viruses is utterly incredible and their genomes, their genetic material, reflect what Juris Grasis terms "reservoirs of genetic diversity".[2] So, in fact, whereas our bodies consist of immensely complicated and very diverse cells, viruses, though nowhere nearly as complex, vastly outnumber all cellular structures. The genomes for the virus HIV, for example, number 10^{16} and there are perhaps as many as 10^{31} on the planet to date. Thus, the words of Richard Horton here are more than relevant when he writes that "we are only one species among many, and we are certainly not a dominant influence when faced with a virus that can destroy life with such ease and facility".[3] Indeed, the virologist George Klein once said: "The stupidest virus is cleverer than the cleverest virologist."[4]

We cannot avoid viruses or the diseases, epidemics and pandemics that they cause. They are clever bastards, and as Louis Pasteur, I believe, once said, will always have the last word. So what is a virus? The Nobel Prize winning biologist, Peter Medawar, described a virus as "a piece of nucleic acid surrounded by bad news".[5] I want to leave any explanation of their nature for the moment but suffice it to say here they are molecular parasites that are capable of reproducing their genetic information once they have invaded a cell. The word "virus" originated during the Roman Empire and meant on the one hand a snake's venom, reflecting its Latin meaning "poison" and, on the other, a man's semen. In more scientific terms, a virus is a submicroscopic entity, in other words, whereas bacteria can be seen under a microscope, viruses had to wait to be seen through the electron microscope when that was developed in the 1930s because they are so miniscule. As unseen forces, viruses affect the whole ecology of our planet, shifting from host to host, from cell to cell, affecting evolution of species, regulating all that they invade. In the *Foreword* to Carl Zimmer's work *A Planet of Viruses*, Judy Diamond and Charles Wood powerfully write: "Every species, from tiny microbes to large mammals, is influenced by the actions of viruses. Viruses extend their impact beyond species to affect climate, soil, the oceans, and fresh water. When you consider how much every animal, plant and microbe has been shaped through the course of evolution, one has to consider the influential role played by the tiny and powerful viruses that share this planet."[6]

Understanding the incredible extent of the virosphere and the intimacy with which viruses and humans have evolved and exist together will, I hope, serve as a warning. Whenever an epidemic or a pandemic outbreak occurs, something is wrong with the balance between the two, and that is so often because humanity has disturbed the environment in some way. Indeed, if I wanted a single thesis for this book it would have to be this factor of human environmental causes of the present pandemic of the coronavirus. I propose to develop that evidence as I proceed. One thing is certain concerning the threat of viruses and that is they are far more likely to occur where there is poverty and social disadvantage.

The interaction between humans and viruses has existed at every phase of human evolution with the human body attempting to fight off the virus enemies, the pathogens, which need the body so that they can exist and thrive. And there has been extensive co-evolution between the two: sometimes the body has won, sometimes a virus and, at other times, they have co-existed for the lifetime of the host. While evolution of human beings has been a slow process from our primate ancestors, the evolution of viruses is much, much quicker as they change, adapt and mutate in order to survive. We know this is the case by the study of the genomes of the human body. When viruses attacked throughout the evolution of primates to humans, those that could withstand the viruses passed on their genetic resistance to their offspring. So in this process of co-evolution, groups of people and larger populations became immune to many viruses, while the viruses evolved to survive but to be weaker in potency. What is certain, however, is that density of population always provides viruses with new hosts, so their co-evolution with humans was very dependent on changes in human habitats and social interactions. If we project that fact into the present, population expansion is a major reason for the outbreaks of new viral diseases such as the present strain of coronavirus. And another major reason is the interaction humans have with animals causing viruses harmless in animals to jump into our own species. The late famous molecular biologist, Joshua Lederberg, is reputed to have said: "The single biggest threat to man's continued dominance on the planet is a virus." And consider Dorothy Crawford's alarming words here: "As soon as we are born, and every day of our lives, our bodies are like castles under siege, surrounded by swarming enemy troops all trying to breach the walls, enter, and plunder the contents. Each enemy carries a weapon to assist it and each tries a different port of entry. But just like fortified castles, we are built to withstand the attack."[7] Or are we? The advent of the more severe coronaviruses in recent times and the mutation of one of these to bring unprecedented changes to the ways in which we live today, should act as a warning that other pandemics are likely to be on the horizon sooner rather than later.

Viruses have shaped history, diminished the strength of armies, reduced native populations, re-shaped geographical populations, caused economic disasters, and decimated populations. Smallpox alone killed about three hundred million people throughout the twentieth century. These major killers are not to be taken lightly and we are now experiencing the effects of one of them – no longer an epidemic, but a *pandemic*. Epidemics, from the Greek for "visit", are regional, and occur when a local "outbreak" begins to affect a higher than expected number of people and a larger geographical area, but usually an epidemic is confined in time and place. Epidemics are often unexpected and account for more unusual numbers of infected individuals. Derived from the Greek *pandemos*, with the meaning "all people", pandemics are global and can be persistent with waves of infections. The National Institute of Allergy and Infectious Diseases at the National Institutes of Health (NIH) came up with eight criteria for the definition of a pandemic:

- ☐ Wide geographic extension
- ☐ Disease movement
- ☐ High attack rates and explosiveness
- ☐ Minimal population immunity
- ☐ Novelty
- ☐ Infectiousness
- ☐ Contagiousness
- ☐ Severity[8]

It is easy to see that these criteria are being met by the current pandemic of the coronavirus: and the major causes – population growth and density; human stupidity; increasing deforestation that challenges natural animal habitats; urbanization; climate change; animal husbandry; and ease of international travel – I shall explore throughout this text. Generally, it would have to be said that humanity is its own worst enemy in creating the suffering brought about by pandemics. It needs to change its views, its habits, its relationship with the planet and the animals that inhabit it. In a rather puckish statement, I read recently that there are two causes of pandemics: (1) How dense the population is, and (2) How dense the population is.

The origins of viruses

There is wide disagreement as to the origins of viruses but complete agreement about their antiquity: they existed well before the advent of humans on the planet, perhaps as early as 4 billion years ago. There are no fossils to help identification, and the speed at which viruses can change makes it very difficult to disentangle them from the hosts that house them. Viruses invade anything that lives, whether creature, plant or bacteria, and with multiple changes, mutations, in so many organisms, finding a beginning is very problematic. It is possible that they predated all other organisms and existed in the primordial soup of the Universe billions of years ago. If this were the case then they would once have been free entities not, as they are today, dependent on the cells of organisms to thrive. If they existed as early as this, they would have needed to survive in extreme and violent conditions during the formation of our planet, but with the right kind of chemicals to encourage their survival. On the other hand, perhaps viruses were part of the sphere of early microbes that were in existence around 3.5–3.8 billion years ago. They would have been the tiniest members of the microbial world. Early microbial bacteria occupied all parts of the evolving planet long before the availability of oxygen, colonizing rocks that provided them with necessary chemicals. They were single-cell simple organisms, lacking nuclei, but primitive life called *prokaryotes*. They had to exist in intense heat and geographical upheavals and were suited to existence in hot deep-sea vents and the vicinities of volcanos. Bacterial organisms of the same nature are everywhere around us and in us today, actually outnumbering the cells of our bodies.

Then, about 2.7 billion years ago, bacteria mutated to use photosynthesis by which carbon dioxide and water were converted by sunlight – the process that produced oxygen.[9] Perhaps just a little later, a symbiosis of different prokaryotes combined to become more complicated *eukaryotes*, important cells with nuclei and DNA. So were viruses part of this process, or did they predate early cells? Arinjay Banerjee and his colleagues have noted this possibility: "In a prehistoric world, viruses might have existed as self-sustaining entities, a sort of ancient machine that could probably reproduce its genetic material. Over time, these prehistoric viruses may have formed complex, organized structures that eventually evolved cell-like entities."[10] A pre-cell origin may, then, be a possibility, but what we know of viruses now is that they cannot reproduce unless within an animal, plant or bacterial cell, so that may perhaps suggest that they would need to have been mutually entwined with cellular life from their beginning – a joint virus and cell origin.

So what about this possibility of an origin of viruses from cells themselves? This is how some see the origins, perhaps an escaped gene, or DNA (deoxyribonucleic acid) and RNA (ribonucleic acid) fragments of genes from a host cell. Once again, since viruses cannot exist and reproduce without a host cell it would seem logical that cells existed before them and this is, indeed, a much shared view of their origins. But note the view of Holmes here: "However, there is no gene shared by all viruses, and recent data are providing increasingly strong support for a far more ancient origin."[11] And Holmes also adds that virus evolution involves a great deal of cross-species transmission and immense diversity as a result, for which minimal gene escaping could not account.[12] Exactly when viruses lost their independent existence and degenerated to become parasites is unclear, but what is clear is their antiquity and their accompanying of all life – animal, plant or microbial – in its evolutionary journey through millions of years.

It is believed that all life – plant or animal – originated with one common ancestral cell, the *last universal cellular ancestor*, or LUCA, as far back as 4 billion years ago. As noted above, simple-cell organisms existed in the oceans of Earth 3.8 billion years ago when organic molecules managed to reproduce themselves and chance combinations of atoms occurred. The transformation of single-cell organisms to multicellular forms provided the basis for the evolution and increasing complexities of multicellular life. It took one simple-cell organism to combine with another to begin this process. But our biological make-up and that of all living things have a common biochemistry and DNA suggestive of the single-cell common ancestor, LUCA, long before multicellular life began, though it was probably not the first and only ancestral entity. LUCA's beginnings would have been very simple: as a single-cell organism with similarities to bacteria but also with differences, the genome of that cellular ancestor exists in an unbroken line within us and all other life. Alongside these genomes are those of viruses.

There are skeletal and molecular similarities between all mammals with only slight variations in DNA – even between fruit flies and humans. Just a tiny variation in genes is sufficient to create a new species. Natural selection – quite separate from chance or randomness – enabled survival in particular surroundings when genes mutated to produce an adapted, advantaged form of life that could survive and reproduce more efficiently. And, again, viruses, providing they had a host, did the same. The early simple bacteria I noted above could survive without oxygen, and early microbial purple slime, possessing a complex ecosystem and suggestive of a source for cellular life, seems to have been present.[13] Did life emerge from this purple sludge? Note, however, the words of Paul Davies here, who said, "the evidence is mounting that our oldest ancestors did not crawl out of the slime as much as ascend from the sulphurous underworld".[14] His view ties in very well with the volatile surroundings of the earliest prokaryotes. LUCA may have existed in what seemed to be "mud volcanos", in hydrothermal vents that bubbled up out of the seas, perhaps with self-replicating molecules that predated the beginnings of living cells with DNA. Could viruses have originated here, or even well before LUCA, in such a "sulphurous underworld"?

The ancient multicellular structures are remarkably similar to any material on Earth: the interconnection is stunning, with the same kinds of molecules. There is now a good deal of evidence for "extremophiles", bacterial life that exists today in the most incredible environments: and they are ubiquitous in many places on Earth. Researchers at Vostok in Antarctica have found a really deep massive subglacial lake containing "a complex web of organisms, including single-celled bacteria, fungi and protozoa, along with more complex animals such as molluscs, worms, anemones and even arthropods".[15] This is an ecosystem that has survived for hundreds of thousands of years and yet shares its DNA with species above the lake. Some of these extremophiles are called *hyperthermophiles* and are microbes that live very close to scalding hot vents over a mile down in the Pacific Ocean away from any sunlight at temperatures way over boiling point.[16] So the earliest microbes including viruses probably began in such a way deep in the oceans, similar to what Davies said above.

Away from Earth, it is not unlikely that early forms of microbiotic life reached us from cosmic impacts. We may yet prove to be descended from Martian microbes if meteorites reaching Earth from the Red Planet contained them. Amino acids, so essential for life, could have arrived here through the medium of meteors that may have had organic compounds on board. Davies claimed that he and Jay Melosh were some of the first to suggest that microbes could travel between planets in rocks ejected from their surfaces.[17] Molecules providing the necessary building blocks for life are likely to have come from such cosmic sources, but the same sources of any size were also subject to annihilation during a time of massive bombardment in the formation of Earth – the Late Heavy Bombardment 4–3.8 billion years ago. Yet some molecules must have reached formative Earth. Can viruses come from outer space? I think it is highly likely, and exploration on the planet Mars may yet discover their even greater ubiquitous existence.

The debate as to whether viruses are pre- or post-LUCA is a vibrant one. Since life evolved post- LUCA – indeed over 2 billion years later – it would be difficult to explain why viruses that infect organisms from the three separate domains of the tree of life – bacteria, archaea (microbes similar to bacteria but with different metabolisms), and eukarya (protists, fungi, plants and animals) that cover all living organisms – show a distinct relationship across the groups, whereas the groups themselves are so divergent. Indeed, some viruses that affect humans *and* bacteria are structurally alike, and that could not happen unless they predated LUCA and maintained distinct lineages despite the immense diversification of hosts post-LUCA. They may, indeed, have their own last common ancestor: because some of the base genes in viruses may have existed for billions of years, this might suggest such a common ancestry for all viruses and account for their common features. Perhaps the virus genomes enabled later cellular microbes to evolve. Our genomes are constructed of DNA, but many viruses – and coronaviruses are among them – have RNA genomes and some believe that RNA was the sort of "master molecule" from which DNA evolved, and not the other way around. Perhaps there was a primordial pool of microbes with genetic elements where the ancestors of cellular and viral structures existed in a communal stage before diverging from each other as life-producing cells on the one hand and parasitic viruses on the other. Searching for a common ancestor may be misleading for there could well have been multiple ancestors of viruses that arose at different times and perhaps independently of each other. There is also the possibility that viruses evolved alongside their hosts, adapting again and again on the evolutionary pathways of the hosts.

The oceans may give us some insight. The oldest traces of oceanic multicellular organisms date back to approximately two billion years ago. Ancient viruses have been found in the permafrost, the frozen ice and snow, in Siberia. In Antarctica, where the snow and ice are frigidly frozen, over ten thousand viruses from a dozen different viral branches have been found in Lake Limnopolar, a freely flowing mass of water deep under the snow. Some of the viruses found there are entirely new. In the Sierra de Naica mountain range in Mexico, miners discovered what is now known as the Cave of Crystals a thousand feet below ground that contained gigantic gypsum crystals. When water from pools in the cave was microscopically examined in 2009, it was found to be swarming with viruses. "There are as many as 200 million viruses in every drop of water from the Cave of Crystals", writes Zimmer, and he prefaces this fact with a remarkable point: "There are no people in the Cave of Crystals for the viruses to infect. There are not even any fish. The cave has been effectively cut off from the biology of the outside world for millions of years."[18] Estimated to have been formed 26 million years ago, to all intents and purposes it seems that there were no hosts on which these viruses could thrive,[19] that they could exist without cell hosts for all that time, and that their origins could be independent of microbial cells and even predate them.

With absolute certainty it can be claimed that viruses predated humans and even their primate ancestors. From the evidence of fossils, our own ancestors, *Homo erectus*, seemed to have been around as early as 1.8 million years ago and lasted until about 250,000 years ago. They were located mainly in East Africa but spread out from there about 1.7 million years in the past.[20] They ate plants and small creatures, and evolved into our true hunter-gatherer ancestors, the Cro-Magnum people, about 150,000 and 200,000 years ago. Alongside the evolution of these peoples was the rapid evolution of viruses. Comparing the two, as I said above, viruses evolve far, far quicker, their genomes mutating at an incredible speed, and the fittest ones reproduce the genes that enable them to survive better, reproduce better and increase more. The role of these viruses in evolution has been crucial. Julia Durzyńska and Anna Goździcka-Józefiat make this point clear: "In the course of evolution viruses emerged many times. They have always played a key role through horizontal gene transfer in evolutionary events and in formation of the tree of life or netlike routes of evolution providing a great deal of genetic diversity."[21] In other words, the evolution of human beings has been dependent on the joint evolution of viruses. Viruses facilitated the genetic diversity of life by the mutations they caused in host genes and by aiding genes to transfer between cells of different species. So without viruses, life could not have evolved.

Before the advent of human beings, viruses coexisted with animals and creatures tolerably well without endangering one or the other. Our primate ancestors in the rainforests of Africa coexisted with their parasitic viruses until early humans came on the scene. These early people were hunter-gatherers who developed increasing hunter as opposed to gatherer skills. That entailed increasing interaction with wild animals and some animals probably became extinct because of that. Consider Crawford's words here:

> By 12,000 years ago over 200 species had become extinct, including giants like the woolly mammoth and rhinoceros, sabre-toothed tiger, mastodon, and giant bison and sloth, all of which had risen to prominence in the Eurasian and African landscapes after dinosaurs died out some 65 million years earlier. Both global warming and epidemic microbes have been blamed for this mass extinction, but although these may have contributed to the disaster, there seems little doubt that human hunters were the main culprit since the timing of the extinctions on each continent coincided with their arrival.[22]

These hunter-gatherers would have carried many viruses, one of which would have been a member of the ancient herpes virus that now manifests itself as chicken pox. Even in remote tribes of present times, despite little contact with the world beyond, natives carry this same virus, indicative of its ancient lineage. The bacterial disease of malaria, too, is probably equally as ancient. The importance of Crawford's words above lie very much in the human–animal interaction through hunting. As hunting increased, we find the beginnings and rise of *zoonotic* infections and diseases where viruses infecting animals jump to humans. Viruses that live in animals and cause them no harm can be fatal when newly introduced to a human host. Here, with primitive hunters, we have the first evidence of the reasons for the spread of viruses, and virus jump from creature to human is as relevant today as it was in the primitive past. When I said there are two reasons for the spread of viruses, (1) How dense the population is and (2) How dense the population is, the former refers to the way humans lived in the past and present, and the second their stupidity in their interaction with animals and the natural world. It will be seen below how both (1) and 2) still obtain in the spread of coronaviruses today. We may have become more "civilized" but we have learned little in the realm of our interaction with creatures and nature. There will be much to explore here alongside Buddhism in later chapters.

Animal viruses often serve to protect animals against humans who invade their habitats, and whereas the animal viruses live symbiotically with their hosts, viruses always need new hosts, and the jump from animal to human passes a completely new virus to the human. As early man passed from hunter-gatherer to agriculture and the keeping of domestic cattle, the chance for that jump from animal to human was vastly increased. This shift of life-style happened about 10,000 years ago, increasing to sedentary farming in larger and larger groups – new hosts for the viruses. It is likely that was the time when some type of malaria began to infect humans – a disease with a vector, the mosquito. The change to a sedentary life-style meant a more static existence in contrast to previous nomadic wanderings. Settlements grew larger, with cramped dwellings that housed both human and beast, providing more cell fodder for the quickly reproducing viruses that must have spelt disaster for crops and inhabitants on many occasions. And here, too, was the beginning of human assault on the environment and the natural biodiversity that had obtained before them. Viruses like filth and the settled and cramped communities supplied it in abundance from their animals and themselves. As trade developed, so viral diseases had easy transport from one community to another and the first epidemics and pandemics occurred. We now know that diseases such as whooping cough, measles, smallpox, diphtheria, mumps and scarlet fever were once animal held viruses and passed to infect humans as early as 5000 BCE. Today, our human genome carries thousands of viruses that first infected our ancient ancestors: these are viruses that no longer harm us though they may well have been fatal to many of those who first experienced them. Crawford writes: "Most would have begun by causing severe zoonotic infections; only once they were established as purely human pathogens could they co-evolve with their host, a process that takes around 150 years and generally results in much milder disease."[23]

And so the more civilization developed the easier it was for viruses to spread: the risks of epidemics of disease increased with the expanded interactions of people, crossing countries, seas, and eventually oceans to infect virgin populations. As we progress through history the mass movements of people from country to towns, where the density of the populations seemed to know no bounds and the filth around overcrowded dwellings no end, towns became viral death traps. And here we would have to include poverty as the medium for the worst of diseases – no less in our contemporary crisis with the coronavirus. In the exploration of the Americas by Europeans, these latter carried viruses unknown to the natives and that had devastating consequences, wiping out whole communities, while the slave trade took viruses harmless to Africans to infect virgin hosts of Europeans and Americans. We hear a good deal about *herd immunity* these days. Usually, any pathogen such as a virus will have been around for some time. Each of us is a diverse individual with a unique response to the viruses that we meet and a unique response from our immune systems to deal with them but whole communities will have genetic herd immunity that will keep them fairly safe in the face of a good many viruses. This is not so for any new communities combating viruses for the first time, which is why viruses often shaped history by depleting armies or conquering peoples newly subjected to a viral force. But once infected, those who survived had life-long immunity except, that is, for children born subsequently to an epidemic. That is why viral epidemics such as measles affect only children.

Bacteria

Some mention here of bacteria is essential since bacteria are very different to viruses. We have seen earlier, in fact, how much smaller viruses are and that an electron microscope is necessary to see them, unlike larger bacteria. Bacteria are shaped like rods, spirals or spheres and, though smaller than body cells, can be seen under an ordinary microscope. Bacteria are single-celled but complex and are free and independent. Of all cellular organisms, they are the most prolific. They invade the body and cause disease, though we have many good bacteria that we need for a healthy bodily system. Bacteria can be destroyed by antibacterial drugs, the first of which was penicillin, discovered in 1945. These drugs attack the outer shell of the bacterium cell without destroying the natural body cell of the host. Viruses, however, are not organic cells and they *have to* invade the body cell in order to reproduce: here, antibiotic drugs cannot usually work. Common colds are mostly from viruses so that general medical practitioners who prescribe antibiotics for colds are offering useless treatment. Such actions mean that bacteria can become drug-resistant and increase in the individual and community. If bacteria can resist destruction long enough they can pass that resistance on in their reproduction of descendants so that anyone infected by the same bacteria will have no defence against them. Then, too, bacteria themselves can act as hosts to viruses but they can also acquire some of their DNA from viruses.[24] Thus, viruses and bacteria are different in almost every way. But bacteria played a crucial role in the pathways to living matter because they were the earliest of all life, "and represent the blue print for cells which make up all other animals and plants", as Crawford points out. As she says, bacteria are the smallest microbes capable of independent existence: "Every day they are busy breaking down dead plants and animals into their component parts ready for re-use. The gases released make up our atmosphere, and simple molecules are rebuilt into new plants and animals. Only rarely do bacteria invade other living things and cause disease."[25] Bacterial cells have their own DNA that ensures their independent survival and reproduction: viruses have no such independence and need living cells, even bacterial ones, to exist and reproduce. Some viruses actually destroy bacteria by way of *phages*, specialized viruses, if bacteria are particularly virulent but, in less virulent strains, viruses simply live within the bacterium's cells.

Characteristics of viruses

The viruses present in contemporary life are a patchwork of different bits and pieces from various sources. As I examine the nature of viruses, it is difficult to avoid giving them characteristics of cleverness, of the ability to plan attack, counter-attack, strategize, and the like. But these tiny, tiny entities have no intelligence whatsoever: they do not think or control what they are doing. Viruses are brainless, inert particles, not cells, and without cells as hosts, they can do nothing. Despite this impotence, viruses can invade all cells, whether animal, plant, fungus, bacteria, protozoa – they have worlds of abundant possibilities for hosts. They need the machinery of cells to activate them in order to reproduce, and to transfer some of that machinery into their own genomes to make that happen. So viruses are *obligate parasites* taking what they need from cells in order to exist and reproduce. In fact, they do not have cell walls and so cannot exist in the same way as cells can unless they invade them. An invaded cell may well die from the invasion of a virus, having been robbed of its essential contents, in effect the protein synthesizing of the cell. They seem nasty entities, as Durzyńska and Gózdzicka-Józefiat graphically put it: "Viruses enter the host cell, utilize cellular resources for creating new viruses and then sacrifice (or damage) their temporary slaves in order to escape the scene of crime."[26] If a particularly virulent virus invades the cell, it is sacrificed, killed: a more temperate virus will simply house itself in the genome of the cells of the host and hang around in a proviral form until a later date when the time is right to reproduce.

Viruses are made up of 95 percent protein and 5 percent nucleic acid, this latter containing the instructions for building molecules, especially proteins. They may have dramatic effects, but the composition of viruses is quite simple, just a protein outer shell (a *capsid*) housing a few genes, some as few as three, and others as many as four hundred, but nothing like the approximately 30,000 genes of a human cell. Even small bacteria have more genes than viruses – between 5,000 and 10,000. So without the genes of host cells, the virus really is impotent. For example, well-known viruses such as measles, yellow fever, Ebola and the human immunodeficiency virus, or HIV, have less than ten genes each, and the lethal smallpox gene, as well as the ancient herpes virus have each somewhere between 200 and 400 genes.[27] The nucleic acid is the genetic material of the virus, either DNA or RNA that I will examine later, and this DNA or RNA contains the information, the code, that the virus needs to reproduce. The whole composition of the virus is termed a *virion*. Examining the total number of genes of a virus, its *genome*, is what renders the specific nature of that virus.

The incredible diversity and proliferation of viruses has come about through *mutations*. These are like experiments done within nature that either work well and are proliferated or do not work well and decrease a virus. Because viruses reproduce very, very quickly and on a vast scale, they make millions of copies of themselves in a very short time: inevitably there are mistakes given the rapidity of the process. These mistakes are what cause mutations, either good ones, new unique genes, that are passed on to the next generation, or not so good ones that fail to make the grade. This is Darwinian natural selection at the level of viruses. If a virus is introduced to a new type of host it may take multiple mutations for it to have any effect, but if this happens – and that may be the case with the present coronavirus – the results can be catastrophic producing a new disease. Note Crawford's words here: "But a few of the offspring will have beneficial mutations, giving them a selective advantage over their siblings. The benefit may result in any number of advantages, including a heightened ability to hide from immune attack; to survive and spread between hosts; to resist antiviral drugs; or to reproduce at a faster rate. Whatever the advantage, it will lead to that particular mutant virus outstripping its siblings and eventually taking over the population."[28] The rapid reproduction of a virus combined with so many mutations and natural selection enable viruses to adapt to a new host environment in an incredibly short time. This is particularly the case with RNA retroviruses such as HIV/AIDS: the virus mutates so quickly that the disease cannot be eradicated.

Human DNA, deoxyribonucleic acid, carries all the genetic information for development, for growth, for the building of proteins and necessary molecules, and for cell reproduction. All organisms including many viruses have such DNA. About 8 percent of our DNA is viral, so our human cells not only work for us but for the viruses too. Human DNA is in two strands of nucleic acid. Viruses also have RNA, ribonucleic acid, genes as does the family of coronaviruses. Viruses will carry DNA or RNA but not both, but because the genomes of either do not have the ability to produce many proteins, viruses need a host cell to produce more. Some RNA viruses insert a copy of their genome into the DNA of a host cell. That cell's DNA is altered as a result and the virus is then able to produce DNA from its own RNA. When the cell divides, the DNA of the virus is then copied along with the cell's own DNA. This conversion of RNA to DNA is done by an enzyme in the virus called *reverse transcriptase*, and is a rather clever way of acquiring the ability to reproduce. Viruses that do this are called *retroviruses* and they can remain in the cells they inhabit undetected by the immune system. It seems the cells of our ancestors were invaded by retroviruses again and again, and the remnants of these can be found in thousands of bits of retrovirus in our DNA sequences, passed on harmlessly from generation to generation.[29] Other RNA viruses are pretty efficient at creating copies of their own RNA and getting them converted to proteins. HIV and influenza are both good examples of RNA viruses.

Viruses are immensely resourceful: they have no brains but they are designed to survive and increase by finding new hosts whenever they can, especially in poor human environments. As Christopher Wills puts it: "How these tiny organisms do this, their resourcefulness in doing so, and the dangers they pose to our species, illustrate a fascinating aspect of the dynamics of parasites. When times are tough for a parasite, it may use all its resources in order to survive and spread.

When times are easy, it may lose those abilities – or, of course, it may never have acquired them in the first place."[30] Viruses must cross barriers to survive and they do this regularly by their frequent mutations. These mutations, if advantageous, are the kinds of genetic modifications and changes they need to become sufficiently different to be new and, very often, more virulent. The influenza virus is of this nature. Then, too, and very relevant to today's outbreak of a new coronavirus, proximity to animals and the penetration of their habitats provide viruses with the possibility of a new home. We now know that viruses do not die when a body – animal or human – is deceased. Social practices of treatment of the dead have been a major source of virus spread.

One obvious characteristic of some viruses is their persistence, persistence that is maintained when the immune system cannot quite overcome the virus, leaving it in the body. Such is the case, for example, with HIV. But all viruses must really move on some way or other, even those that remain alongside a host for a lifetime, otherwise the virus will die out. To exist persistently in a host, a virus really needs to tone down its effects, otherwise its home is lost if the host dies. That is why a virus may be asymptomatic for many people. The balance between virus and host here is a delicate one, giving the host no problems, though it could result in disease if that delicate balance were to be interfered with. Viruses are cunning: they may cause an epidemic and then lie low, subsiding for years before re-emerging.

So what do viruses look like? Well, they are very, very small and very, very tough. Thousands of viruses would fit into the full stop at the end of this last sentence: "life stripped to the bare essentials" as Crawford depicts them.[31] As Crawford says, three million *bacteria* would comfortably sit side by side on the head of a pin but viruses are five hundred times smaller.[32] Covid-19 virus is 120 nanometres (billionths of a metre) across, and according to Michael Mosley; "You could fit a hundred million viral particles on the head of a pin."[33] And later he says: "Despite being so tiny (they are a million times smaller than a human cell) together they weigh more than every living thing on earth, including all plants, insects and animals. In fact someone with time on their hands calculated that if you were to string together just those viruses that live in the oceans they would reach to the planet Mars, and back again, more than twelve trillion times."[34] Imagine, just one sneeze sends out billions of virus particles that could infect thousands. And yet, scientists are beginning to discover comparatively giant viruses, as ones found in the Siberian permafrost that were frozen as long ago as 30,000 years. Such large viruses are called *mimiviruses* and they have far more genes – over a thousand – than other viruses and even more than some bacteria. Then, too, an even bigger virus has been found and given the name *mamavirus*. Subsequently, these giant viruses have been found to be ubiquitous on our planet and present as well in humans and animals. As to their shapes, these are varied – bullet-shaped; brick-shaped; rod-shaped; many-sided.

So is a virus alive? Wills believes they "inhabit a twilight world between life and non-life",[35] and Matti Jalasvuori describes them as "a genuine form of life that can exploit foreign cell-vehicles for preserving their genetic information".[36] But most claim that viruses are not alive. Crawford says they do not have the necessary metabolic and molecular processes and machinery to make proteins, though they can reproduce with aid from host cells.[37] They are not cells, which are, and have, the building blocks of life, but they are remarkable in the ways in which they invade and use cells to reproduce. Viruses cannot think, cannot plan, but their genetic mechanisms of invasion and infection make them seem remarkably *as if* they are living entities. And while Mosley depicts them as "mindless scraps of genetic material, brilliantly adapted by evolution for one purpose: to spread as far and as fast as they can",[38] it is impossible to write about these incredible viruses without using compellingly intelligent descriptors.

Access to cells

Viruses usually have a number of possible routes into the body. The skin is one route, particularly if there is an abrasion or cut exposed to the air. But they also invade the inner body through pathways such as the respiratory tract (the nose and mouth), the genital routes (vagina, penis), or the urinary tract. These areas all have sufficient secretions for viruses to embed themselves, multiply, and spread to other areas of the body – their aim, to infiltrate cells. But attacking cells is not that easy. On the surface of cells are *receptor molecules*, which are just like locks that can only be opened by a chemical with the correct receptor-binding molecular key. And here, viruses manage to produce exactly the right key to unlock a cell, each virus carrying a different key. Once inside a cell the virus gets rid of its outer shell and releases its genes in a specific way in order to reproduce, or *replicate*, its genome by producing multiple copies of it. This is usually done in the nucleus of the cell, utilizing the cell's genome to create the necessary proteins for replication. These replicated copies get out of the cell either by killing it and freeing the thousands of virus particles within, or by altering the host cell and the way it functions. Some viruses create new particle buds on the surface of the cell that will burst and emit the newly-formed virus progeny.[39] The virus is then able to spread through the blood and nerve channels. Viruses also have the ability to transfer from one cell to another destroying or polluting each cell as it travels.

Replication

Viruses have one thing on the mind they do not have and that is to reproduce, to replicate. The whole process of evolution of viruses has made replication more and more effective with poor mutated genes dying out and successful ones surviving. The better they can create disease, the more profitable the replication. But they can only replicate well by hijacking the cells of hosts. And their replication is incredible: just one virus invading a cell can reproduce a thousand viruses in that cell in 24 hours and in a number of cells, thousands more in just a few days. We have to remember that viruses cannot reproduce as cells do by dividing into two (binary fission). They do not grow or have energy, or expel waste, but they are brilliantly designed to reproduce once inside a cell host. They carry their own components ready to combine with the genomes of as many cells as they can as soon as they enter them, and before the immune systems of the hosts kick in. They have to reproduce and get out of the host as quickly as possible, finding a new host before they become inactive in transmission. The sheer rate of replication and production of thousands or millions of new offspring is the reason that viruses are very prone to mutation in the replication process. Some mutations work well and others do not, but if they work well, this is an advantage in spreading the effects. RNA viruses such as HIV are particularly prone to mutations and errors in replication, which makes treatment in the sense of cure impossible.

Reassortment

Sometimes, two similar viruses can combine by what is termed *reassortment*, and is just one way whereby a new virus can be formed. Reassortment happens when two viruses invade a cell at more or less the same time. A host cell is hijacked by one virus to manufacture the necessary matter for its replication and then has another virus to contend with, ending up mixing the two together, shuffling them, and exchanging some of each other's gene segments so that newly formed virus particles will have genetic content from two viruses – a "viral version of sex" as Zimmer terms it.[40] That is what happens with flu viruses. What Zimmer has to say here is important:

A quarter of all birds with the flu have two or more virus strains inside them at once. The viruses swap genes and gain new adaptations, such as the ability to move from living in wild birds to chickens, or even to mammals such as horses or pigs. And sometimes, on very rare occasions, reassortment can combine genes from avian and human viruses, creating a recipe for disaster. The new strain that results from this combination can easily spread from person to person. And because it has never circulated among humans before, no one has any defences that could slow the new strain's spread.[41]

An example here is the human/swine flu that broke out in Mexico in March 2009. Rotaviruses, of which coronaviruses are a good example, change genetically in such a way as to be quite different from the original strain. So someone who becomes immune to the first strain will not be immune after such a genetic shift by gene reassortment has taken place and the nature of the virus has changed: a new virus emerges. Of course, sometimes these genetic shifts will not make much difference to the effect of the virus but at other times the shuffling of genes is radically successful and will permit that new virus to infect widely, leading to an epidemic or pandemic.

Infection and transmission

So once a host cell has been attacked by a virus and the virus has replicated and dispersed its new virus particles, how are they transmitted to other hosts? The precarious existence of a virus outside its host is put rather well by Crawford when she writes, "this is a process that viruses have to leave entirely to chance as their particles are completely inert. Add to this the fact that after infection with a particular virus all vertebrates, and several more primitive organisms, are immune to re-infection, and it seems rather surprising that viruses can survive at all."[42] Some of the genes of the virus will produce proteins to protect the virus particles in the precarious journey from host to host. However, viruses have to attack, infect, replicate and quickly find other appropriate hosts, and they want a *large* group of such hosts. Crawford again: "Given the right conditions a microbe will rip through a population, infecting and perhaps killing until it runs out of people to infect. When all are either dead or recovered and immune to further attack, the microbe will move elsewhere and only return when there are again enough susceptible people to sustain the chain of infection."[43]

Droplet fluids from a host are a very efficient way of transmission of virus particles. One sneeze carries thousands and thousands of them ready to fall on surfaces, on skin, up noses and in throats. Rhinoviruses, the causes of common colds, actually have mechanisms to tickle the nose, causing the host to sneeze and send out its particles. Flu is also transmitted by such droplets. Other virus particles are airborne and are breathed in by new hosts. In many cases, a *vector*, a carrier, is involved in transmission. Malaria bacterial infection, for example, is carried by one type of female mosquito as the vector. And female mosquitos are also the vectors of dengue and yellow fever viruses, sucking infected blood from one host and biting another to transfer the virus there. A virus now mostly eradicated from the world, though only very recently from Africa, is the polio virus that is spread via water. But there are also viruses like the smallpox virus that can actually survive without a host, waiting for a long time for new hosts to come on the scene. Saliva is the medium for transmission of the Epstein-Barr virus, the virus that causes glandular fever, unkindly nicknamed "kissing disease". In some cases viruses contaminate blood – anything from blood used in transfusions to the dentist's drill – to transfer particles from one host to another. Our skin is the most exposed aspect of our bodies but it is covered with layers of dead cells that cannot be used by live-cell-needing viruses. One cut, however, can create exposure of the live cells that viruses need.

One of the most important means of transmission and infection – and very much relevant to coronaviruses – is *zoonotic* means of infection. Zoonotic infections derive from animal sources and will be an important part of the remainder of this chapter and of the chapters relating to Buddhism that follow. All mammals carry zoonotic viruses and many of today's infectious diseases derive from animals, birds and other creatures. Often, the virus in the animal causes it no problem at all but the ways in which we treat and interact with animals today are responsible for the epidemics – and, indeed, the coronavirus pandemic currently besieging us. As Jonathan Quick says about the recent Ebola and Zika viruses, they sometimes kill animals but we do not pay that any attention until they pass to humans who eat infected meat or who are bitten by vectors. He has these stark words to say on this point: "The Ebola, AIDS, and Zika epidemics have much to teach us about the ways viruses from the African jungle – combined with human lassitude, denial, and ignorance – can unleash hell on an unprepared world."[44] And I think it is worth citing Quick's experienced words concerning the ways in which so many people get their protein:

> In the poor villages of the steamy, massive West African rainforest, you can't sit down in a restaurant and order a juicy, USDA-inspected filet mignon. You're lucky to get chicken or goats stew. But there isn't

much of that kind of meat to go around, so the next-best source of animal protein is bushmeat. If you're lucky you can occasionally bag monkeys or squirrels; otherwise, you can hunt down a colony of bats that have migrated from deep parts of the jungle. You can chop up the bat meat, mix it with some root vegetables, and stir it into a spicy stew. Otherwise, you can pick up bat meat from a market vendor who roasts the animal over an open fire, the smell of the meat mingling with that of burnt fur."[45]

The outbreak of the Ebola virus began with these practices and this is a classic case of just how zoonotic viruses begin in the animal world and are transmitted to humans mostly through appalling treatment of animals. And as Quick points out in his remarkable book: "Mammals of all kinds are a happy host for zoonotic pathogens. Since the year 2000, 75 percent of new human infectious diseases have originated in animals, the majority of these from wildlife."[46]

The usual route of a zoonotic virus is from bird > pig > human where a genetic shift in the virus enables it to cross a species. China has a particularly bad profile here since the three species of the triangle live so closely together and, as we shall see in later chapters, conditions for animals are so horrendous that the crossing of a virus to another host species is inevitable. Birds, especially waterfowl, carry the different types of flu virus in all kinds of combinations of flu 15 HA and 9 NA. Thus, as Crawford says: "So birds act as the melting pot, throwing up large numbers of different flu strains which are excreted in profusion in their droppings."[47] The birds (usually ducks in China), act as factories for the reassortment of genes. As Crawford explains, only a few of these viruses can infect humans directly but their droppings are eaten up by pigs who are hosts for both pig flu and human flu. If both of these virus flus, pig and human combine, reassert their genes, then passage to humans for a new strain of flu is set up for the virus. Crawford points out that the 1957 Asian flu pandemic resulted from a human virus mixed with three bird virus genes, and the Hong Kong flu pandemic had a human virus mixed with two bird viruses.[48] There is also a possibility that the great flu pandemic of 1918, the so-called "Spanish flu", was a pig > human direct transmission.[49] More certainly, the 1997 outbreak of a new H5N1 flu virus killed hundreds of chickens in Hong Kong, and infected humans: there was no piggy in the middle.[50]

The other zoonotic source of viruses is bats, and reading Quick's graphic account of their cooking and ingestion does not lead to wild imaginative thought to see their obvious possibility to infect. Human activity has long invaded the territory of bats so it is no surprise that the viruses they carry have passed to humans. Quick's quotation above very graphically illustrates this, and bats here were the source of the Ebola viral outbreak. In fact, humans give viruses exactly what they need, new situations in which they can spread, reassort, and wreak havoc in a new kind of host. And new hosts have nothing in their immunological arsenal with which to fight a new virus hence, if a virus reaches a new, virgin community, it will decimate the population.

Symbiosis of virus and host

Viruses are symbiotic partners in our existence. Like us, they have had to evolve genetically and battle to survive against all kinds of odds. There are many occasions when that survival has resulted in a permanent relationship with us as their hosts that is beneficial for both virus and human – a true *symbiotic* relationship. This symbiosis between host and its viral environment is termed the *holobiant*. Animal and human health is often dependent on the functional dependency between the two reflecting their joint evolution and the sharing of environmental resources – namely, each other's genomes. It is surprising how many bodily functioning processes *need* viral assistance to avoid disease. There are even instances of *symbiogenetic relationships* whereby genes of both are fused for mutual evolution whether in microbes, insects, plants or mammals. Sometimes such fusion can create a new species. It must have been at a very early stage of the evolution of life that parasitic microbes found a home in hosts. Crawford gives the example of cows here: "On occasion, a comfortable symbiotic relationship developed, like, for example, the microbial communities that form self-sustaining ecosystems in the guts of their hosts. For ruminants such as cows the advantages of this partnership are obvious; the microbes are bathed in nutrients and protected from the outside world while they digest the cellulose in plant walls which cattle are unable to do for themselves."[51] The inhabitants of the guts of cows, as much as our own, are more bacterial than viral, but the latter are also there as part of the community of microbes.

Viruses are, therefore, part of the evolutionary backdrop that, through the mixing of genes with their hosts, have been an enormous aid in generating the rich diversity of life on this planet – diversity of bacteria, plants, insects, and animals, often being beneficial friends of their hosts, especially since they force cells to develop differently and evolve. Their continued presence in all species is essential. The retrovirus ERV-L (or HERV-W), for example, originates and exists endogenously, internally, in mammals and provides the gene for the protein syncytin for the production of their placentas. The protein makes a barrier of cells in the outer layer of the placenta that stops the foetus being rejected by the immune system of the mother. Viruses are also able to restore normality through modulating bodily processes that have become partially dysfunctional. In the world of insects their activities regulate the ecosystems of species, and the effects of other microbes and pests relating to plants. Viruses that use bacterial hosts in our bodies actually encourage the growth of *good* bacteria, giving those bacteria the edge over unwanted bacteria. So rather than think of viruses as deadly enemies and disease-causing agents, they do a lot of good.

In a remarkable statement, Durzyńska and Gózdzicka-Józefiat state: "Therefore, the real question is whether viruses and their hosts may form a symbiotic relationship that can increase the fitness of the whole organism within a large-enough evolutionary frame. In other words, we can ask, for example, if the virus host symbiont could invade a population of virus-free hosts because of the advantages that the virus provides to its hosts."[52] This is, indeed, an interesting remark that turns a virus from an enemy to a remarkable friend. In host cells, viruses can influence the stimulation of the immune system against another invading virus. While two viruses invading a cell about the same time can reassort, a long-term symbiotic relation between host cells and virus could actually inhibit the invasion of another virus.

The residues of past viruses are embedded in human chromosomes, many inactive but some appear to have been active for more than tens of millions of years.[53] Others do not resemble any known viruses, as the 90 percent of viruses found in healthy humans' lungs.[54] In the long process of evolution of viruses and their hosts the body has had to battle against the effects of viruses, and viruses, for their part, have had to withstand attacks of the immune systems of the body. This constant tug-of-war strengthened both, refining them through mutations and gleaning advantages from natural selection and the survival of the fittest. Herpes viruses are a good example here and were here long, long before the advent of primates, over 220 million years ago.[55] We would not have the efficient immune systems we have today were it not for the incessant tug-of-war between viruses and the bodies of our ancestors. In all aspects of life, viruses have the capabilities of transferring DNA between host cells, and that sometimes helps the host to adapt to a new environment. Over hundreds of years peoples have built up resistances to long-standing viruses, so minimizing the severity of infections they cause. In all, most viruses have little or no effect on us at all: we provide shelter and food for them, keep them safe, and the intimate relationship is generally not harmful, especially if the host is healthy, though that friendly nature is not guaranteed for the life of the host. But persistent symbiotic viruses actually protect a host by infecting other species that are a threat to the host. Indeed, one of the main reasons why a harmless, symbiotic virus in an animal host will spread to other species is that it acts as a means of protection for the animal: Hanta and Lassa viruses have performed this function. If we do not interfere with the animal ecosystem, parasitic viruses within them will cause little harm. Of the multitude of viruses that travel with us in our bodies, Wills writes: "They spend most of their time minding their own business, dining off what they can get, and keeping a commendably low profile. Most of these parasites trouble us very little and go to uncounted and unrecorded graves by the trillion."[56] So rather than the immune system disposing of these harmless viruses, it seems to take no notice, but that is probably because the viruses have evolved ways to hide themselves from the immune system of the host over the countless years that viruses and hosts have evolved together: the symbiotic balance between the two has been sophisticated to the extent that both can live with each other, sharing their genes and the cell products necessary for them both to exist.

Viral friends

The symbiosis between viruses and their hosts is expressive of how necessary both have been for the evolution of the other. We would not be here today if our ancestors had not used some of the virus DNA to adapt and survive. When we consider the endogenous retroviruses that produce the protein syncytin for mammalian placentas the fact is staggering. Zimmer puts this starkly: "Over 100 million years ago, an ancestral mammal was infected by an endogenous retrovirus. It harnessed the original syncytin protein, and evolved the very first placenta. Over the course of millions of years, that original placental mammal gave rise to many lineages of descendants."[57] Common colds have been evolving with us for centuries. They are a nuisance but not usually serious. Caused by different strains of rhinoviruses that all share core genes, but that mutate quickly, the cold may, in fact be a friend in that, as Zimmer puts it: "Human rhinoviruses may help train our immune systems not to overreact to minor triggers, instead directing their assaults to real threats. Perhaps we should not think of colds as ancient enemies but as wise old tutors."[58]

Inside our bodies are millions of bacteria, some good, and some damaging to the body. As I mentioned above, some viruses are *bacteriophages*, or just *phages*, from the Greek "to devour": they are viruses that eat up and destroy harmful bacteria. There are millions of these in what we eat, as well as in our bodies. Without the phages our bodies would be plagued by harmful bacteria. Marine bacteria are also controlled by marine phages; as many as 70 percent of marine bacteria are infected with them. In seawater they have an important role in crossing genes from one bacteria to another, but also in controlling the number of bacteria, which have considerable benefits for the marine ecosystem. If, as Crawford says, 10 percent of all the photosynthesis, so important for the production of oxygen on Earth, is produced by viruses: "Breathe ten times, and one of those breaths comes to you courtesy of a virus."[59] In all, we should not consider viruses as totally harmful. They have given us life and helped us to survive. As Zimmer puts it: "There is no us and them – just a gradually blending and shifting mix of DNA."[60]

Viral enemies and their causes

We have now seen that viruses have been around for far longer than we mortals have and that, when our primate and human ancestors evolved, viruses evolved alongside us for tens of millions of years, challengingly but also often symbiotically. We know, too, that transitions in human life-styles, particularly concerning interactions with animals and increasingly compacted and unsanitary existences, gave viruses all they needed to multiply and spread. Some have been very old enemies: the ancient Egyptians, for example, suffered from colds, the rhinoviruses. Many viruses stay hidden, latently waiting for the right time to reactivate in new hosts. They manage to avoid the immune system and may live a long, long time in their hosts, often with a fairly stable relationship. And while some are harmless, others are the pathogens, the causes of diseases that kill and bring immense suffering. Looking at statistics mainly for the twentieth century, but also onwards, deaths from viruses are incredibly high:

- **Smallpox** at least 300 million in the twentieth century.
- **AIDS** 35 million by 2015 and 78 million infected globally; 700,000 die each year.
- **Influenza** 500 million [**Asian** 2 million; **Hong Kong** 1 million; **avian HPAI** [2003 and 2016] kills 50% of those it infects; **Spanish** 50 million and half a billion infected; **swine** 575,400.
- **Ebola** 11,325
- **Lassa** fever 5,000–10,000 deaths annually
- **Measles** 8 million in 1970, 134,000 in 2015 and 70,000 in

countries today where the vaccine is not taken up. 20.3 million deaths have currently been avoided due to vaccination.
- **SARS** 8,000 cases and 800 deaths in the first four years of the twenty-first century.
- **MERS** 1,917 infected, of which approximately 36 percent died.

So let us have a look at some of these viruses and establish how far humans, like their early ancestors, are the causes of their own suffering through viruses.

Smallpox

Oldstone comments that smallpox is interwoven with human migrations, particularly throughout wars.[61] It infected human beings as long as 5,000 years ago and killed 30 percent of those who caught it. But Oldstone thinks this *variola* virus is even older, infecting early agricultural settlements as long ago as 10,000 BCE.[62] The hideous scarring created by the virus means it can be traced archaeologically on, for example, Egyptian mummies. Smallpox could destroy large sectors of communities, killing and disfiguring double the number of people in the twentieth century than its wars, including World Wars I and II.[63] Its source was animals. It probably jumped from domestic animals to humans more than 5,000 years ago. It used to be thought that smallpox was related to cowpox, but it seems the virus is better matched with the pox viruses of camels and gerbils. It is now thought to have originated from a pox virus in rodents in that period 5,000 to 10,000 years ago when humans began to live a more settled farming existence,[64] jumping from rodents to camels and humans. Human interaction with animals, then, is the prime cause of its origins. As an airborne-spreading virus, inhaling the virus through mouth or nose is the means of easy infection. 90 percent of the Aztecs and Incas were wiped out when this devastating smallpox was brought to them by travelling Europeans.[65] And in Central America, smallpox killed 90 percent of the natives after the arrival of the Spanish conquerors. The spread of smallpox was no different in origin than when it began thousands of years ago. Humans gave it its impetus with urban overcrowding, filth and poverty, particularly in the late eighteenth and nineteenth centuries. In 1980, the World Health Organization (WHO) declared smallpox to be totally eradicated in the world. Could it return? Yes, it certainly could as a biochemical weapon, and since the virus has been long gone for most of us, our immune systems would have no memory of it. Russian and American laboratories have covert stores of smallpox, and overt stores for research. Considering how

Russian experiments at one time were combining smallpox with Ebola, we have much to fear.

Measles

Measles is a retrovirus with RNA genes as opposed to DNA ones. It has been around for about 2,000 years. It has a virulent spread to about 90 percent of all with whom it comes into contact, and its RNA genome means it mutates much faster than its DNA counterparts. It may have an ancient ancestry because its closest parallel virus is the rinderpest virus, which causes plagues in cattle. This probably suggests, again, an animal source originally infecting humans when they came closer to their domesticated cattle in the early period of settled agriculture over 5,000 years ago. But 2,000 years ago, it looks as if a common ancestor existed that was the source of today's strain of rinderpest and of the present superior and more virulent virus of measles. But earlier strains of measles were around much, much earlier, when sizable towns grew up of about 500,000 inhabitants. This, according to Crawford, is about the right-sized community for measles to circulate well: "The first towns of this size evolved around 5000 BC in the Fertile Crescent, and so from this time onwards, viruses like measles could break the link with their animal hosts to become entirely human pathogens."[66] Again, we have human changes in lifestyles to town living with dense populations and animal proximity. Measles is another airborne virus, with droplets being carried by coughing and sneezing, and even just by talking, the droplets reaching cells in the nose, mouth, throat and eyes. Just one individual can infect fifteen others. Those who have had measles are protected from the virus for the remainder of their lives and that is why just one vaccine works. This is a horrific disease that can result in brain infection, severe brain damage and seizures.

Rhinoviruses

We are all familiar with the nuisance of the "common" (as it is called) cold for which there is no real cure. It is a nuisance but rare to die of it. The old rhyme, "coughs and sneezes spread diseases" is more than apt with the current coronavirus pandemic and the importance of everyone protecting others by remembering this old slogan. There are as many as several hundred viruses that cause colds, not just the 100–150 types of rhinovirus, for many other viruses cause cold symptoms.[67] One set happens to be coronaviruses – NL63, HKU1, OC43 and 229E – that do not cause severe illness. The last of these, HCoV-229E, has close genomes with the MERS coronavirus that I shall explore below. This cold-causing coronavirus originated in camels just like MERS. But other cold viruses were crossed to humans from birds about two hundred years ago. Again, the cold virus is another zoonotic infection. Having invaded the body via the nose the rhinovirus has evolved to the extent that it can actually tickle the nose and force a sneeze, sending out a massive number of infected droplets of daughter viruses not only far, but also widely, to take up residence in the cells of other noses, or on surfaces ready to be picked up on the skin and transferred to noses. They also cause the throat to be inflamed and produce more mucus-laden virus ready to be coughed out. Viruses causing the common cold have mutated sophistically enough that no vaccine could ever really be effective against them: there are simply too many strains, too many rapid mutations, and our immune systems could never identify them all or the new strains they throw up. Most of us do not give up working because of a cold; children continue at school; people travel on public transport; the cold virus being a mild infection supports its own easy spread.

Influenza

There are three flu strains, A, B and C and the A strain is the only one that is a zoonotic virus and one that will return again and again, very possibly as a pandemic. The A virus, apart from infecting humans, also infects many birds, seals, horses and pigs. It is found in wild and domestic birds, especially water birds like gulls, terns, ducks and geese. Domestic birds such as chickens, turkeys, pheasants and quails also carry the virus. And pigs are, once again, another medium for viral mix.[68] Quick describes this cunning virus rather well when he writes: "Like HIV, influenza is sneaky. It lies hidden; it's easy to underestimate; it's devilishly mercurial' it's uncontrollable; and it's impossible to eliminate. The flu virus changes so fast that it outraces scientists' ability to develop potent vaccines against it."[69] The word "influenza" comes from the Italian for "influence", with reference to the influence of the stars: it is a word that has now been respectably shortened to flu. Flus are designated according to the balances of the proteins *hemagglutinin*, H, and *neuraminidase*, N, on the surface of the virus particles. Every single genome of a flu outbreak exists in birds, and there are flu viruses waiting in the wings that have not infected humans yet. Working with poultry on farms and in markets is the source of the jump from bird to human, and management of global animal markets has a lot to answer for in causing outbreaks and deaths from flu, as we shall see in later chapters. The Chinese are easily the main culprits here with their longstanding domestication of water fowl reaching back many thousands of years. Again and again since then, the flu viruses have jumped to humans. Contemporary footage of bird species in Chinese markets with creatures packed together in squalid conditions for Chinese to buy live for cooking is upsetting to view. In these conditions there are so many opportunities for mixing of gene viruses across these domestic birds, particularly through their droppings, and the inevitable passing of that new virus to other animals – horses, and pigs that eat the droppings, as well as humans.

I shall return to these points in later chapters. Suffice it to say here that new strains of flu are produced in the gene-swapping arena of creature markets, when different strains of viruses are mixed; strains of which our immune systems know nothing, so providing new flu viruses with virgin territory for infection. In addition, challenging mutations increase the number of hitherto unknown new strains. Crawford gives interesting statistics here that exemplify well the gene swapping that occurs: "Over the last one hundred years, there have been five flu pandemics: in the H_1N_1 Spanish flu of 1918, all eight genes came from birds; the H_2N_2 'Asian' flu of 1957 acquired three new genes, including H and N from birds; and the H_3N_2 'Hong Kong' flu of 1968 acquired two new genes from wild ducks."[70] So the flu virus is able to change its genetic profile very frequently, something called *antigenic shift* or *drift*: in one year, that may mean drifting two or three times every year, creating a new virus strain and necessitating a new vaccine. Many scientists have always felt that a new strain of flu would be the next highly serious pandemic; no one knew what Covid-19 was going to bring. After all, flu pandemics seem to occur fairly regularly – three times in the last century – but with a sufficient gap between pandemics for a large number of the population not to have any immunity.

The flu pandemic that stands out as memorable, was the "Spanish" flu of 1918–19 and it was global. It was a strain of H_1N_1 proteins. The name "Spanish" has nothing to do with the origin of the flu, but because Spain could enjoy uncensored journalism as a neutral country in World War I, it reported widely on the disease and its effects. It seems the virus was circulating in the terrible conditions of World War I, in the trenches, and amongst the armies, and after the war, servicemen took the virus back to their homelands and to celebrations with massive groupings of people. The flu killed more than all those who died in the war, especially teenagers and young adults. It seems the particular mixture of genetic drift in the 1918 virus was especially potent and virulent. What is more, the 1918 flu appears to have been the ancestor of four subsequent human and swine flu virus strains. Swine flu is, like Spanish flu, an H_1N_1 strain started by what Quick aptly calls "animal kitchen chemistry",[71] whereby the guts of pigs provide the mixing bowls for the droppings of infected chicken or wild birds, adding a few other genes in the process. I shall be examining the Concentrated Animal Feeding Operations conglomerate in chapter 4 where profit far outstrips animal welfare and how it contributed to swine flu and other potential virus infections. In following the swine flu outbreaks, scientists have found that gene reassortment had happened in each case. Pigs herded together in large enclosed barns were the melting pots for gene mixing.

Bird flu, the H_5N_1 virus was first found in chickens but mutated to become a virulent virus, first jumping to humans in Hong Kong, killing more than half the people it infected, but only those working with poultry. It is an example of a zoonotic virus that could, one day, become a highly human to human pathogenic. The source was, again, China, with its cramped conditions in which birds were kept. And now there are other mutated bird flu viruses, H_5 but with unknown N. As Crawford says: "Their transmissibility to humans is low, but the threat of a human pandemic remains as a genetic drift or shift could at any time generate a human transmissible virus."[72]

Chickenpox and shingles

The *varicella zoster* virus, or VZV is one that likes to hide in the system of the host, tucked away in the nerve cells as persistent or latent. At the first infection, it causes chickenpox and then retreats to the nerve cells usually for decades. The infected body is immune from chickenpox throughout life, but the virus sometimes quits its nerve-cell home and causes a skin infection nearby. That infection is *shingles* or *herpes zoster* and the rash it causes follows a line of nerves. The Greek meaning of herpes is to creep like a snake, as does the rash in a clear wavy line of nerves, and zoster is the Greek for "belt", since the shingles rash sometimes encircles the body. The painful tiny blisters caused by the rash are packed with the virus, ready to break and infect anyone who has not had chickenpox, but shingles itself cannot infect another person to pass on shingles. Both chickenpox and shingles belong to the *herpes virus* group of viruses that cause genital sores and cold sores. Herpes virus is exceptionally ancient and is found in remote tribes all over the world, suggestive that the earliest tribal hunter-gatherers must also have succumbed to it in some form or another. The viruses may even be around 400 million years old, present when the first creatures left the seas for the land.[73] Nearly every creature since has some mixture of herpes viruses. Chicken pox and shingles are not zoonotic diseases, though it seems to infect some apes and gorillas. Given that these are ancient and mild diseases, it may be relevant that they are not zoonotic, suggestive possibly that those that are zoonotic infect more potently.

Papilloma virus

The papilloma viruses are very common and have over a hundred different types. They cause warts and verrucae, but some are also the cause of cervical cancers. These viruses too, are ancient, even more so than the herpes virus group, because they infect so many species – mammals, vertebrates, birds and reptiles. In fact, the viruses could be as ancient as 300 million years, present when vertebrates first crawled onto land to lay eggs, and evolved with the different branches of species thereafter, existing symbiotically with their hosts down the centuries and millennia.[74] While for a minority some strains of papilloma virus develop into cervical cancer, now treatable by vaccination, these ancient viruses are mainly harmless. They like to be latent in the stem cells in the inner part of the skin reproducing alongside the DNA of the cells. As the cells gradually move up to the surface of the skin and die, they carry the viruses ready to be dispersed on the outside of the skin.

Yellow fever

Yellow fever is an arbovirus, one spread by flying insects, and is indigenous to Africa and South America. Female mosquitoes are the vectors, sucking infected blood from one host – monkey or human – giving the virus scope for reproduction in the mosquito ready to be passed to a new host when the mosquito bites elsewhere. Crawford notes how climate change has affected the increase of these vector mosquitoes in that warmer and wetter climates have enabled them to extend their territories.[75] Such human-made global warming is having its effect on yellow fever. In West Africa, the source for yellow fever is monkeys, who carry the virus symbiotically and therefore harmlessly. These monkeys live normally in the tree canopies along with mosquitoes that is, until jungle deforestation began to disturb the habitats of both monkeys and mosquitoes creating the damp conditions for the latter to breed more. Those who worked in the jungles clearing the trees were highly susceptible to virus-laden bites from the mosquitoes. So Africa was the home and provenance of yellow fever, but it probably arrived in South America through mosquitoes carried on slave ships – the mosquitoes keeping the virus safe and well, multiplying in their guts – as well as with the African slaves transported on the ships. Many black Africans today have had such a long relationship with the virus that it only presents in mild symptoms or, even if more severe, they recover. But for Native Americans and Caucasians who have not lived so many generations with the virus, yellow fever can be fatal, producing the yellow skin from liver jaundice from which the virus gets its name.

Zika virus

Another virus with the same insect mosquito vector of yellow fever is the Zika virus, named after the Zika forest where it originated in Uganda. And again, the cycle here was monkey > mosquito > monkey, and occasionally human, but by 2007, it spread rapidly to humans and to the Caribbean, the Pacific Islands, South America, Colombia, Venezuela, and particularly Brazil. While not being fatal, the virus had the ability to pass through the placenta of pregnant women and affect the development of a foetus, so causing birth defects, in particular, microcephaly, a characteristic small head. Even males once infected with the virus can pass it to women in their semen. It is highly likely that global warming with temperatures in these countries reaching all-time highs provided the perfect conditions for an increase of the virus-carrying mosquito, the *Aedes aegypti*.

HIV/AIDS

If we wanted a classic example of a zoonotic virus that has been caused by bad human intervention in the world of animals, HIV (*human immunodeficiency syndrome*) is certainly the most obvious. It emerged in the 1980s as an incredibly powerful and complex virus, an awesome killer that could affect the whole system of its host, though it may have been present as early as the 1930s. It is a maleficent, silent virus with a long, long period of incubation so that it remains latent and unrecognisable with any symptoms. Crawford's words here are stark for she says it was "aided by despotic leaders, corrupt governments, civil wars, tribal conflicts, droughts and famines. Carried by undisciplined armies and terrorists, the virus infiltrated city slums, infected commercial sex workers, was picked up by migrant workers and passed on to their wives and families. While malnutrition accelerated the onset of AIDS (*acquired immune deficiency syndrome*), breakdown of healthcare services in the political turmoil of Africa excluded any possibility of medical support for the millions in need."[76]

This incredible virus is ultra-elusive, capable of hiding in the body without detection by the immune system, and at the same time replicating at an enormous speed and mutating frequently to make new proteins that sustain it and evade the immune system. HIV viruses are retroviruses carrying RNA as opposed to DNA. There are two basic HIV viruses that are fairly distinct from each other with clearly different genomes: they are HIV-$_1$ and HIV-$_2$. They have become distinct through the phenomenal speed at which they evolved. Oldstone comments aptly that: "Compared with the genes of our chromosomes, all these retroviruses seem to be in a kind of evolutionary overdrive."[77] And AIDS viruses do not have to wait until the hosts' cells divide to get into them, they can insert copies of themselves into cells that are not dividing. These are viruses that can outwit and dismantle the immune systems of their hosts. That is why HIV is a *human immunodeficiency virus*, a virus that silently increases in the body of the host as it battles with the immune system's antibodies and T-cells, especially CD$_4$ T-cells. T-cells are produced on a huge scale in our bodies all throughout life and are the body's major tool for counteracting foreign bodies. But the HIV virus is continually eating away at the body's defence systems and all the time mutating in ways that improve that process. The host has no symptoms for perhaps a decade or more. Then, HIV morphs into *acquired immunodeficiency syndrome*, AIDS: the CD$_4$ cells run out of steam – indeed, run out – the immune system collapses and death follows.

Fortunately in today's world there are antiviral drugs that can be introduced at the HIV stage – hence the importance of early testing for the disease – and these prevent or delay the progression to AIDS. But even AIDS is now not the killer it was with antiretroviral drugs available – that is, if the sufferer happens to be in a position to receive the treatment. In poorer areas of Africa, few are ever relieved of the death sentence that HIV/AIDS brings. There are more than 75–78 million individuals infected globally with an HIV virus: most of these individuals – 70 percent – are in southern Africa. But wherever the virus is, it will target underprivileged areas of the world and those poorer and socially marginalized in societies. So when and how did it begin? HIV was probably around at the turn of the last century, since scientists have traced back two HIV-$_1$ viruses, group M (the major one) and group O (there are also two other rare groups, N and P), to the early 1900s, but it was not until 1983 that it was first identified for the virus that it is. Its origins are clearly African for chimpanzees there carried HIV-$_1$ viruses widely without much risk to themselves. But at some time the chimps must have passed the viruses to gorillas. When apes were killed for their meat, no doubt the virus passed to humans also but in the early twentieth century there was little travel outside villages and the virus was not able to spread to any effect. These viruses were identified as *simian immunodeficiency viruses*, SIVs, retroviruses that were common to primates and must have passed widely through the ape species and occasionally to humans. When migrations of people from villages to towns gradually increased, the viruses had their necessary increased numbers of hosts, mutating rapidly as they infected more and more. The pattern is so reminiscent of the hunter-gatherer migrations to settled dwelling and onwards. We now know that it was the chimpanzee SIV HIV-$_1$ M group, and the gorilla HIV-$_1$ O group, that passed to humans. HIV-$_1$ has spread throughout the world leaving HIV-$_2$ to infect West Africans, probably originally from sooty mangabey monkeys. But it is in Central Africa that nearly all the different strains of HIV are to be found.

HIV and AIDS have had a massively detrimental effect on Africa. Wills puts this very starkly, I think:

> AIDS has stabbed at the very heart of the poorest countries in Africa and Asia, causing the potentially most productive members of these societies to be struck down in their middle years and paralysing these countries' already inadequate health care systems. There is no doubt that the disruption and fatalistic carelessness that is engendered by the high probability of dying of AIDS has contributed to the virtually complete societal breakdown in war-torn countries like Uganda, Rwanda and Somalia. It is difficult for most of us to imagine living in a country in which a large fraction of the population, very likely including ourselves, will be doomed to die young from a wasting disease. In such a society it is not possible to see a future.[78]

SIV retroviruses have probably co-evolved with primates over many centuries. The problem is that once they pass to humans they change and wreak havoc on the human immune system. The characteristic of retroviruses being latent for a long time during replication is the killer aspect. They are clever, using the special enzyme *reverse transcriptase* to make copies of themselves in the DNA of the cells they invade. The reverse aspect comes in because the usual DNA > RNA flow is reversed to RNA > DNA so that the cell is recognized as normal. Every time the host cell divides, so does the virus. The virus uses the new DNA in this way to replicate itself again and again, and it is during this replication process that the virus is latent, just reproducing itself and remaining invisible to the immune system.[79] In fact, the HIV virus replicates so quickly it makes trillions of copies of itself each *day*. Every time a cell divides in the body it is reproducing more copies of the virus to infect other cells. And it is always ahead of any responses of the immune system because it throws out new forms of itself again and again, mainly because, with so many rapid replications, the chances of mistakes, mutations, are very high indeed, even in its primate sources. That makes the virus very difficult to overcome once humans are infected.

The interaction between humans and primates is ongoing in Africa. Crawford says that between one and five million tons of "bushmeat" is consumed in the Congo alone.[80] And HIV viruses will not be the only viruses carried by the butchered animals. The viruses are transmitted by blood and semen, so those engaging in killing primates are at risk of infection. Transfusion of blood from an infected person to another is also a means of spread for the virus. It can also be passed from pregnant mother to baby in the womb. But the main source of infection is through semen. Repeated unprotected sex is risky, whether that is heterosexual or homosexual, and it has to be remembered that the virus lays hidden and latent in the body for a decade or so. I said it is clever: its ability to infect others while it is latent is the key to its survival and an individual who looks and feels perfectly healthy may be HIV positive. *But*, HIV does not have a virulent transmission rate in comparison to other viruses such as measles. In fact, Oldstone puts the infection transmission rate as low as less than 5 percent,[81] yet about 50,000 Americans, for example, contract the virus every year. No vaccine is available for HIV though there are antiviral drugs at the HIV stage – if it is discovered, and financial constraints mean they are unavailable for many: HIV is permanent in the body and treatment for those who can get it, is lifelong. It is a travesty that there is still a stigma about HIV/AIDS for that prevents any hope of limiting its spread by preventive measures. At least people with the virus are living longer and with fewer symptoms because antiretroviral drugs, especially protease inhibitors, are targeting parts of the virus' cycle, though the drugs are lethally expensive: at least deaths from HIV have been reduced by over 67 percent.[82] And yet, HIV resistance is a big issue given the rapid mutation of this particular virus. It is unremarkable that treatment is mainly confined to the West: for the poorer societies in poorer countries, there is no hope of treatment, and the words of Wills above are sadly very pertinent. Some fortunate gay men, female sex workers and one percent of the population in the world carry a gene that protects them from infection and have immunity.[83]

Ebola

Another RNA virus, Ebola, named after the local African river, broke out in 1976 in the Democratic Republic of Congo, Zaire as it was then. Then, in 2014, it broke out in Guinea, West Africa, from where it spread to Sierra Leone and to Liberia, becoming an epidemic. But then it spread to Mali, Nigeria, Senegal, and beyond Africa to the USA, the UK, Italy, and to Spain. 40 percent of those who were infected died. Ebola is easily spread because it is passed in any fluid of the body – blood, urine, faeces, vomit, saliva, semen, and even breast milk. And since the virus causes bleeding with a haemorrhagic fever, vomiting and diarrhoea, it is spread to anyone in contact with an infected person. The virus has evolved to produce exactly the symptoms that can help it to spread. Ebola is probably a zoonotic virus originating in bats, though research here is ongoing. But something passed this dangerous retrovirus to humans. It is so virulent that it is even more potent in a deceased body so caring for the sick, and the deceased rites that follow death, serve to spread the infection. What is devastating about Ebola is that it remains hidden in the body even after someone has recovered. It can affect the eyes or the brain but, as a hidden and cunning virus it stays in the male genital tract ready to infect any woman with whom an infected male has intercourse. The Ebola virus kills its host in a short time, short enough to create epidemics, but since direct contact is necessary, if recognized for the virus it is, can be overcome through isolation of the infected individuals. Nevertheless, Ebola is a patient virus that can lie quietly in wait for the opportunity to infect and spread.

Lassa Fever

The zoonotic carrier of the Lassa virus is the African brown rat or, rather, the mutimammate mouse (*Mastomys natalensis*) found in the villages and towns of southern Africa. The virus does not cause the rats any harm, but when the rats excrete or urinate the virus close to humans, especially when they move into buildings in the rainy season, infections break out frequently. The virus may cause just mild symptoms for many, but about 15–20 percent die of the disease and it is lethal for unborn foetuses, as well as for women in the third trimester of pregnancy. But the virus does not die in its animal host: it has a good symbiotic relationship with the rodents who carry it.

Hanta viruses

The USA is home to Hanta viruses that, like Ebola, cause a haemorrhagic fever. These RNA viruses may be old ones and probably originated in Korea but, apart from the USA, Hanta virus has been found in Japan, Scandinavia and Russia, as well as in Europe. Again, Hanta viruses are zoonotic, their host being mainly the deer mouse (*Peromyscus maniculatus*), but they have been found also in other types of rodents. As RNA viruses, the rate of replication and associated mutation is remarkably high, so this is a virus to watch.

Creutzfeldt-Jakob disease (CJD)

Creutzfeldt-Jakob disease is better known as mad cow disease and I am including it here because it will be highly relevant in chapter 4. Mad cow disease began with cows and passed to humans: in either species, it destroys brain cells, memory, neurons, personality, and causes dementia, hallucinations (hence the "mad" label) and seizures. In cows it turned their brains into sponges leading to what has been termed *bovine spongiform encephalopathy* or BSE. With real justification, I think, Quick calls this disease that hit the UK in the 1980s "the first man-made epidemic" and a "Frankenstein disease."[84] We know that cows are herbivores and definitely not carnivores and yet, in an act of perplexing stupidity that is hardly credible, some complete idiot came up with a protein for cows made from deceased cattle, using their meat and bone meal – MBM as it was called. Sheep suffer from a disease called "scrapie", so called because they shake, lose balance, and rub their flanks on whatever they can find to ease itching. The dead sheep that were used to produce MBM made the transmission of scrapie from sheep to cattle inevitable. Quick writes: "Feeding MBM to herbivorous cattle effectively turned them into carnivores, to horrific and unforeseeable effect. That change in cattle feeding habits allowed an age-old animal pathogen to enter the human food chain."[85] And this was another virus that had a long incubation period so it was not until 1996 that the virus raised its lethal head in overt human disease, long after MBM was being used widely. Human stupidity was at the heart of this disease: indeed, what I have tried to show by including all these viruses is that human behaviour lies at the centre of their emergence and spread. There are so many times when it seems we have not travelled much further than did hunter-gatherers in the move to socially closer encounters. But I must now come close to home and, bearing in mind what I have said in relation to viruses, present some insight into our present threat of the new coronavirus.

Coronaviruses

While we know that the present pandemic of 2020 is coronavirus, it is more correctly *a* coronavirus for there are other coronaviruses that infect humans with the common cold, for example, as well as animals, especially camels, bats and cats. These are probably the earlier zoonotic carriers of the viruses that jumped across to the human being in the recent past. Humans infected with coronavirus colds were first identified in the 1960s. Interestingly in terms of immunity today, those who picked up the 229E coronavirus cold of the 1960's were no longer immune to it two years later. Four of such coronavirus colds have now been identified, two seem to have emerged from bats, and two from rodents. They cause only mild symptoms much as other colds. The main symptoms of these coronaviruses are respiratory infections – as we know from the present virus – and also gastrointestinal symptoms that are also present in some of those infected by Covid-19. Coronaviruses are RNA viruses and their genomes contain more RNA than any other RNA virus, genomes designed to infect and be carried symbiotically by certain animals for hundreds of millions of years. From all that we have seen above about the jump of viruses to humans, it would have to be claimed that it is usually human interference in the natural environments of creatures that has provided the basis for the cross-species infection. As we shall see, this, indeed, is the reason why we have the present pandemic of a virulent and often lethal virus: we humans created its causes and are responsible for the suffering it brings. Aside from the mild coronaviruses that create colds three are much more serious – SARS, MERS, and our present Covid-19.

SARS

Severe acute respiratory syndrome, SARS, is a more lethal member of the coronavirus family of viruses labelled SARS-CoV. Coronaviruses have projections like spikes protruding from their outer surface giving the effect of a "corona", a crown. The SARS virus probably jumped from animals to humans a number of times, and the provenance here was China, with the first identifiable outbreak there in 2002–3, in Guangdong, southern China. Its source were the animal markets where live animals were kept in cages in the most appalling conditions ready for someone to buy, have the creature slaughtered and dismembered, to be taken home and cooked. These horrendous markets are a hive of humans and animals, incredibly unhygienic and teeming with all sorts of microbial matter. Analysis of the virus identified it as a coronavirus but uniquely comparable to the RNA genomes of masked palm civets in the animal markets. Civets resemble cats, and are kept live in the same cramped conditions as other animals ready for sale/slaughter/dismemberment to be taken home raw for cooking. Then SARS broke out again in 2003–4, though China's political shenanigans are probably the reason that infections were not, in fact, completely under control with the earlier outbreak.[86] Fortunately, the World Health Organization (WHO) acted quickly and the epidemic was suppressed though only after it spread to thirty-three countries including as far as Toronto in Canada: but this was not a pandemic. No new cases have been reported since 2004; the disease disappeared as suddenly as it came. But China has a poor track record in reporting the outbreaks of new viruses and is decidedly guilty of allowing the spread of SARS, and of being complicit in the suffering and many deaths that resulted. It will be the same, as we shall see, with Covid-19. Horton's words here are remarkably apt concerning not just the SARS outbreak in China but the present pandemic of Covid-19 that began there: "China performed poorly. The country's weak public health and primary healthcare systems, its turgid and authoritarian bureaucracy, excessive respect for political authority, poor coordination, suppression of evidence, repression of the media, reluctance to ask for external assistance, and fear of internal instability all contributed to a less than optimal response. Chinese officials simply refused to share information with WHO. They practised a systematic deception."[87] And such a harsh criticism is no less justified in China's behaviour in the light of Covid-19.

SARS was a zoonotic virus, a new RNA virus, whose animal microbe as a *zoonosis* jumped to a human host in the live animal markets in Guangdong. The original source was the Chinese horseshoe bat that must have infected civets through its droppings in the squalid animal wet markets. So the civets were the medium of passage to humans but not the natural reservoir of the virus. Indeed, when the bats were tested they were found to have antibodies against SARS-CoV. Oldstone believes that the bats passed on the virus to the civets through their saliva. Apparently the bats are partial to fruit but eat from it what is necessary and spit out the remainder – to be eaten up by civets.[88] The pattern of SARS pathogens being animal originated is found here again, and not when hunter-gatherers move to settled living but in the so-called civilized world of the twentieth century. While the virus is spread by coughing and is therefore airborne spread, it is also spread through watery diarrhoea – two symptoms present also in Covid-19 infections. As to the airborne transmission, Quick writes: "Once transmitted to a human, an airborne virus could pass from that one infected individual to 25,000 others within a week, and to more than 700,000 within the first month. Within three months it could spread to every major urban centre in the world. And by six months, it could infect more than 300 million people and kill more than 30 million."[89] Quick was writing these words in 2018 and could not have realized then how soon his words would come true with Covid-19.

The symptoms of SARS apart from the dry cough and diarrhoea are fever, loss of appetite, muscle pains and weakness, but also show marked respiratory failings because the virus is mainly produced in the lungs. It infects the cells that line the lungs causing breathing problems, a decrease in lung oxygen output, and pneumonia, similar to Covid-19 symptoms. Because it is based in the lungs, infected mucus is coughed out, but that means this heavier mucus cannot travel far. SARS also infected the kidneys, the liver and the small intestine. Covid-19 also affects other organs of the body in some patients. The elderly are particularly at risk with SARS and about 20 percent of those infected were hospitalized with half of those dying of the disease. The SARS virus – as Covid-19 – had two to fourteen days incubation in the body with massive replication of the virus before any symptoms appeared. Yet it seems the virus was only spread when symptoms showed, not during the incubation period or after recovery. We know that with Covid-19, the incubation period is one when the virus really does spread – a time when it is hidden and extremely likely to be passed on.

MERS

The other serious coronavirus alongside SARS was MERS, Middle-East Respiratory Syndrome, that broke out in Saudi Arabia in 2012. It spread in the Arab world, and in 2015 to Korea. In comparison to SARS it was nowhere near as serious in so far as its spread, but it was far more lethal in terms of its infection, killing one in every three it infected and causing severe respiratory problems for many. The source was once again bats but this time from Africa, and the medium of infection was camels. The link between African bats and Middle Eastern camels was an odd one. It may well be that an infected camel reached the camel markets of North Africa and passed on the virus to other camels in that route: camels now are rife with the MERS virus. If a camel gets sick, mucus oozes from its nose and infects others.

Covid-19: A new virus

The coronavirus that we are experiencing now in 2020 is related to SARS and MERS but is new. To give it its proper name, it is SARS-CoV-2, *Severe Acute Respiratory Syndrome Corononavirus 2*, belonging to the *Sarbecovirus* subgenus of the *Coronaviridae* family,[90] and is the seventh known coronavirus type. Just as SARS-CoV, it is a severe respiratory illness that can range in effect from a mild cold to severe viral pneumonia and acute respiratory distress and in very severe cases can lead to multi-organ failure, sepsis and blood clots: this tiny, tiny virus can be lethal. There were, in fact, originally two strains of the virus identified at its source in China: one of these, the *L* type as it is called, seemed to have been prevalent early on, but seems to have given way to the second type, the *S*. The disease is called Covid-19 because 2019 was when it first broke out, and Covid-19 is the official name given to the virus by the WHO: from now on, I shall just refer to it as Covid, as many contemporaries now do. And in the weird world of Covid in which we now live, some are referring to the virus as the twenty-first-century world war. That is perhaps not an exaggeration since no country has escaped it completely and some scientists believe that probably everyone is going to get Covid at some time or other. The ubiquitous nature of the virus may well prove these words to be true. When Covid had spread to 118 countries, the WHO declared it a pandemic on 11 March 2020.

The similarity to the 2003 outbreak of SARS is obvious, but Covid is clearly a new virus, a new strain of coronaviruses, especially now in an age when new viruses seem to be increasing in frequency. In fact, new viruses have been emerging at four times the rate they were back in the 1980s.[91] Two characteristics that are completely new are first, the way in which it infects the throat and travels down through the body perhaps as far as the lungs. Throat swabs of those infected show 1 billion per millimetre of the virus in the throat and nose. The other new aspect is called *shedding*, the shedding of the virus *during incubation and replication* by those who may have very mild symptoms or may have no symptoms at all. That makes this new virus a huge danger. There is no doubt of the potential severity of Covid: undertakers are saying that the numbers of deaths they have had to deal with is unprecedented. Right at the beginning of 2020 in January the virus had spread to nineteen countries months before it was declared a pandemic. In January there were 17 deaths globally, by the end of February, 2,979, and by mid-March, 4,970. Early in the next month, April, 70,917 people had died, by the end of that month, 221,140, and by June, 371,888. Half of the individuals admitted to intensive care units to be ventilated died. In many countries, mortuaries filled up and additional mobile units had to be used – something previously unknown. By February in New York, 21,000 people had died and by April crematoria could simply not cope. More people died in New York than in some whole nations. Now, approaching the end of October 2020, more than 39.4 million have been infected by Covid worldwide and over a million have died.[92]

Characteristics of Covid

Covid is a retrovirus with an RNA (ribonucleic acid) not DNA genome. Its genome, released by the Chinese in January 2020, is not very complicated, just one strand of an RNA molecule with about 30,000 bases that contain just 15 genes – a miniscule reproducing machine in comparison to the highly complicated DNA of human cells that have double helixes, and each about 3 billion bases and 30,000 genes. Covid is a tiny virus and about 600 could fit across the width of a human hair. There is some conjecture that it could in fact be two viruses conjoined.[93] Covid's strand of RNA has an outer membrane that is weak and the advice given to wash hands carefully and fully with soap and water is more than apt, since that membrane is destroyed in the process. The front cover of this book shows the Covid virus with its characteristic corona, the spikes like tiny clubs that are the keys the virus uses to get into our cells. On the outer part of many human cells are enzyme receptors called ACE2 (*angiotensin-converting enzyme-2*) and these spikes on the outer shell of the virus are the very "keys" that fit the ACE2 enzyme receptors to get access into cells. The virus is spread by droplets and attacks the ACE2 cells in the nose, throat and eyes and, if serious, also the lungs. Once in the cells, the virus is able to sabotage the cells' DNA functioning in the nuclei to reproduce itself a million times in just one day: and while that is happening, the body immune system is *not* alerted. This is something of a unique infection mode of Covid, for the virus is multiplying at an incredible rate without any symptoms to show for it in an infected individual. That is the key to the success of the virus and to the virility of its spread: it can remain hidden, incubating, and no one will know. And even though no one knows he or she has the virus, they can still shed it, infecting many of those with whom they come into contact.

Social distancing is a critical factor in avoiding infection. Since Covid is spread by droplets, a sneeze or a cough can shed out 3,000 droplets containing 200 million virus particles at a speed of 50 mph into the air. Most of the larger droplets can be avoided at a distance of 2 metres but it seems smaller ones are able to hang around in the air for almost three hours.[94] Those that do not hang around in the air or make it into the throats and noses of new hosts, will fall on surfaces ready for someone to touch and transfer the virus to their faces. Indoors, the virus survives longer than outdoors. As to wearing a protective mask, if an individual is infected *and does not know it*, the mask will stop that person being a super-spreader of the virus: it makes sense to wear one. The virus is clever with this novel incubation period that throws up no symptoms, and the danger of unsuspected shedding is even greater indoors. Alarmingly, viral shedding seems to be ongoing "between 8 and 20 days *after symptoms resolve*. However, the virus has been detected for up to 60 days in various samples," and it is not necessarily true that the duration of viral shedding correlates with duration of infectivity:[95] this is, indeed, a clever virus. The mutation rate in a retrovirus is usually very rapid and this seems to be the case, too, for Covid-19. In fact, since the summer of 2020, a variant strain of Covid is now widely evident in Europe. It originated in Spanish farm workers and is now the major source of Covid infections – over 80 percent of those infected in the UK and Spain; 60 percent of cases in Ireland; 40 percent of cases in Switzerland and France. This mutated virus is called $_{20}A.EU_1$ (or 20A for short) and has six distinctive mutated variations.[96] So how did that virus spread? Clearly, many researchers blame those travelling to Spain for the purpose of holidays – holidays during which social distancing was not diligently maintained, and the wearing of masks and washing of hands less observed. Those are the people responsible in the main for the present revival and spread of the mutated virus. These new mutations will have a serious impact on the development of a vaccine against Covid.

Common symptoms are fever, cough, fatigue, anorexia, dyspnoea, myalgia, sore throat, nasal congestion, headache, diarrhoea, nausea and vomiting and loss of taste and smell, but for some, all or none of these may be present in infected individuals. For the 20 percent of people who have more severe symptoms and those with underlying health conditions, as well as elderly people, males, black, Asian, and minority ethnic individuals BAME), critical illness could be, and has been, the outcome. Notably here, such a statement obtains *even when social factors are taken into account*. BAME individuals are more likely to be infected by the virus with severe consequences and even death, and this fact obtains for those not coming from deprived social backgrounds. But – and it is a huge but – too many BAME individuals live in deprived areas, so there is clearly also a structural race issue underlying the statistics. Covid causes mini blood clots in the lungs in small vessels of the lung tissue and this stops oxygen getting into the bloodstream: that has an effect on the heart. Damage to the lungs from the virus can be extreme and to the point when nothing can be done. For some, Covid is a multi-system disease, affecting so many organs of the body alongside many of the symptoms just noted. It can cause brain issues – bleeding and inflammation, as well as increased strokes. In the heart there may be diffuse swelling and inflammation leading to low oxygen levels in the body.

So if you develop Covid will you be immune from it afterwards? If we think back to the four strains of coronaviruses that cause mild colds, it is known that immunity in those cases lasts only for a few months, and it looks very much as if there is no guarantee that there will be long-term immunity against Covid for those who have had it. Increasingly, there are more individuals being discovered who have been re-infected. While tests on monkeys suggest there *is* immunity, it is too soon to tell how long that immunity would last. It is, indeed, a clever virus. Very recently, a very fit 25-year-old USA man has been shown to be re-infected. He had two positive tests for Covid on 18 April and 5 June 2020 but the two follow-up tests done in May were negative. Richard Tillett and his colleagues had this to say about the case: "Genomic analysis of SARS–CoV-2 showed genetically significant differences between each variant associated with each instance of infection. The second infection was symptomatically more severe than the first."[97] The researchers conclude that the second virus was "genetically distinct" and that "previous exposure to SARS–CoV-2 might not guarantee total immunity in all cases". That point, and the variant nature of the present virus, has considerable implications for future vaccines and, given that it is not an isolated case, for continued protective measures for those already infected. Researchers at Imperial College, London have found that after infection immunity is likely to wane in the same way as with seasonal coronavirus colds. There is already evidence of a small number of cases of reinfection according to Dr Helen Ward, who says that the level of antibodies in a large study of post-Covid individuals "dropped significantly".[98] The virus has not been around long enough to know whether antibodies will fail to be effective perhaps after a year or so.

The source and causes of Covid-19

Covid is not a human-designed virus in the sense that it has a laboratory origin, though some wish to claim this latter. But it is human orientated in that it is human behaviour that lies at the root cause. It began probably as early as November 2019 in China, the provenance of a good many viruses, and the country in which new flu viruses are expected to arise. Covid began in a live seafood and animal market in the centre of Wuhan city in the province of Hubei, and spread throughout China before any lockdown took place.[99] On 31 December doctors in Wuhan claimed to the authorities that the patients they saw with the disease had all visited the live animal market. The Chinese authorities in Beijing first notified the WHO of the disease on 31 December 2020 but, though aware of the potential problem, there was no curtailment of the massive movements of Chinese people for the New Year, celebrations that took people not only to all parts of China but also abroad. But on 1 January, the animal market, which was dealing not only with live animals for the table, but also with illegal trading of wild animals, was closed. While these actions were taken by the authorities, there seems to have been a deliberate attempt to conceal the true number of cases.[100] In an acerbic attack on Chinese actions over Covid, a special edition of *The Epoch Times* has a catalogue of accusations against China – sitting on information; arresting those who spoke out about the disease; censoring media news; incarcerating people with the disease in inhumane conditions; delaying the announcing of the disease for a whole month; denying that the virus was passed between humans, which prompted the WHO to reiterate that incorrectly on 14 January, 2020; allowing mass movements of Chinese people at New Year; under-reporting case numbers and deaths. Then, too, while the three top gene-sequencing Chinese companies isolated the genome in December; that information did not get out to the world until 12 January 2020.[101] Following the notification of the virus to the WHO at the end of December, the WHO later announced the virus to be a new one and on 30 January 2020, declared the virus to be a public health emergency of international concern: it was eventually termed a pandemic by the WHO on 11 March 2020.

Just as with SARS, the source of Covid is horseshoe bats, the *Rhinolophus affinis*, whose genome sequences are similar for both viruses. So while Covid is a relatively new virus, it has been extant in bats for thousands of years without killing the bats. Present research suggests that the medium of transmission from bat to human is the pangolin, a scaled creature that is abundantly killed in China for its scales to be used in Chinese medicine. In the appalling conditions of the animal markets, the pangolins would have picked up the virus from the bats and passed it to the humans who handle or butcher them. Certainly, the Covid genome is very closely matched to that carried by pangolins. Alexandre Hassanin believes that Covid is a combined new virus from *two* viruses of bat and pangolin, not just a single virus passed from bat to human through the medium of the pangolin. In this case, Covid would be a recombination of two viruses, where two viruses infected the same host simultaneously.[102] The bottom line here is the fact that new viruses are accidents waiting to happen when animals are herded together in overcrowded conditions in farms and markets – different species in close contact with each other.

When the cruise ship, the *Diamond Princess* was quarantined for a short time with its 3700 passengers because of an outbreak of Covid, its passengers really gave the world a closed experiment similar to laboratory conditions. It was an ideal situation for researchers if not for passengers. Since the virus can incubate for five days, or even a few weeks without symptoms being evident, these passengers on board could shed viral particles without even knowing they had the disease. 46 percent of the passengers tested positive for Covid but *had no symptoms*. This is the real problem with this virus: many of those infected are asymptomatic and shedding the disease without knowing.

The immune system

Our immune systems have been battling with viruses for as long as humans have inhabited Earth and viruses have done us the favour of forcing our immune systems to counteract anything foreign that gets into our bodies over thousands of years. On the whole, the immune system wins, while the virus has to be in, replicate and get out before the full blast of the immune system's defences. The word "immunity" comes from Latin "uncommon", or "privileged" and Paul Klenerman thinks this meaning may have stemmed from the idea that average people would succumb to disease, whereas the uncommon one would not.[103] Once sections of a population have been infected with a virus, they *should* then be immune to other attacks, for the immune system "remembers" the virus and quickly overcomes it: the virus will then have to go elsewhere for its hosts. But it may return if there are sufficient people without immunity to infect.

Covid as a new virus affects the immune system of individuals differently and some of those individuals will be asymptomatic and will continue to be so without ever being ill. As I said above, this is the danger of Covid because these asymptomatic cases are still shedding the virus. So there are far more people out there carrying Covid than have overt symptoms. And for some reason, children do not seem to be readily infected, nor is there much evidence that they pass the virus on to others. Human bodies have trillions of different cells with different functions and each cell has a nucleus that contains the DNA – 6 feet of it – of chemical genes and all the instructions for its replication. Our immune response mechanisms obtain in all the cells of our bodies with each cell having its own means for protection, but there are also more specialized immune cells that play a major part with the immune system as a whole being sophisticatedly integrated and in communication. Some reactions of our immune system are innate and are ancient, even in plants and insects; others have been *adaptive* to threats of viruses already known to the system – its "memory" part – but the whole is constantly operating to control all the various microbes that are part of our bodies' systems, and to counteract any alien *antigens*, virus and bacterial proteins that might invade cells. Evolution of the immune system has made it extremely effective and the most powerful immune cells to fight infection are *T cells*, *B cells* and *antibodies*. Since Covid is a new strain of coronavirus, our immune systems have no memory of it, which is why in some cases it can have devastating effects.

So when infected with Covid, the innate immune response is the first to attack. Then the adaptive response sends out T lymphocyte cells and billions of antibodies from B lymphocyte cells, but these have to be exactly the right shape in order to attack the virus and it will take some time to get this right.[104] T cells (of two types, CD4 and CD8) are known as "killer cells" because they are able to attack a virus before it gets into the body cells and replicates, or destroy any virus that has already invaded host cells. They are always circulating in the body looking for anything foreign that does not belong. Every day, the body creates 5×10^{10} B and T cells whether or not they are needed and each one of all these has a different function of attack. Sometimes the immune response is so strong – as happens in some Covid cases – that it becomes a danger to the body causing excessive inflammation: then the immune system becomes a destructive instrument. What results is *immunopathology* when the immune system is actually harming the body's organs. For some severe cases, the immune system causes the lungs to be filled with fluid and grossly inflamed: it is then that the cases are critical and the patients end up on ventilators. In cases where individuals have had a bone marrow or organ transplant they are given drugs to suppress the immune system from overacting, so these people would have immune systems not capable of fighting Covid. In cases of HIV, the virus actually attacks the immune system by overcoming the CD4 T cells and managing to hide in some of them ready to reactivate in the future. And for those who are malnourished in so many parts of the world, the immune system under-functions and the appropriate level of T cells, for example, cannot be produced.

What of herd immunity; would this inhibit the growth of Covid? It is sometimes used in farming contexts when farmers do not vaccinate their entire herd but allow the majority immunized to protect the remainder of the herd. Those not immunized would be thinly spread out and the infection unable to spread further. "The resistant majority protects the still susceptible minority", writes Wills.[105] Would this work with humans? It is unlikely in the context of Covid. We do not know for sure that those who have had the virus are immune from future attacks. The virus seems to affect the production of antibodies and they would be needed for future immunity. Herd immunity would be hard on the elderly as the susceptible minority, and it would overwhelm the health service in treating them. The UK government seems to have courted the idea at the onset of the virus, though they completely deny this today. Perhaps the issue of herd immunity was why the UK government was so late in putting the country into lockdown. Certainly, the chief scientific advisor, Sir Patrick Vallance, advised that communities would become immune if 60 percent of the people contracted the virus. It was not until 23 March that the UK went into lockdown – somewhat late. But the bottom line here is that there is no guarantee of future immunity for those who catch the disease and it is not known whether a positive test for antibodies means it could not return a second time. When students were allowed to begin or return to universities, those students testing positive for the virus rocketed: this was certainly the case in the UK. In many ways, this provided a herd immunity situation where young people, who are mainly only affected by Covid in minor ways, could propagate the virus amongst themselves. By self-isolating in their groups and accommodation cohorts most of the students will hopefully end up with immunity. The problem here, of course, even setting aside possibilities of re-infection, is their shedding of the virus to older individuals in the population during the incubation period of the virus when no symptoms are evident.

Antiviral drugs

Since there is currently no vaccine available, antiviral drugs have been tried to fight the virus, not to cure it but to slow down the infection. So drugs used to fight other viral infections are the only course of action at present. Some of those with severe lung infections have been given *interferon beta* to boost the immune system. The HIV drug *ritonavir* is believed to inhibit one of the proteins needed by the virus to replicate. The malaria drug, *hydroxychloroquine*, despite Donald Trump favouring and taking it at times, has mostly failed, though *remdesivir*, a drug used for Ebola, seems to reduce the time taken to recover by inhibiting a number of different enzymes needed by the virus for replication. This drug has been so stockpiled in the United States that it is difficult for other countries to get hold of. Then, *dexamethasone* seems to reduce the death rate in the severely ill and so is partially useful. When Trump contracted Covid, it seems he was given both dexamethasone and remdesivir. Globally, there are hundreds of such drug trials being tested. There is certainly reduced risk in sunshine, so being outdoors or at the equator is a bonus. *Monoclonal antibodies*, also given to Trump, are yet unlicensed. The drug is a combination of two antibodies with the aim of attacking the spikes on the outer surface of the virus. This combination may work but without clinical trials it is impossible to know whether an individual improves because of the drug or not: only clinical trials can verify this.

Vaccination

As I write now in October 2020, there is no vaccine against Covid available though over a hundred are being explored globally. The usual method of creating a vaccine is to use a very weak (*attenuated*), or killed virus to introduce to the body and preserve memory of that virus in the body's immune system. Dead vaccines are laboratory produced, the virus being chemically inactivated and then injected into the body but this type has been found to have less impact over time. Weak vaccines are weakened live virus particles that generally work well, but not so well in the case of elderly and vulnerable cases. Either way, both approaches give the immune system something on which to practise. The Englishman, Edward Jenner, was the pioneer in such experiments in the 1790s with live vaccine against smallpox, but it was not until viruses were discovered in the early part of the twentieth century that vaccines against viral diseases began to be used, especially against smallpox. An additional vaccine is a protein antibody type that stimulates the body to produce the antibodies necessary to counteract a disease. Vaccines stimulate the immune system so that it produces the necessary antibodies, and those important B and T cells that locate and cling on to the outer wall of a virus so that it is neutralized.

The production of a vaccine of any kind is a very slow process and it would usually take about five years for one to be tried and tested with prolific animal testing before being tried on humans: many such vaccines fail. But today's pandemic means a vaccine is exigent. Five are perhaps leading here in the race for a vaccine. Research at Oxford University's Jenner Institute is promising and is currently at the phase of human trials. The team here has concentrated on attacking the "keys", the club-shaped spike proteins, on the surface of the virus that open up the cells of the body. They are taking the gene sequence from the spikes and genetically modifying a cold virus that affects chimps to produce the same spikes as the virus but without the ability to replicate. Injecting this into the body should deliver an immune response and immune memory for the real thing. Experiments with (probably countless) macaque monkeys were successful, which is why human trials are now taking place. And the biopharmaceutical company, Astra Zeneca, is standing by for large-scale production of a vaccine, but Oxford has also engaged other companies in addition to ensure maxim vaccine production.

Imperial College London is also in the race for a vaccine. Researchers here are also working on the protein spikes with the idea that just that part of the virus would be introduced into the body without the rest of the virus, causing the body to react to *part* of the virus but not the whole. The part that would be injected into the body – the viral spikes – will still get into cells and will still reproduce, but only produce the spikes, and not whole viruses. In effect, this type of vaccine would be a synthetically produced bit of the virus, not the real thing, but enough to provoke immune response. There are many other attempts to provide a vaccine – too many to list here. The Chinese company Sinovac has started human trials after success with mice, rats, and monkeys, of purified and inactive Covid virus taken from people who had been infected – a more traditional approach to vaccine production – and the pharmaceutical company Sanofi, is working with the flu vaccine to see if that can fight Covid. Whatever the outcome of the race for a vaccine, when it comes, it would supply the *right* kind of herd immunity. Science has a lot to do and there is unlikely to be just one answer to the pandemic despite media broadcasts that refer to *the* scientific advice: scientists rarely agree. There is no *single* answer to Covid: I do not think you can have *the best* scientific advice, so to "follow the science" as we hear so often is an impossibility, and SAGE, the Scientific Advisory Group for Emergencies in the UK, seemed reticent to be too precise in its advice. Covid is still not fully understood and science has a long way to go yet. It has to be remembered, too, that in clinical trials, however sick someone is, 50 percent of individuals would be given the trial vaccine and the other half a placebo that does nothing: such are the ethics of placebos. One novel treatment is the use of the BCG vaccine for tuberculosis. (BCG is Bacillus Calmette-Guérin, named after the two scientists who developed it.) The vaccine is by no means a cure for Covid but it is believed it might buy time in helping to prevent or lessen some symptoms.

There is a sinister side to the production of vaccines since covert development of biological weapons can easily be masked. In rather alarming words, Crawford spells this out starkly: "Although new restrictions are in place, seed cultures of many dangerous micro-organisms can still be obtained from national collections, with no questions asked, and since making vaccines is a legitimate reason for growing microbes on a large scale, biological weapons factories can masquerade as vaccine production plants."[106]

Measures for protection and prevention

I recently watched the film *Contagion* produced in 2011. It was unbelievably relevant to today's pandemic, especially in the measures advised in order to avoid a deadly virus. And all the advice we are being given today was there in the film. I have seen extracts from the film cited in a number of academic sources simply because of the accuracy of the film in portraying how deadly a virus pandemic can be. At the end of the film, a bat flew above the heads of a pig herd in a barn, its droppings immediately eaten up by a pig: how prescient was that! In Britain today, October 2020, Covid infections are increasing and the R_0 rate is now over 1 in the UK. R_0 is the reproductive rate of the virus that shows how one case infects others: anything greater than $R_0 1$ is indicative of increase of the virus: less than $R_0 1$ means the pandemic is under control. Imagine what would happen if the $R_0 1$ rose to $R_0 2$, which would mean one infected individual infects two others; then those two infect four others; and then those four infect eight and so on. So how can this be prevented? Travel restriction is crucial. Had the Chinese restricted the movements of people after the first outbreaks, the pandemic may never have spread globally. In our world today, the faster we travel, the faster we spread a disease. We need better entry and exit testing at airports, and efficient quarantine of infected individuals. Collectively, we can all help eradicate the virus by maintaining social distances, and if social distancing means closing public places then that is sensible. We are woefully poor in the UK for testing. Even a close friend who is a National Health Service Consultant Anaesthetist has repeatedly *failed* to get a test for Covid. Testing is one sure way of identifying the asymptomatic individuals who are unwittingly shedding the virus everywhere. Wearing face masks, whereas at one time a disputed and discretionary policy, has now become the norm in many countries, though President Trump did his best to avoid wearing one and mocked those that did. Unfortunately, Trump's diminishing of the dangers of Covid subsequent to his succumbing to the virus and emerging from it seemingly unscathed is not helping Americans to take sensible precautions against infection, despite the deaths of over 200,000 in the USA.

The new normal

We are now several months into the Covid pandemic, long enough for it to have had a marked effect on the way in which we think and behave: Covid is, in fact, *forcing* us to think differently. Horton so aptly says of this virus: "COVID-19 invites us, calls on us, requires us to rethink who we are and what we value."[107] There has been little impact where I live in a corner of Monmouthshire in a fairly isolated area but those in towns and cities have been badly affected. The nearest town to me, Newport in South Wales, had one of the highest infection rates in the country, where the real trauma of the illness for those hospitalized and those mourning the deaths of relatives and friends were sucked into a completely new unimaginable experience. So we are now in no doubt that there is a second wave of Covid – or even of a mutated variant – in Europe. In reality, the first one never ended and now, in October 2020, cases of infection are seriously rising again: the virus never went away. Many people use the word "weird" to describe how they view this strange event that is casting a shadow over our lives and will continue to do so for many months, even years, to come. There is really no "new normal" yet on the horizon, and Horton's words are again rather prescient here when he writes: "Perhaps COVID-19 represents an impermeable boundary between one moment in our lives and another. We can never go back."[108] To reiterate the global statistics now in the autumn of 2020, over 45.5 million individuals have been infected globally and over a million have died.

From a positive point of view, lockdown brought many changes: pollution decreased so that we can breathe again in towns and cities, road accidents declined in large numbers, and wildlife has been safer and has enjoyed the lack of human threat. Climate change has also benefited from decreased carbon footprints of humanity. Collective support for the vulnerable during this pandemic has brought people closer together – whole communities of individuals who previously had not known each other. Sadly, closeness between countries and governments has not obtained, and more than ever we need a globalized response to this virus and to any that await us in the future because there is a high likelihood of future pandemics of one sort or another. Countries with a high-density population in city areas, encroachment into animal habitats with deforestation, wild-life traders, the exotic animal trade, are all major areas of concern. Geographically, Central West Africa, South Asia, South-east Asia, and China are the areas where future viruses are likely to emerge. China has a bad record here with its live animal markets. The virus has no respect for national boundaries, for different religious faiths, for male or female (though it infects more of the former), or young and old (though the former here are relatively safer), and a globalized response is exigent. I think it unlikely that life will return to the *status quo* of pre-Covid times and we have many adjustments to make for the future. Subsequent chapters will be devoted to early Buddhism and the ways in which human beings have a responsibility to evolve personally, socially and nationally in order to cope with a new kind of living, a new kind of world.

3

The Noble Truth of Suffering

The Four Noble Truths

At the core of the Buddha's *Dhamma* were Four Noble Truths that he taught as his first sermon to a group of five ascetics following his enlightenment. The Truths were what he saw as the essence of all life, and he presented them as a physician would to a sick patient – diagnosis of the symptoms; the cause of the symptoms; the cessation of the symptoms; the methodology for cure. So fundamental are these *four* Truths that they cannot be added to or one taken away without the whole Truth collapsing. They are important enough to delineate here in their Buddhist form:

- The First Noble Truth – suffering, *dukkha*
- The Second Noble Truth – the arising of suffering, *samudaya*
- The Third Noble Truth – the cessation of suffering, *nirodha*
- The Fourth Noble Truth – the Path for the cessation of suffering, *magga*

These four Truths are believed to encompass all possibilities of the nature of existence and are at the heart of Buddhist spirituality and wisdom. They are believed to represent the nature of conditioned reality though, importantly, the Buddha did not invent them but awakened to them. Such Truth was not meant to be either pessimistic or optimistic but, as Walpola Rahula pertinently remarked, the Truth was *realistic*: "It looks at things objectively (*yathabbutam*). It does not falsely lull you into living in a fool's paradise, nor does it frighten and agonize you with all kinds of imaginary fears and sins. It tells you exactly and objectively what you are and what the world around you is, and shows you the way to perfect freedom, peace, tranquillity and happiness."[1] Understood fully, the Four Noble Truths are deemed to bring the Buddhist to the kind of enlightenment experienced by the Buddha himself. That experience is of *nibbana* (Skt. *nirvana*), a complete "blowing out" of misconceptions about life and about the self.

Nibbana, in its Sanskrit form *nirvana*, has become a word in everyday usage to depict an experience that is superlatively exquisite, indescribable, unforgettable and utterly sublime. This is a description not that far removed, I think, from its original meaning in Buddhism. But it was not an everyday experience even for monks well trained in meditative procedures. *Nibbana* was the ultimate goal as total awakening to the Truth that the Buddha experienced, and it was not to be realized without immense meditative effort as well as wisdom, and could take many lifetimes to experience even for the most committed of monks or nuns. The *Dhammapada* said: "There's no meditation in one without wisdom, or wisdom in one who doesn't meditate. The one in whom are both meditation and wisdom is close to *nibbana*."[2] It was a subject that the Buddha resolutely refused to discuss and so *nibbana* was open to a good deal of interpretation in the past and is still so in the present. Steven Collins gives a most apposite comment on this point when he says: "Instead of supplying a verbalised notion of what *is* the sphere of ultimate value; Buddhism simply leaves a direction arrow, while resolutely refusing to predicate anything of the destination, to discuss its relationship with the phenomenal person, or indeed to say anything more about it."[3] While the word "*nibbana*" means something like "blowing out" or "extinguishing", this was not the blowing out and annihilation of the self *per se*; it was more the extinction, the cessation, of the *egoistic* self, the cessation of the Five Aggregates (with which I shall deal below) and, most importantly, the extinguishing of the three fires, poisons or evils, of greed, hatred and delusion.

While *nibbana* itself was uncaused, the pathway and causal process to it was set out for monks and nuns fairly clearly in the monastic praxis for living life, the concomitant meditative and contemplative praxis that focused the mind away from the senses and inward to wisdom, and eventual abandonment of ego-consciousness. In particular, the three evils or poisons, the fires of greed, hatred and delusion, were overcome as part of this process. But *nibbana* itself remained causeless and not the effect of anything, so the path to it was not in many senses causative. Rahula explained this thus: "The only thing you can do is to see it, to realize it. There is a path leading to the realization of Nirvana. But Nirvana is not the result of this path. You may get to the mountain along a path, but the mountain is not the result, not an effect of the path. You may see a light, but the light is not the result of your eyesight."[4]

Thus, the overall textual descriptions of *nibbana* point to its unknowability. The Buddha is reputed to have said: "There is, monks, a domain where there is no earth, no water, no fire, no wind, no sphere of infinite space, no sphere of nothingness, no sphere of infinite consciousness, no sphere of neither awareness nor non-awareness; there is not this world, there is not another world, there is no sun or moon. I do not call this coming or going, nor standing, nor dying, nor being reborn; it is without support, without occurrence, without object. Just this is the end of suffering."[5] Again, there was no indication whatever that *nibbana* was nothing, that it was the complete annihilation of the enlightened being: it was, instead, the annihilation of the conditioned being and of the delusion of a permanent self. *Nibbana* is often depicted as "the other shore", this earthly shore being the one without wisdom. But, just as a raft is constructed to get from one shore to another and is then abandoned at the other side, so *nibbana* is the abandonment of everything, of all *dhammas*, conditioned phenomena, including the self.

It is not important to my purpose in this book to dwell on the concept of *nibbana* but, since it is the goal of the serious Theravada, conservative, Buddhist I need to include it briefly. But the goal should be set aside for the majority of us ordinary mortals. What was so important to the Buddha was pragmatic living and thinking in the right way. This we shall see in chapter 6 when I examine the Noble Eightfold Path, the fourth of the Four Noble Truths. The pragmatism of the Buddha means that the Truths are focused on *us* as human beings, on how *we* are in any one moment, not on some philosophical tenets that are hard to grasp mentally and must be approached intellectually. No, the Four Noble Truths are rooted in the realities of life as we live it and in the ways in which we answer some of its difficulties, especially those pertinent to today's pandemic of Covid: that is why the Four Truths are "Noble".

So let us return to this first of the Four Noble Truths, suffering, *dukkha*. I am going to retain this Pali term throughout, mainly because it has no exact translation into English. *Dukkha* is not just one of the Four Noble Truths but is also the second of what are called the "three marks" or "three characteristics", the other two being the theories of no-self and impermanence that will take up some space in Chapter 4 of this book. *Dukkha* has very wide meanings in Pali, anything from physical pain to mild unpleasantness. If we divide the word into its compounds, *du* means something like "difficult, bad", and *kha* means "empty", or "hollow", and this latter part suggests that *dukkha* hints at something missing, an incompleteness, unsatisfactoriness, impermanence or insubstantiality. Its opposite is *sukha*, "happiness", but even that can never be *completely* so because of the very fact of its impermanence: we know that any happiness we experience is not destined to last fully forever. The idea of being unsatisfactory and incomplete suggests a measure of dissatisfaction and disappointment, and perhaps such dis-ease comes close to the meaning of *dukkha*.

The Buddha had these often-cited words to say about suffering: "What, Bhikkus, is the Noble Truth of Suffering? Birth is suffering, decay is suffering, death is suffering; sorrow, lamentation, pain, grief and despair are suffering. To be separated from the pleasant is suffering; to be in contact with the unpleasant is also suffering. In short, the Five Aggregates of Existence connected with attachment are all suffering."[6] Really, anything that is not *sukha* is *dukkha*. If we think of our world today in 2020, we have seen dreadful floods, raging fires, earthquakes, racial persecution, wars, and now, coronavirus, where the impermanence and instability of life are so evident. In the natural world, life preys on life and we, too, have to destroy animal and plant life in order to feed our bodies. There is considerable social and economic injustice, and statistics concerning Covid suggest that it is far more rampant in underprivileged areas. We know that natural disasters create suffering on large scales but how do we react to such things? How far do we immerse ourselves in our own existences and turn a blind eye to the plight of others as long as we ourselves are OK? And are we blind, too, to the more localized and immediate suffering of the kind we can actually witness and sometimes ignore? I was amused by an incident a few months ago while I was shopping. A man in the street was asking for any odd change passers-by might have for him. Few people actually carry coins these days, and the few who stopped had to turn him down. However, I found some for him. Entering the shop I was aiming for, I was approached by a lady brandishing a charity box and asking for money. I replied that I had just given all the coins I had to the man around the corner. "Oh him", she said, "he's always there asking for money; I just ignore him"! My point here is that suffering seems to be something that we do not generally think about, and that we avoid as much as we can.

The Buddha saw *all* life as suffering and attitudes to it totally misguided. It is a universal phenomenon that is applicable to all of us. Who at this very moment is totally free of dis-ease, that is to say, in *perfect* physical health, in *perfect* mental and emotional health, in a *perfect* state of economic and social stability? If we asked each other whether there were something troubling us and answered honestly, we would probably find there are elements of present-day and present-moment dis-ease or unsatisfactoriness affecting all of us. So is this a pessimistic view of existence? If we left it at that then, yes, it is perhaps a pessimistic view. But the Buddha did not leave it at that. Like a physician, he found the reason for suffering, stated that it could be cured, and provided a pathway for cure. In this sense, the message of

Buddhism is *optimistic*. It does not suggest that joy and happiness are wrong, just that the mind is programmed to expect and search for the pleasures of life and disregard the fact of suffering as a universal facet of it. His was a realistic and objective view of the world that stands opposed to subjectivism and selfishness. Fear, discontent, envy, covetousness, ambition, and the like are endemic in many parts of the human psyche and are indicative of individuals who constantly feel things lacking in their lives. But the *Dhamma* is a hopeful message, though the first step of cure is to understand the nature of the ailment – the universality of *dukkha*.

We all understand the meaning of ordinary suffering that befalls us simply because we have been born. We get sick from time to time, we have to get old and die; we have to face unpleasant things or persons; we may be separated from those we love or fail in getting what we want in life. Any kind of adverse physical or mental conditions fall under this kind of ordinary suffering, though the term "ordinary" should not belie the pain such things may cause. We can become disturbed, irritated, worried, anxious, fearful, vulnerable, dejected, and most human beings will experience such emotions at some times in their lives. The Buddha's experience of suffering as old age, sickness and death was widened at his enlightenment to the whole of human existence, but let us take each of these in turn. As we pass through youth and middle age we rarely give old age a thought until, perhaps, we are faced with parents and grandparents who, in old age, begin to suffer more serious decline of body and mind. I confess to not having really understood the full meaning of "old age" aside from elderly members of my family with, for example, Alzheimer's Disease. My mother recently died not of any specific condition, but of "old age" so her death certificate states. She was ninety-eight and at the end of September 2019, she contracted a urinary tract infection from which she never really recovered. For five months she was bedridden nursed by wonderful carers in a nearby nursing home. Mum was not in any pain, but we had to watch the process of old age to the point of death, and that took five months. My mother's body became skeletal; her eyes were sunken in their sockets and she barely opened them; her skin was dreadfully thin and greyish yellow; her skull was so obvious with its thin covering of skin. We expect persons to die of some sickness, of a heart attack, stroke, or cancer, but dying of old age is a real possibility for us all and it is a grim prospect. Maybe this end-of-life old age is what the Buddha saw on his first excursion from the palace.

The Buddha's other two experiences of sickness and death are more than ever present with us in 2020. The coronavirus has killed more than a million people globally and continues to kill thousands of individuals each day. Whatever our age – child, youth, adult, middle-aged, elderly – we are faced daily with the threat of this disease, one that, if we are lucky, we will avoid, catch and survive, even get off lightly: if not, we could find ourselves extremely sick and facing death. And watching the news daily we witness the suffering of those who have lost ones they loved to this incredible virus. Most of the individuals interviewed after such loss, it seems to me, bear that loss with immense dignity and courage despite their sorrow. And in such sorrow, it is hard to let go of he or she who was lost. The Buddha believed that such sorrow can develop into darker emotions of lamentation, lamentation into grief that will not depart, and grief into despair, where the mental state is totally overcome by the loss and, here, thoughts may become suicidal. According to the Buddha, such emotions may accompany more worldly events such as the loss of money and wealth when individuals plummet into despair through such loss: here, we can see a little clearer that letting go of the effects of the loss is the way to find comfort, and the Buddha would have said that the same should be applied to loss of a loved one. One Buddhist text has a good analogy: "Sorrow is like the cooking (of oil, etc.) in a pot over a slow fire. Lamentation is like its boiling over from the pot when cooking over a quick fire. Despair is like what remains in the pot after it has boiled over and is unable to do so any more, going on cooking in the pot till it dries up."[7] What we shall see in later chapters is the Buddha's means for overcoming the depths of despair.

The success of lockdown in so many countries throughout the world is suggestive that there is sufficient fear of the coronavirus for peoples to abide by restricting regulations, and rightly so. But there are some with other illnesses who are so fearful of, say, ending up in hospital where they might contract Covid that they do not take action soon enough and become desperately ill consequentially. Others are fearful because they cannot actually get into a hospital for treatment – even for cases of cancer – given closures of surgical wards and a backlog of past patients needing attention. Medical suffering through post-modern illnesses – obesity, high blood pressure, heart attacks, stomach ulcers, and the like – are perhaps indicative of underlying social and economic stresses. Some refuse to look such medical suffering in the face, will not accept that they are ill, and convince themselves that all is well. This kind of fear of hospitals, doctors, and a severe "white coat syndrome" is a radical refusal to entertain the idea of suffering even for cure. Close to home, it meant the death of a dear friend of mine who refused to accept anything was wrong until it was too late and a primary cancer had metastasized into his whole body.

In present times, so many individuals and families have to suffer economic deprivations because they are unable to work. Social isolation has meant immense loneliness for those who live alone, though there is such heart-warming news of the kindness and generosity of those who are doing their very best to seek out and help the lonely. It may be that when this crisis is over the warm-hearted behaviour of so many will continue. But boredom and suppressed restlessness are bringing their own levels of suffering. The human being is by nature one that is ever changing. Restlessness as a result of confined home spaces, and restricted activities can bring their own kinds of suffering with agitation, frustration and irritability, even anger. And in the dark corners of societal life domestic violence against women and children has risen dramatically in the lockdown situation. At least 15 million more cases were estimated by the United Nations Population Fund during the pandemic.[8] But, on a positive note, I spoke recently to a close friend whose husband died just over a year ago. Her suffering through the loss was tangible and she said how lonely she had felt. In having to self-isolate, she found consolation in the fact that others shared in her loss through deaths from the coronavirus, and she now feels part of humanity and no longer the lonely, grieving widow.

Lives are ruined by epidemics and pandemics not only because so many lives are cut short but also because of the grief that is left behind. In countries where there is deep poverty and overt likelihood of diseases taking over communities the economic effect is a massive burden. Young men die in droves, children have to come out of education, and the knowledge of how to effectuate changes for a better existence is eroded, if it existed at all. I was impressed with the accuracy and relevance of the 2011 film *Contagion* that I mentioned in Chapter 2 with its portrayal of our own present predicament and the suffering a pandemic causes: it was, indeed, a remarkably prescient piece of creativity that resonates with our contemporary challenges and suffering posed by Covid. Witness Jonathan Quick's words here: "Meanwhile, the virus spreads with geometric internet speed from hand to lung and from city to city. Days pass before anyone understands the gravity of the situation; some suspect a bioterror attack. Society begins to break down. Kids can't go to school; nobody goes to work; streets and airports are empty. Supermarket shelves are stripped bare; chaos ensues as people fight over resources and a snake-oil salesman's useless herbal remedy."[9] Quick is describing the film *Contagion* here in words written long before the outbreak of Covid.

At present we are experiencing a so-called "second wave" of Covid, though the first one hardly departed, and while the elderly are believed to be more susceptible to serious effects of the virus, a significant number of young and fit individuals experienced severe symptoms when the virus first emerged in our societies, though under the age of 30, the chances of dying are less than 1000 to one.[10] Perhaps this is why younger people have rather readily flouted restrictions on numbers gathering together and have not been afraid to have parties and raves. As I write now in October, 2020, global deaths from Covid have reached more than a million, and over 45.5 million have been infected by the virus. In the United Kingdom we were subjected to daily briefings by the government about such statistics, and they are still being delivered. I have some sympathy with Richard Horton's words about these statistical summaries with lives being "transformed into mathematical summaries" for comparisons with other nations. He writes with some force: "But those who died must not be summarised. They must not become lines on squared paper. They must not become mere rates used to argue differences between nations. Every death counts. A person who died in Wuhan is as important as one who died in New York. Our way of describing the impact of the pandemic erased the biographies of the dead. The science and politics of COVID-19 became exercises in radical dehumanisation."[11] I certainly agree here: numbers do not generally move us in the same way as individual suffering.

In Chapter 2, I took time to examine how human behaviour was often the source of its own suffering through its lack of any sense of animal welfare or their natural habitats. Again and again, the viral diseases that besieged humanity in the past and now in the present have originated in such a way, and the result has been terrible suffering through the diseases. Take smallpox, for example that, at its worst stage, has a bleeding rash starting as red spots that fill with fluid and pus, eventually rupturing spreading their virus contents. The characteristic pocks that scar the sufferer are the result of virus-laden scabs that remain after the spots rupture. But apart from the visual aspects of the virus on the skin, the smallpox virus invades the body's organs: the pain from this virus is excruciating. The influenza virus can curdle the blood,[12] and with Spanish flu, the lungs and organs collapsed in severe cases with the body turning a hideous blue-black. Ebola causes internal bleeding and septic shock while the internal organs of the body shut down. Full-blown AIDS destroys the body's immune system so that the individual is highly susceptible to any infections and to cancer. The Zika virus causes microcephaly and birth defects in new-born babies, and the Creutzfeldt-Jacob (vCJD), or "mad cow" disease causes the gradual death of brain cells leading to dementia, hallucinations, loss of memory and personality. So let us be certain about viruses, they can be lethal and utterly horrendous in the suffering they cause. The President of the United States, Donald Trump, played down the virus in a hardly believable manner, rarely being seen in a face mask and not exactly giving much encouragement to Americans to undertake sensible methods of protection: "The end of the pandemic is in sight", he said on 3 October 2020, just before he tested positive for the virus himself, which was surely a message to all that viruses do not differentiate between the powerful and the lowly. It demonstrates how wrong he was to ridicule the use of face masks and to play down the virus especially at election rallies where his supporters abandoned social distancing and the wearing of face masks. The virus is not "behind us", as he claimed the day before he had Covid; it is very much in front of our faces.

The symptoms of Covid can be no less severe in the incredible level of suffering it can cause. Those who have complications of severe Covid disease may have multi-organ failure, septic shock and blood clots in addition to the severe respiratory problems. Pneumonia, where the tiny air sacs of the lungs become full of fluid so restricting breathing, is common for the more severe forms of Covid. Unfortunately, the body's own immune system goes into overdrive and destroys healthy tissue alongside alien invaders. When severely ill patients end up on ventilators, their chances of surviving are curtailed with long-term health problems for the few who survive: at least half of patients on ventilators die. The virus can affect the whole of the body – gut, kidneys, brain, heart, liver – with all the concomitant ill effects on each body organ. The elderly are critically at risk. Here in the UK, more deaths occurred in care homes in England than elsewhere and accounted for 40 percent of all deaths with over 70 percent more deaths than in the same period the previous year. This shows not only the virulence of the virus but the susceptibility of the aged.

Aside from the suffering of those with severe Covid, medical staff, especially those in intensive care units, had to witness the many deaths, and it is clear that some were terrified of the virus. The need for oxygen to treat patients was in short supply and what previously lasted a whole month was depleted in two to three days. That meant oxygen had to be rationed even for severely ill patients. Here in South Wales where I live, the nearby city of Newport, about 15 miles away, has a major hospital, the Royal Gwent. The intake of Covid patients there was higher than the capital city of Cardiff and was half of the total for the whole of Wales. Staff on intensive care units struggled to keep going and many staff dreaded going to work. The level of protective clothing was such they could hardly recognize each other. Their masks cut into their faces and made their skin sore so that they looked scarred when they took them off. There was no fresh air and it was hot, very hot, so that staff were dehydrated when they came off the wards. They had the emotional pressure of dealing with relatives who were unable to visit their loved ones, and of trying to help the sick, their disembodied voices not always able to give patients the assurances they needed. These medical staff battled with shortages of equipment, space, standard drugs that were running out, and 24-hour shifts. It was not until 20 April 2020 that the numbers of patients began to decrease at the Royal Gwent: now, in the autumn, they are rising again. For those patients who were very ill with Covid there may well be a long road to recovery for post-Covid symptoms are usual and after leaving the intensive care unit the recovery for them is long. Some patients present with confusion and delirium because of effects on the brain; others have problems with heart circulation, the kidneys, the lungs, the gut and strokes. It may take months or even years for a patient to recover. When we face the fact that 50 percent of those who found themselves in an intensive care unit died, the suffering of the virus is a stark reality. Even for some not hospitalized, the term "long-Covid" is now being used for those who are not recovering after months.

One factor that has emerged concerning viral diseases and the suffering they cause is that the poor suffer most. It is so often in deprived areas where there is little space and little economic scope to change lifestyle in order to improve it. Countries like China with no employment benefits, no health care system, no resources for the poor, little social protection, and real concrete jungles of living areas, there is little chance of avoiding infections from viruses. Horton writing of Chinese poverty says: "If anything, it shows how deeply the population has been culturally and politically suppressed, and how the voice of the really poor in China gets completely buried and forgotten. This just isn't right."[13] And what really is not right is that these poor, deprived areas are the sources of many of the viruses that have plagued us globally, that have caused untold suffering and innumerable deaths. As Horton continues to say: "COVID-19 exploited and worsened already existing inequalities in society." He justifiably writes of a "steep social gradient to this disease".[14] Closer to home, we know that unemployment has a detrimental effect on people's health physically and mentally: lockdown – whether total as it was earlier, or partial as it is now in the autumn of 2020 – is going to have serious consequences for the economic future of many individuals. Whereas we may have viewed physical suffering as something that is in the periphery of our thoughts and something that we can mostly avoid, Covid has forced us to look closer at what it is, at its different dimensions and, I so hope, at its causes. That is an issue I raised in Chapter 2, and it will resurface a number of times through this book in different contexts. But I think we now understand the nature of suffering because of Covid and that will help in our exploration of the Buddha's perspective on it.

So there are many, many facets of suffering and the reader may now understand a little of the way in which the Buddha saw suffering as endemic to all life. In more general terms, *dukkha* is a certain unsatisfactory feeling about facets of life, a dis-ease of body, mind or environment, a general discomfort perhaps from working too hard or not enough, a lack in contentment because there is too much to do or because of not being satisfied with present life conditions. So though death is for most the ultimate in suffering, and something many put to the back of the mind – for some, as far back as to be oblivious to it – daily lives bring their own stresses and strains that come into the range and scale of *dukkha*. The Buddha was so apposite in placing *dukkha* as the first of his Noble Truths because if you do not *see* that there is a problem; if you do not *understand* its nature, then there can be no cure for any dissatisfactions in life. Thus, the wide spectrum of suffering that I have shown up until now is meant to go some way in demonstrating the Buddha's perceptions here, but now I want to look at suffering from a completely different dimension in our desires and aversions.

Desire and aversion

So many eastern religions deal with desire and aversion as inimical to a healthy mental well-being. Desires are of what we like, would like to have, or like to be, and aversions, are what we do not like and want to avoid, though we may often be neutral. And, of course, we do not like suffering of any kind, mild or serious, short term or long term. With the present coronavirus we are having to exercise avoidance from a different perspective that is not a voluntary one – avoid being closer than two metres from other people, avoid leaving the home except for short exercise, medical reasons or essential shopping, and avoid seeing those we love in the family. We have to take practical measures here to avoid becoming sick and suffering, even dying. The aim is the search for happiness, *sukha*, the exact opposite of *dukkha*, and the opposites of sorrow and happiness are juxtaposed more vividly in the face of Covid than they would normally be in life. Because of Covid we are witnessing daily the way in which suffering can enter life and impinge radically on happiness. In reality, we can only know what suffering is because we can compare it with its opposite of happiness. Both suffering and happiness are necessary contrasts in order for us to understand the nature of both and the variety of gradations that swing like a pendulum from one to the other. Neither of these two opposites can ever be complete: there can be no perfect happiness that is not subject to change; nor can there be any complete sorrow that is permanent and unaffected by change. We need both happiness and sorrow to be balanced human beings.

But happiness is elusive, even if we try to create it in our lives as if it were the answer to everything. Our search for happiness is generally a selfish desire, a search for something individually satisfying, though there are so many within the caring community who at present are acting thoroughly *un*selfishly: perhaps, in the face of so much global suffering, humanity is able to put others first. But the motivation for happiness is a general trait of the human being. Natasha Jackson wrote: "The crucial point is that our motivations are always the same. Whatever we do – whether a man robs a bank, or commits murder, or gives his life in defence of a principle, or becomes a monk and gives up the world – behind each and every one of these actions is the belief that it tends to promote the happiness of the individual so involved."[15] And as Jackson went on to say: "To obtain happiness, or freedom from Dukkha, is the seeming paradox of Buddhism. No one can be happy who still cherishes and hugs to himself the idea of separateness, of grasping at a personal private fulfilment."[16] Having the goal of *personal* happiness, satisfying the self in some way, is the wrong perspective on happiness according to the Buddha, and he sought to correct the misapprehensions of those with such a wrong views.

Aversion is less elusive: we know what we do not like. There are many things about which we feel utterly repugnant, angry, disdainful, and those sentiments may on occasion lead to evil or unkind actions. Each human being has his or her own pathology, blends of positive, negative, conditioned and genetic factors that make him or her different from anyone else. Environmental influences, especially, reinforce those psychological factors, maybe lessening some and developing others. The resulting pathology of an individual will create his or her unique desires and aversions. When it comes to suffering, however, few would welcome it, desire it, or see any benefit in it. But fighting it and railing against it, allowing it to radically affect mental health does not help. Rahula poignantly wrote: "Thus it is wrong to be impatient at suffering. Being impatient or angry at suffering does not remove it. On the contrary, it adds a little more to one's troubles, and aggravates and exacerbates a situation already disagreeable. What is necessary is not anger or impatience, but the understanding of the question of suffering, how it comes about, and how to get rid of it, and then to work accordingly with patience, intelligence, determination and energy."[17] Indeed, there is a lot to be said for mind over matter. Should we have an aversion to Covid? That would be a natural reaction, but to turn that into fear is irrational and fear often turns to panic. Quick's advice here is apposite: "Scared people overpersonalize the news, and their worries increase. Fear is a warning system intended to alert us to impending danger, just as it is in animals. When we let it override our rationality, we make things much worse."[18]

So ingrained is the psychology of human need for pleasure and happiness that the brain produces dopamine when an individual is allowed to talk at length about his or her self: we are selfish creatures! I am always amazed at how few questions people ask in conversation, but they are so very happy to answer questions put to them about themselves – what they do, their hobbies, what they think about something. It was a foolproof means for me to alter the demeanour of a very grumpy old male friend of mine many a time! Many such drives for pleasure are unconscious, but that is exactly what the Buddha was saying: *understanding* the nature of desires and aversions is the beginning of recognition of the problem, the sickness that he wished to cure. With the advent of the coronavirus we have had to reckon with our levels of need, sacrifice the things we most like to do, the places we love to visit, the grandchildren we love to hug, for the safety of the greater number and to play an important part in making sure health services can cope with the mounting number of sick to treat. It seemed we were over the worst in the summer months but autumn has reinvigorated the virus and necessitated societal restrictions once again.

Dis-ease for many individuals stems from all kinds of subtle incidents that lead to dissatisfaction in life. We may feel dissatisfaction with our employment, or some of the individuals in it. We can be tired yet have to fit in so much in the day. There may be jobs needing attention for which there is little or no time. Family members may be exerting pressure or have needs with which one has to cope. Life can be very difficult. Some individuals tell me that they enjoyed lockdown because they had *time*, time to do the things they cannot normally fit into their lives. So here there are signs of satisfaction in life. But others struggle for basic needs, struggle to feed their families, struggled to live in a tenement flat with no access to a garden and fresh air. We are now dealing with present vicissitudes that affect *us*, affect our*selves*, our needs and desires. That does not mean to say that global issues have or should disappear. The planet is still suffering – many species in danger of extinction; thousands of acres of forests being felled to provide farm land and food crops for locals as well as timber supplies for a greedy world; global warming is melting the ice at the poles – all because of the unreasonable desires of huge numbers of humanity.

A major aspect of the Buddha's teaching was *impermanence*, and I shall take up this point in Chapter 4. Here, in relation to suffering, sorrow or happiness – *none of these can last*. Whether happiness, unhappiness or neutral emotions occur at any one moment in life, they are subject to change and transience. They *cannot* last and, as such, are subject to being unsatisfactory, *dukkha*. The happiness so desired by all can only be fleeting for that is the nature of all life. Similarly, suffering must also be fleeting; it, too, cannot last. It may take as long as two years for this virus to vanish from the planet, or for a vaccine to defeat it but it, also, cannot last. In this connection of impermanence, the Buddha categorized three types of suffering associated first with mind and body, then with what are called the *Five Aggregates*, and then with change and transience.

Mind and body

We do not need to be eminent physicians to know that suffering is a facet of the mind, or the body, or both. Given what I wrote above in connection with the impermanence of suffering or happiness, we would have to accept that suffering of the body is transient, something we all experience from time to time: the body, too, is subject to change. But what about the mind, is that also a transient phenomenon? The Buddha would certainly have depicted it so. We tend to think of the mind as that permanent kind of entity that belongs to us and over which we have control. But what we call the mind is, from a chemical point of view, the electrical charges of the brain that make sense of incoming data past and present. We locate *consciousness* – one of the most difficult and complex aspects of the human being – as being in the mind. The fact that we can think we are conscious of consciousness might suggest some entity, even a self, that consciously observes the mind and knows what is in it. However, the mind is nothing short of billions of neurons formulating complex networks as a result of sense stimuli reaching the brain *but*, all the previous data fed into the brain will build up unique neurological patterns, a unique brain for each individual that will have its own unique perspective of reality, and that perspective will inform how thought functions in the present and future. We create our own brains, our own pathological instincts, idiosyncrasies, fears, dislikes – the whole gamut of what we call the "self".

So Mark Csikszentmihalyi describes consciousness as "a clearing-house for sensations, perceptions, feelings, and ideas, establishing priorities among all the diverse information",[19] and thinks that material provided by consciousness permits our actions, thoughts, volitions and reactions, all of which arise from our individual subjective views of reality. Our brains, in fact, even carry out reasoning processes without our knowledge. And neither can we rely on consciousness to present the correct information: we can be deluded into thinking we are right about something only to be proved completely wrong. Susan Greenfield defines consciousness as "that world that only you can access, and that makes you feel special and different to those around you".[20] The critical question here, however, is how a purely objective and biological brain built up through biological processes can give rise to subjective experiences and yet it obviously does so: I can reflect on myself, on others, and convey to others my thoughts, albeit subjective ones.

The consciousness that is "me" is brought about by millions of neurons formulating in the brain to give rise to my consciousness of something. But Susan Blackmore dispels the notion of any centre of consciousness in the brain:

> To begin with, there is no centre in the brain which could correspond to this notion, for the brain is a radically parallel processing system with no central headquarters. Information comes in to the senses and is distributed all over the place for different purposes. In all of this activity there is no central place in which 'I' sit and watch the show as things pass through my consciousness. There is no place in which the arrival of thoughts or perceptions marks the moment at which they become conscious. There is no single location from where my decisions are sent out. Instead, the many different parts of the brain get on with their own jobs, communicating with each other whenever necessary, and with no central control. What, then, could correspond to the theatre of consciousness?[21]

The brain absorbs multiple narratives before we are conscious of the one outcome of them: "We have a single idea of self despite these multiple narratives because we have an inbuilt system for self-definition which involves telling a narrative of who we are. Our 'self' is a narrative spun out of these multiple narratives. The winning narrative is the one that is consciousness."[22] These words of Al-Chalabi, Turner and Delamot explain rather well the myth of "self" and the cause of consciousness as arising from the interplay and interconnectivity of neurons.

Thus far, we have not found much to suggest that the so-called self is anything other than neural activity in the brain. Reacting to what the brain presents to us means that we focus our attention on something and become conscious of it often to the exclusion of other things. Once attention and consciousness are focused in such a way, it is easy to see how a sense of self develops and how repeated attention to certain stimuli, to particular memories and the like, create a personality. Experiences of an individual create meaningful personal existence by configuring brain neurons in certain ways. And each further experience is assimilated into the brain into the configurations of neurons already set up by similar experiences of the past. The brain has a mechanical job to do in gathering information, sorting it, storing it, and delivering up the appropriate neurological configurations applicable to each moment of life. Simon Blackburn usefully describes consciousness as our "animation" in the world,[23] which suggests that the outcomes and choices we make are those of our associations of neurons in any moment: how is rational thought capable of dealing with that? We are left with consciousness being the subjective personal experiences and behaviours of neurological assemblies we have created for ourselves, not in a static way, but in a way that creates a different perspective of reality for each and every one of us. That perspective of reality is not exactly stable, bearing in mind that we cannot always accurately recall something from the past: forgetfulness is a certain facet of the human mind. So our minds consist of transient processes with different configurations of neurons from one moment to the next. This fact is critically important for the first of the Four Noble Truths, *dukkha*, because if the mind and consciousness are flexible, changeable, transient, then *it is possible to change the state of the mind*.

The Five Aggregates

The Buddha's analysis of the empirical self was as a conglomerate of Five Aggregates or groups, *khandhas*. Critically, each of these is *conditioned*, that is to say is dependent on causes that arise and disappear, making it subject to change and impermanent. These five are *dukkha* in that they cannot be avoided; we cannot run away from them, for they are what compose us. Understanding them is key to understanding the first of the Four Noble Truths, that all life is *dukkha*.

1. **Matter** is everything that we can see and includes earth or solidity; water or fluidity; fire or energy/heat; wind or motion; the sense organs and their relative functioning; also the mind, this last accepted as a sense in most Indian systems. Matter is form, shape, phenomena or *dhammas* in Buddhism (not to be confused with the *Dhamma*).

2. **Sensations/feelings**, both physical and mental, are experienced by sense organs. These include the *functions* of the mind, which is responsible for processing not just the sensations of the physical world but also abstract thoughts and ideas. Here there are pleasant, unpleasant or indifferent sensations.
3. **Perceptions** involve recognition and classification of sensations – more determinate accurate or inaccurate cognition of what the senses have processed. Apperception is perhaps the better term since it incorporates mind processes rather than simple sense contact. I shall be looking closely at this aspect of the self and the sensations that precede perceptions when I examine Dependent Origination in Chapter 5.
4. **Mental formations** are volition, the activity of response to sense stimuli and perceptions. This is when we react to what we see or hear and when we can run wild in the wilderness of our likes and dislikes, our desires and aversions and neutral feelings. Memory and imagination are included here. At this stage characters are formed by the way in which we react to sense stimuli and it is here where *kamma* is created, where the causes of the future, near or distant, are made: indeed, the Buddha equated volition with *kamma*.[24] In the first verses of the *Dhammapada* we find the following:

   All that we are is the result of what we have thought: it is founded on our thoughts, it is made up of our thoughts. If a man speaks or acts with an evil thought, pain follows him, as the wheel follows the foot of the ox that draws the carriage.
   All that we are is the result of what we have thought: it is founded on our thoughts, it is made up of our thoughts. If a man speaks or acts with a pure thought, happiness will follow him, like a shadow that never leaves him.[25]

   All impulses belong in the aggregate of mental formations – desires, greed, hatred, wisdom or lack of it, determination, energy, ignorance, and the like, as well as the positive drives for personal enlightenment. But it is important to visualize the mind as a *sense*, simply a tool for assimilating and interpreting what the senses present to it. Change the perceptions and it is possible to *change the mind*.
5. **Consciousness** occurs in relation to the senses and their faculties, as noted above. It is a *conditioned* flow depending on the way it arises so it is *caused* by the other four Aggregates and the flow of ever-changing things presented to it becoming a state of mind, a developing, but changing, character. V. F. Gunaratne aptly likens consciousness to the flow of a river that is never the

same from one moment to the next: "The river one crosses in the morning is not the river he crosses in the evening. Each time, each moment, it is a different set of waters that flow. Similarly where the mind is concerned, each time is a different sensation or perception or volition or consciousness that exists, only to pass away giving rise to another."[26] Consciousness cannot be permanent for it is part of a process of flux. It can never be a permanent self.

According to this analysis of the self, all the suffering that is incurred by human beings is a result of their fixation with the idea that their self is permanent. And all the *kamma* they reap is the result of their volition, their will to relate all things to what is, in truth, an impermanent self. *Ego* develops as a consequence of the Aggregates, though it is present in none of them, and ego perpetuates the idea of an independent self that desires and grasps at things in life to feed its perpetuity. Here is the real cause of all suffering. The five interrelate, are insubstantial and impermanent and, therefore, unsatisfactory or, to put it stronger, suffering, the basic premise of the Buddha. Since they condition each being, it really is nonsensical to claim any or all of them together as constituting a real "self". The Aggregates are only the *conditioned* self and its suffering. Because of this equation the Buddha knew suffering could be alleviated: get rid of the notion of ego and self, see the Aggregates for what they are, and suffering can be annihilated. And so the Buddha said:

> Cut off five, give up five,
>   Develop five to the highest.
> The monk who has gone beyond the five bonds
>   Is called "crosser of the flood."
>
> Whenever he contemplates
>   The arising and passing away of the aggregates
> He gains joy and happiness.
>   That is the "deathless" for those who know.[27]

The interplay and transience of the Five Aggregates inform all of life. What we call life as far as our so-called selves are concerned is nothing but a series of thought moments, and this leads to the third of the aspects of suffering related to impermanence.

Change and transience

Every moment and all things are in a state of perpetual flow, of the coming into being of moments before their passing away. No two seconds are ever the same, though we expect them to be because we are unaware of the transience of all things and all times. We will suffer, said the Buddha, if we do not understand this and try to cling on to what can never be permanent: there is no stability anywhere. It is impossible to be happy forever so there is an unsatisfactory nature to life that needs to be understood. Thus, the Buddha is reputed to have said: "Where there is change there is *dukkha*" and this must suggest a condition of insecurity in life. Happiness is as changeable as the person who experiences it, as is sorrow. I want to leave discussion of the impermanent nature of the self until the next chapter but consider Story's words here, "the conscious being is in reality a cause–effect continuum flowing through space and time, his existence in the moment of conscious awareness a cross-section of an eternal process. The suffering of the Aggregates is inherent in their mutability; the process of coming-to-be which never attains the fulfilment of perfect being."[28] So there must be deterioration, decay, in each moment of existence, not just the decay of the body and mind into old age, but the decay of nature, and if we lift our eyes from ourselves to the bigger canvas of world events, we should be able to see the deterioration of the planet too.

So is Buddhism pessimistic? If we left the analysis here, it would have to be admitted that it is, but the Buddha wanted his hearers to understand more fully the nature of the dis-ease so that he could cure it. We never really focus on suffering unless it is something with which we become personally involved, but with the coronavirus we are faced with it daily when we hear of the many who are so sick and the thousands who have died. The Buddha would have wanted us in this life situation when suffering is brought to the fore to analyse ourselves carefully and look for the more subtle areas of dis-ease that we have in our own lives. And we have had the space and time to do that, the space and time to look closely at the lives we lead and at the conditioning factors that are the hidden facets of our personalities. Analysis in this way is the first step to cure because, as the Buddha pointed out, if you can see *dukkha* you can see how it comes about, how it can cease, and the way, the path, for that cessation. The Buddha gives us that choice of a change of view by understanding the first of the Four Noble Truths as the foundation for cure.

4

The Second Noble Truth of the Cause of Suffering

The Buddha's Four Noble Truths are set out in the same way as a physician would diagnose a malady, discover the source of the malady, find a cure, and administer it. The second of the Four Noble Truths takes up the second part of this process, the stating of the cause of the malady, the cause of suffering. In the Buddha's words: "What now is the Noble Truth of the cause of suffering? Truly it is that craving which gives rise to fresh rebirth, and, conjoined with pleasure and lust, finds gratification now here, now there."[1] So here we have the cause of all the suffering in the world as craving. The epitome of suffering in the Buddha's day was incessant rebirth. That is a topic I want to leave until Chapter 5, but it is worth bearing it in mind throughout this present chapter while we explore this concept of craving.

Craving, *tanha*

Buddhism is widely described as a way of life and, therefore, it is intimately concerned with human nature. And if human nature singly or collectively is unsatisfactory in some way it can only be cured if the correct cause is known. This is precisely the point of the second of the Four Noble Truths. The cause of all suffering, the Buddha said, is *tanha*, craving, a malady that encompasses all the delights and greed that characterize humanity. *Tanha* means something like "thirst", or a very strong desire, particularly if that desire is unreasonable or excessive. Thirst is a particularly good translation since it is well illustrated as a thirst for wealth, for possessions, for another person, or even for an ideal or a religion. As Walpola Rahula very pertinently remarked: "According to the Buddha's analysis, all the troubles and strife in the world, from little personal quarrels in families to great wars between nations and countries, arise out of this selfish 'thirst'. From this point of view, all economic, political and social problems are rooted in this selfish 'thirst'."[2] While *tanha* may well include the meaning "desire", there is always a negative connotation to *tanha* so desire here would be an unwholesome one. Thus, *tanha* as "craving" has an element of selfish gratification and misguided goals.

The link between craving, *tanha*, and suffering, *dukkha*, is totally symbiotic, a point Rahula made when he wrote: "A being, a thing, or a system, if it has within itself the nature of arising, the nature of coming into being, has also within itself the nature, the germ, of its own cessation and destruction. Thus, *dukkha* . . . has within itself the nature of its own arising, and has also within itself the nature of its own cessation."[3] Thus, *dukkha* has a psychological genesis that manifests itself as craving, greed, grasping, longing, yearning, affection, and more negative emotions such as lust, aversion, dislike and hatred. These emotions are mostly the result of sensory stimuli and experiences that encourage attachment and clinging to what is believed to be good, and aversion to what is not good. Happiness is believed to belong to the former providing at the same time the latter can be avoided. Any sensory stimulus that occurs, instantly provokes a positive, negative, or neutral response. With a positive response come attachment and clinging and a rather futile attempt to hang on to the desirable thing, person, or idea. But since nothing can be permanent in life, such attachment is doomed to failure and to bring suffering. Rupert Gethin puts this well: "At this point it begins to become apparent just how and why craving leads to suffering. There is a discrepancy between our craving and the world we live in, between our expectations and the way things are. We want the world to be other than it is. Our craving is based on a fundamental misjudgement of the situation; a judgement that assumes that when our craving gets what it wants we will be happy, that when our craving possesses the objects of its desire we will be satisfied. But such a judgement in turn assumes a world in which things are permanent, unchanging, stable, and reliable."[4] Human beings base their lives on this kind of unreal assumption, living lives with expectations of happiness acquired through craving for things that are transient and impermanent.

Such is the way of life that fulfilment of desires, wants, are believed to be the measure of happiness. Grasping, clinging, craving are deeply rooted in the human psyche; they are what Buddhism terms the "nutrition" of life, the fuel for life. However, the world is in fact always in a state of flux, always changing, always transient and never perpetually stable. There are just connected similar moments without anything ever being permanent. Since *tanha* is a thirst for life, for enjoyments and happiness in life, that craving is somewhat misguided and doomed to be largely unfulfilled: here is the heart of the unsatisfactoriness that is *dukkha*. As we shall see in the next chapter, *tanha* is not the independent cause of suffering but is itself conditioned by other factors, but for our present purpose, it is the most obvious, proximate and immediate cause.

When desires result in craving – whether that is overt or subconsciously psychological – the individual tries to *own* that which is desired; it has to become *mine* and be related to *me*, so there is a profound level of selfishness in craving. The Buddha in his famous Fire Sermon used the analogy of fire to describe the passion of clinging. Wood is the fuel for fire and permits the fire to burn and engulf what it feeds on, spreading rapidly and consuming all in its path but never being satisfied. Fire burns now this and now that but is never completely fulfilled until it destroys everything in its path until its fuel runs out. Just so is craving, wanting so much without satisfaction at any point and fuelling suffering as a result. The poor crave to be rich; the sick crave to be healthy and want solace; the wealthy want more and desperately want to hold on to what they have. Such is the struggle in life to have what is not obtained and to avoid what is not wanted. Psychologically, such craving is mostly instinctive – a pattern of life conditioned from birth, from interaction and competitiveness with others and from the desires for material enhancement. In short, craving is a powerful motivating factor for existence with a concomitant selfishness in achieving goals, and craving begets more craving. So suffering, *dukkha*, is due to the actions of individuals, due to the *my* nature of behaviour and desires in the case of each individual.

Three forms of craving

According to the Buddha, craving has three dimensions, sensory craving, craving for existence, and craving for non-existence. The first of these is easy to understand because it involves contact of the senses with objects of desire and pleasure and the greater the gratification, the more the longing and craving increases. Whatever is seen, tasted, smelled, heard, touched provides the fuel. Equally so, in the mind's incessant wanderings with its ceaseless imaginings, its ideas and thoughts, and its bombardments from sensory stimuli, the creation of positive or negative responses results in desires and aversions: pursue those desires, and thirst for the positive sense objects results. But none of these pleasures can last. The Scottish poet Robert Burns in *Tam O'Shanter* wrote:

> Pleasures are like poppies spread
> You seize the flower, its bloom is shed;

> Or, like the snow fall on the river,
> A moment white, then melts for ever.

Craving here will also include goals individuals set for themselves in life. Wanting to be the best in a skill or discipline is thirst, competitive drives are a thirst to win, and being jealous is a thirst to have or be what another has or is. Seen in these dimensions, thirst or craving is often a psychological and mental drive to be better but, so often, to be better than someone else: there is a strong element of self-love in such psychological drives.

The second dimension of craving, the desire for continued existence is a much more complex kind of craving. It may well be that such a deeply-rooted desire for continued life has been prevalent from the advent of humankind. We are programmed as human beings to survive and to fight the odds against survival. Most religious expressions have some kind of belief in an afterlife and the very earliest of burials of primitive humankind had graves that showed expectation of life after death. These were ubiquitous with the graves bearing items for future post-death existence. The thought is no less prevalent today with fairly elaborate beliefs about a Heaven (or even Hell) where those who die will be waiting for those who are still living. Early Buddhism accepted, not a rosy world of Heaven as a final resting place, but incessant rebirth life after life after life in order to reap the results of causes made in the previous and collective previous lives.

Conversely, there are those individuals who turn away from any kind of forward ambition, who wish to stay only in the background, often despising life and spending it in depression with thoughts of suicide. These are the individuals who see no value in life, who do not want life and wish it annihilated. They live in self-doubt and in a sense of failure in life. The Buddha tried to emaciate himself in intense austerity after leaving his palace but came to realize that such negative attitudes to the body and mind were fruitless. For those who do not value life, death is mostly conceived of as the end with no life beyond. Then, too, whenever something unpleasant befalls an individual he or she generally craves to be rid of it. Think of the coronavirus here where those who hang in the balance between life and death will either try to keep fighting to live or will want to die. It is interesting that the Buddha rejected both eternalism, the idea that life could continue permanently without any end after death, and annihilationism, the belief that after death the body and self were totally destroyed. That was another dimension of his Middle Way. To crave for non-being and view death as the only good outcome to end a depressed life is as bad as believing there is a happy hunting ground where one can live for ever in peace and tranquillity. The Buddha's message is always the same, *nothing* can ever be permanent and *everything* is subject to change, transience and impermanence: the only exception here is *nibbana*, something I shall look closer at in the context of the third of the Four Noble Truths. Both eternalism and annihilationism can only be understood from the idea of the continuous flux of all matter, including the human body and mind. But by continuous flux is meant not only a present life but a continuation of the constantly changing conditioning processes in future rebirths.

Four causes of existence

Existence and re-existence in the form of rebirth in the beliefs of early Buddhism was informed by four causes, termed "nutrients". The first is the obvious nutrient of material food, without which the human being or any creature could not survive. The second nutrient is the contact of the sense organs with the world around, including the mind as the sense organ that synthesizes all stimuli. The third nutrient is consciousness, which I discussed a little in the context of the Five Aggregates in Chapter 3. But it is the fourth nutrient that is critical, and that is volition. In reflecting on these nutrients they supply a clear process. I see something pleasant with my sense organ the eye. My mind processes the perception to provide consciousness of the object. But it is only *then* that reaction to the conscious moment occurs. I *like* what I see; I *want* that cream cake; I *long for* that cream cake; I *must have* that cream cake; and here volition, will, is where *kamma* – again something I shall return to in Chapter 5 – is created. And if consciousness relays what is disliked, something for which I have an aversion, I will crave to get away from it or even to destroy it. Deeper than these sensory perceptions that create volitional responses are stronger psychological impulses of the will to live, to exist. In fact, the Buddha defined volition as *kamma* so each volitional reaction, whether negative or positive will become part of the complex process of building up the appropriate *kamma* for an individual. Such volitional activity will create wrong views of life, fetters – of permanent individuality, desires, aversions, rigid regard for certain views or no regard at all, pride, anxiety, agitation – all of which create *kammic* fruits for rebirth. When a fetter such as desire is not satisfied, it is easy to see how agitation and anger can set in and a "well I didn't want it anyway" attitude prevail. And in many, many ways, we are fettered by the conditioning of our own societies, by our environments, our peers, our family outlooks. Such conditioning may well be misguided and prevent a broader perspective of humanity as a shared and interrelated existent for whom we all have responsibility.

So volition is the root of rebirth but it itself is conditioned by so many processes. In every moment of existence interrelated causes come into play only to disappear and other causes take their place. Those newer causes may well be very similar to those of the previous moment, as may those of the next moment, but they can never be exactly the same, even though they provide the continuity we experience in life. Volitional desire acts in the same way to provide a momentum for rebirth, so craving, thirst, and desire keep the continuum of life going from birth to birth – rebirth being the worst of all suffering according to the Buddha. Since volition takes place in the mind, the mind has to be a significant cause of suffering and rebirth, though the interrelation of causes in constant flux means there can never be just one first cause. But the mind has a big part to play. Gethin writes that: "The suggestion is that deep in the minds of beings there is a greed or desire that manifests as an unquenchable thirst which is the principle condition for the arising of suffering."[5] The process by which this happens in the mind I shall leave until the next chapter where I shall examine the Buddha's very important teaching, Dependent Origination. But it is crucial to say here that craving is a process of the mind, and control of the mind is the means to stop it: since it is craving that causes suffering, controlling the mind to stop craving should help to alleviate suffering. This was the Buddha's message.

Craving and self-centredness

We are witness to a strange time when normal life as we have always known it has disappeared. Our lives are in danger from a hidden enemy, an enemy that, thus far, is only gradually being understood, and cannot be stopped without radical changes to the way we live. All individuals in all countries are being asked to do their part in counteracting the potent life threat of this particular coronavirus and this means that everyone has to act without selfish concerns. The things and events to which we are attached must be put aside for the general well-being of humanity. Holidays have had to be abandoned, and pleasures such as sport or visiting friends had to be set aside as we were asked to self-isolate or live under lockdown. We hear of so many noble causes now, of so many individuals and groups who are setting aside their own desires and working for the health of others. At the outset of the outbreak, indeed minute by minute, many in the health care services put their lives at risk. In the United Kingdom where I live, their selfless noble efforts were being applauded in a literal manner by the clap-for-carers weekly ritual at exactly 8.00 p.m. each Thursday evening when almost the whole of the country emerged at their doors and windows to clap and clap and clap for the many individuals in caring roles – the doctors, nurses, carers, refuse collectors, postmen and women, shop assistants, cleaners, transport workers, police. In New York, the same was done every single evening.

The Buddha would have so endorsed the lessening of attachments to the things we would normally desire. Four kinds of attachment are prolifically mentioned in Buddhist texts, the kinds of attachments that stem from the senses; attachments to ideas, ideologies, religious beliefs; attachment to the rules and regulations of monastic life in the days of the Buddha; and attachment to the idea of a permanent self. In all four there is an idea of self-centredness, a sense of *I*, *me* and *mine* about the attachments. So we find ourselves talking about *my* house, *my* job, *my* hobbies, *my* religion, *my* idea, *my* knowledge, and so on. And on the negative side there are *my* faults and failings, *my* aches and pains, *my* illness, *my* sadness, and the like, and on the broader perspective, we have *my* country, *my* nationality. When the *my* of self-centredness is deflated, perhaps through inability to fulfil goals, achieve levels of attainment, or because of challenges to superiority, then there may be feelings of inferiority and considerable disappointment that bring mental suffering. Self-love is a powerful force for promoting feelings of happiness and, generally, people love themselves more than others. The Buddha is reputed to have said that you can traverse the whole world in every direction with your thought but you will not find anyone dearer to a human being than his or her own self. In today's challenges, one facet of the world in its suffering with Covid is that there are so many cases of sacrifice of self-love for the benefit of others and true altruism in the face of the virus has so often shown the very best of human selfless endeavour. Will it last when we get back to real normal and not the "new normal"? We shall have to find out in years to come. Will those who have lost employment because of the virus cease to be concerned about *my* job? Will economic recovery hit people hard with higher taxes and cause them to become heavily self-centred in order to protect their properties, their families, their possessions? Fear is a real driver of psychological desires, whether fear of disease, old age or death and, now, the very real fear of contracting Covid and facing possible death. Such fears are difficult to abandon, but the Buddha's message was definitely one that they should be abandoned, for they are nothing more than attachments to fears. We probably all know that if we have something about which to worry, it is so hard to let the worry go, so much so that it disturbs our sleep, our thoughts when awake, and our interaction with others.

One theory that is repeated again and again in early Buddhist texts is that of the Five Aggregates – matter, sensations/feelings, perceptions, mental formations, and consciousness – that I dealt with in Chapter 3. Since all five are always dependent on combinations of causes and on each other in fluctuating conditionality, they make the human self also a being of fluctuating conditionality. And yet, each human being wants things and events to be static, unless, that is, those things and events are unpleasant. But the very fact that the self that is made up of the constantly conditioning Five Aggregates means that no permanent picture of the world is sustainable, and no attachment can be permanent. Where is the self that can permanently maintain ownership of things and events to which they are attached? Francis Story described the Aggregates of personality as arising "by way of antecedent and co-incidental conditions, both mental and physical, that are the cause of clinging to life".[6] So who suffers here? The constantly changing Five Aggregates that compose a personality do not suffer, only their combination in any one moment in the form of a so-called self can suffer. But since the Aggregates are changeable, changing the mental formations resulting from them in particular should, at the very least, make possible changes to attitudes to suffering, prevent the worrying and anxious mind from grasping and clinging to problems, and so avoid mental suffering. The problem really is that we have a tendency to take *ownership* of difficulties, make them *ours*, something *we* own. But the Buddha's view is that there is no point in attaching oneself to such difficulties if there is nothing more to the personality than constantly changing, moment to moment, Aggregate formations to inform a self that really does not exist. In the *Digha Nikaya* the Buddha is reported to have said:

> Transient are formations all,
> Their law is to rise and fall.
> Arisen – soon they disappear.
> To make them cease is happiness.[7]

And again the Buddha said: "Suffering only arises when anything arises; suffering only ceases when anything ceases."[8] Of course *feelings* play a huge part in how we are mentally. If we have a pleasant feeling about something, we usually fail to live in the moment, simply experience that feeling, and leave it there: instead, we become attached to it and want it again. Similarly, when an unpleasant feeling occurs we become miserable and distraught and become attached to the idea that we must get rid of it. It is difficult to get the measure of the arising of the feeling as an impermanent experience that is a fluctuating condition of multiple changing causes. With diligence and concentration however, as we shall see in chapter 7, the possession of feelings and ownership of them can be lost for a more balanced and freer perspective.

The Buddha's attitude to desires and aversions was not one that disregarded the normal individual and the kind of morality that was important in the interaction with others. On the Buddhist pathway to the *ultimate* goal of *nibbana* there was nothing wrong in having *proximate* goals. In the context of *karma* and rebirth, good actions contribute to a more wholesome future birth and life and, conversely, repeated evil actions result in an unwholesome future existence, even to one that is in an inferior life form. We shall see this in Chapter 5. In the context of Covid and the sheer selflessness of so many people, the desire to help, to do good, to care, to sacrifice one's own health for others, we are surely living in a time that will be remembered for its heroes and heroines in all walks of life. The whole world came to know Captain Tom who wanted to walk a hundred laps of his garden before his hundredth birthday. He just wanted to raise a little money to help the National Health Charities in the United Kingdom. Such was his beauty of soul that the world warmed to his endeavour and he raised over thirty million pounds. His selfless attitude and the selfless generosity of the millions of individuals who donated money for his cause are the kinds of *good* actions, *good* desires that are so necessary in life, and that are so needed at this time of struggle in nations throughout the world. Thus, today we need *positive* desires. Damien Keown is so right when he writes: "Having positive goals for oneself and others . . . desiring that others should be happy, and wishing to leave the world a better place than one found it, are all examples of positive and wholesome desires which do not count as *tanha*."[9] It is hoped that when this huge crisis is over – and that may be far in time from now – that nation leaders will reflect on the need for positive goals to reinvest the world with good. Suffering can be minimized if it is realized that no one can hold on to the things he or she wants, because everything is subject to change and transience: everything is impermanent. Craving and impermanence are completely incompatible and suffering can only be overcome when this is realized.

Impermanence, *anicca*

From all that has been said, it must be clear that impermanence, *anicca*, lies at the heart of the Buddha's message. As such, it is the first of the three marks, the three characteristics of all life. As I sit here typing, I look out of my study window right in front of me and I see my garden, one of my meadows, my huge oaks hundreds of years old that I love so much I give them names – Gandalf, Frodo, Baggins – and the special oak, Barclay (because it has branches everywhere). I refer to the birds I feed daily as my little sparrows, and the beautiful brightly feathered male peacock that I feed, I call my special bird. I refer to my house, my study, my husband, my dog, my books – my, my, my . . . . My huge ash trees are intact, except for one, and I fear it may have contracted ash dieback and will not survive, and that one tree reminds me that nothing is permanent. In a rather beautiful passage, Phra Khantipalo wrote:

> If impermanence meant change all the time towards better and happier states how excellent our world would be! But impermanence is allied with deterioration. All compounds break down, all made things fall to pieces, all conditioned things pass away with the passing of those conditions. Everything and every-everybody – that includes you and me – deteriorates, ages, decays, breaks up and passes away. And we, living in the forest of desires, are entirely composed of the impermanent. Yet our desire impels us not to see this, though impermanence stares us in the face from every single thing around. And it confronts us when we look within – mind and body, arising and passing away.[10]

It is worth adding Khantipalo's following words here since they seem so relevant to the present day. He said: "So don't turn on the TV . . . read a book, seize some food, or a hundred other distractions just to avoid seeing this. This is the one thing really worth seeing, for one who fully sees it in himself is *Free*."[11] The television that I see, which is admittedly little in comparison to most, seemed at the beginning of lockdown to be full of advice on how to manage the day – plan the day from beginning to end; exercise; play games; have quizzes; devise interactive pastimes with others on social media; have targets and goals; compete with others online. This frenetic advice is quite the opposite of Khantipalo's wiser words. Now really should be the time for taking stock of who we are, of the important things of life, of thinking about just *being*, letting the mind be still, and building a more holistic individual. I shall be returning to such ideas in Chapter 7. Those in lockdown have a chance to step aside from the normal stresses of life and exist in a calmer environment before, at some time, we must all return fully to the stresses of life out there in a truly normal existence.

The impermanence within all existence is unnoticed simply because we find continuity from moment to moment. In fact, this moment is different from the last one and has already disappeared into the next one. That rising and falling of moments in rapid succession gives the impression of static time: but that can never be. In much reverence to the Buddha, people offer him flowers to remind them of the passing of all things, and they light oil lamps before images of the Buddha to represent impermanence in the dying of the flames. We cannot make a sunset static; it will have to fade into darkness, just as day follows night. The beautiful song of a thrush singing in one of the oaks here at this moment, will soon lose its spring song and concentrate instead on raising a brood of young. Multiple mutating conditions inform each split second of life in a fleeting series that suggest permanence to us but in fact are but vanishing conditions that rise and fall never to be the same again. Covid, too, is subject to the same conditioning rising and falling: it is never static and cannot be forever.

As the first of the three marks, impermanence, *anicca*, informs the other two. According to the Buddha: "The five aggregates, monks, are *anicca*, impermanence; whatever is, that is *dukkha*, unsatisfactory; whatever is *dukkha*, that is without *atta*, Self. What is without Self, that is not mine, that I am not, that is not my Self. Thus should it be seen by perfect wisdom as it really is. Who sees by perfect wisdom, as it really is, his mind, not grasping, is detached from taints, he is liberated."[12] And in the same text, the *Samyutta Nikaya*, the Buddha said: "The perceiving of impermanence, monks, developed and frequently practised, removes all sensual passion, removes all passion for material existence, removes all passion for becoming, removes all ignorance, removes and abolishes all conceit of 'I am'".[13] The importance of the doctrine of impermanence can be seen clearly from these words of the Buddha. He believed that to have a true perception of the nature of reality for just one day would be better than a whole century of life without that knowledge.

Anicca is simply a compound word of *a* "not" and *nicca* "permanent", though there are other possibilities that need not concern us here. The *Dhamma* of the Buddha states that there is nothing at all in the Universe or beyond it, whether divine or human, animate or inanimate, organic or inorganic that is permanent, unchanging and everlasting: *all* is impermanent. Such a theory runs completely counter to substance theories, particularly those of the time of the Buddha in the Hindu acceptance of a permanent divine Absolute: there could be no such permanence, only progressions of conditioned elements coming into being and disappearing. As we shall see below, the human being is no exception to this rule of existence. We know now that random change and perpetual fluctuations are facets of the behaviour of quantum particles in a vibrating whirlpool of reality where observable cause and effect as we would have expected no longer obtains.[14] Matter is now known to be unstable and composed, as the Buddha believed, of changing conditioned states of energy, events that change from one moment to the next. Paul Williams writes rather appositely then: "The world truly is a torrent of cause and effect with no stability in it, save the stability we try to make for ourselves as a refuge from change and inevitable death. That stability only exacerbates suffering because it is a fictional stability created by our desperate grasping after security."[15]

There is no self-reality in anything at all: *everything* is conditioned by multiple factors that change from moment to moment, instances of conditional sequences in constant flux and flow, "a congeries of ever-changing elements in a process of ceaseless movement", as G. P. Malalasekera put it.[16] As dependent existences, everything is subject to previous causes. The Buddha put it this way: "If *this* is then *that* comes to be; in the absence of *this*, *that* does not come to be." So in the conditioned world in which we live, even causes themselves, the *this*, are impermanent: the theory obliterates any substantiality in the whole Universe. The Buddha also got rid of the concept of a divine being, God. In a world of causal contingency, there was no need for any divine being to direct events, to create effects; the world operated from natural cause–effect processes in constantly changing, transient and evanescent conditionality. And nothing arises *and stays the same*: at every stage of an existent, there is change and nothing is ever static. *Anicca* is causal *becoming* but nothing can ever actually *become* for it changes from moment to moment.

In being conditioned and lacking any permanence, everything is really unsatisfactory and when we look at the nature of the self, below, its unsatisfactory nature will also be pertinent: that unsatisfactory impermanence produces suffering when we try to make things stable and lasting. David Kalupahana sums this up so well: "The realization that such phenomena are impermanent and unsatisfactory, and that all experienced phenomena are non-substantial and dependently arisen, constitutes the cessation of suffering and the attainment of freedom and happiness."[17] So whatever is impermanent is unsatisfactory and what is unsatisfactory cannot be the basis of happiness. To become attached to the impermanent is to court unhappiness and sorrow; to detach oneself from the impermanent is to be free of unhappiness and to be free of craving for all that cannot and does not last.

The three evils/poisons

The Buddha spoke of three poisons or evils that conditioned the human being. These unwholesome evils are greed, hatred, and delusion or stupidity. They are interacting facets of the mind that processes the information from sense stimuli and responds to the environment. The three evils/poisons seduce us into a life that can never be a happy one, concomitant with the feeling that however much we have, *something* is missing; *something* eludes us so that true happiness is not experienced.

Greed

Greed is very close in meaning to *tanha*, craving, but it has a connotation of not being satisfied, of wanting more. In the United Kingdom in 2020, a very well-known television personality committed suicide. She left a message to her many fans, "be kind". The media had not been kind to her so she asked for that change in human outlook. And she got it for a while, her "be kind" message iterated far and wide. And then the coronavirus hit and people feared a shortage of food. Her be kind message became: "Sod being kind!" as people pushed and shoved in supermarkets to clear the shelves of produce. That was sheer greed, taking as much as possible for one's own self and family and not caring in the least about others. A nurse cried publicly on television as she bemoaned the fact that she had done a long shift in hospital and found nothing healthy left to buy in the supermarket after work. Shopping for groceries online became equally difficult because of the rarity of available delivery slots. So to stock up on just about everything possible as if the supermarkets would run out of food is just an expression of the greed in human beings. Greed is unnecessary wanting of more, wishing to possess something, being self-indulgent, wanting wealth, desiring fame, becoming attached to some thing or person.

There is a far more sinister aspect of greed that is responsible for widespread suffering, and that is the more corporate kind of greed. Take measles, for example, and the decline in the number of parents taking up the offer of MMR (measles, mumps and rubella) vaccines for their children after a 1998 article in the British Medical Journal, the *Lancet*, linked the immunization to autism. It was a massive deception prompted by greed. The paper in the *Lancet* written by Dr Andrew Wakefield was discredited, as was his greed in accepting payments from lawyers who benefited from claims by those blaming the immunization for autism. As a result, the suffering caused by the rise in cases of measles was the inevitable result. It took until 2015–17 to offset the negative rumours,[18] and it took twelve years for Dr Wakefield to be found guilty of dishonesty, to be proved unethical, and to be struck off the UK Medical Register.

Many corporate businesses are equally guilty of massive greed. Jonathan Quick's book, *The End of Epidemics* is a very brave and remarkably stark examination of the corporate greed and lack of political will to engage with issues that will offend businesses. At present, the world is racing to find a possible vaccine against Covid but if one is found, will it reach the poorest and the most deprived in the world? Quick's words here are stark even in the pre-Covid time when he wrote: "How many vaccines never get developed because poor people can't pay for the drugs that pharmaceutical companies could develop? How many times do governments and leaders plead that there is no budget for preparedness? How many disease-fostering agribusiness companies line the pockets of politicians who conveniently overlook threats bubbling up from factory sewage? Greed is the bottom line, and when it comes to exchanging dollars for human lives, greed is unforgivable."[19] The shareholders of pharmaceutical companies are greedy for rewards and the big pharmaceutical companies regularly overcharge for their medicines and vaccines. As an example of the greed close to home here in Wales, I mentioned Creutzfeld-Jacob or "mad cow" disease in Chapter 2. Here, where herbivore cattle were being fed animal meat and bone meal (MBM) protein, the result was a horrific disease in the cattle that passed to humans. The lack of political will to deal totally with the problem allowed the circulation of MBM long after nearly 4 million cattle had been slaughtered and human deaths had ensued. And, unbelievably, the animal feed trade was given five weeks to use up its stocks after MBM was banned so that even more animals were affected. It is still in use in the Third World.

Given what I wrote in Chapter 2 about lethal viruses emerging from the ways in which animals are farmed, fed, kept in close proximity to each other and to humans, Concentrated Animal Feeding Operations, CAFOs, in California, Iowa and Idaho find animals "buried deep in urine and feces".[20] CAFOs are perfect examples of corporations that are allowed to proceed with barbaric conditions for animals while politicians fail to act. And that is, at the end of the chain, because consumers want the beef, pork, poultry, and dairy products that these multi-million businesses produce. It is important to think of how we are responsible for the viruses that make us suffer if we accept such practices. Again, Quick puts this starkly:

If you've ever taken a drive through central California or the American Midwest where CAFOs are common, you can't possibly miss them. You can recognize them from a distance by their enormous green silos, but what really stamps them is their awful stench. The feedlots are packed with thousands or tens of thousands of beef and dairy cows, hogs, chickens, and turkeys, all squished together in concentration camp conditions as they're fattened up for milking or slaughter. Meanwhile their waste and attendant genetic material is stored and mixed into a viral soup in gigantic, reeking lagoons.[21]

That great conservationist, Bill Gates, said of this situation: "We've created, in terms of spread, the most dangerous environment that we've ever had in the history of mankind."[22] Added to the greed of companies that produce these horrendous situations is the greed of companies for more and more land, forest land that is regularly destroyed around the globe bringing humans into close contact with the animals whose habitats they have destroyed. And that greed provides the means for the viruses – that do little harm to the forest animals – to pass to humans with devastating effects. And for those tourists who want the "bush meat experience" in Africa, hunting primates for enjoyment, the dangers of contracting a virus from an animal–human virus jump are obvious. We are an increasing population on this planet, all the time destroying habitats, invading and disrupting delicate ecosystems with that increase. The greed now manifest globally is out of control with huge industries annihilating millions of acres of forests annually so altering the delicate balances of the ecology of the planet and opening the door to viruses like Covid and others that will surely follow.

Hatred

Hatred, the second of the three poisons/evils is profound aversion for something or someone. It produces rancour in the mind, prevents sleep and good health, and is inimical to sound interaction with others and relaxed living. But both greed and hatred are fed by delusion as to the nature of life, especially the delusion that concerns the self as permanent. Greed is probably motivated by a deep-rooted fear in human beings, fear of not having enough to eat, of not having a warm and protective home or people around to give support. But few are satisfied with a basically comfortable life and want more and more and more – an insatiable greed for so much that is believed will provide happiness, whereas in reality it makes life unsatisfactory and leads to suffering. Selfish greed on a national scale and a desire to shift blame elsewhere prompted Donald Trump to destroy any confidence built up in US and Chinese relations by outright blaming of China for Covid. As cases of Covid rose beyond a million by May, and with more than 64,000 deaths, the President of the US ramped up the hatred of China. Richard Horton writes on this point: "Business, financial and scientific ties started to be severed. The president instructed his intelligence agencies to continue to search for evidence that the pandemic had its origins in a deliberate or accidental leak from a laboratory in Wuhan. Trump claimed to have already seen such evidence, although none has been published and all reputable authorities have dismissed the idea."[23] Trump also attacked the World Health organization, the WHO, as being complicit in the Chinese cover-up. There is no doubt that the Chinese suppressed any rumours or evidence of the virus in the first instance, but Trump's delusional blame game to enhance his own status shows a remarkable level of egoistic greed. On 14 April 2020, President Trump ceased contributory funding for the WHO – an act that Horton believes is a crime against humanity.[24]

Delusion/stupidity

The Pali word for delusion, the third of the three poisons/evils, is *moha*, which means not only delusion but also stupidity and dullness of mind that lead to bewilderment and dithering thoughts and actions. From a strictly Buddhist perspective, the delusion and stupidity here refer to the total absence of a grasp of reality, but in the wider context of life it can be extended to the ways in which life is lived, the egoistic goals and drives of life, encompassing also the whole aspect of greed. In the context of the present pandemic we have witnessed a good deal of such stupidity, not least in the dithering of governments to take control of the situation in many nations. With Covid, dithering cost lives. Consider Quick's apt criticism of government stupidity here, written long before Covid reared its head: "The toxic trio of denial, dithering, and distrust characterized the early phases of the AIDS epidemics in the US, SARS in China, Ebola in West Africa, and Zika in Brazil. In each case, failure to heed alarms and to invest in preventive measures paved a road to disaster."[25] In the case of the AIDS epidemic there is plenty of blame to be levelled at those governments who deluded themselves into believing there was no problem or who, as Christopher Wills writes, believed it "irrelevant to their own segment of society, and who obstructed educational and public health measures that could with relative ease and low expense have slowed or even prevented its spread. And much more blame . . . will be laid at the doors of those who encouraged the societal destruction and upheaval, particularly in Africa, that first gave this rare virus its opportunity to become more common."[26] Was there any difference with Covid-19? Not really, and the failure to face issues is palpably obvious in daily news. The UK has been totally deluded in the way in which it has handled, and is handling, test and trace of the virus. As to Donald Trump's super-spreading event both in the Rose Garden of the White House followed by a gathering inside the building on 26 October 2020, that was unbelievably delusional. Footage of the event shows no social distancing and no one wearing a mask. This is governmental stupidity at its most obvious and a total failure of the President to face the issues at stake with the pandemic. His succumbing to the virus does not seem to have changed his attitude. I wonder how history will portray the stupidity and deluded mindset of this president in relation to Covid-19. The rising number of infections in the US he blamed on the increase in the number of people tested! This is a man who was more concerned with being re-elected than with the exponential rise in infection rates and the 220,000 families that had lost someone to the virus.

The WHO was somewhat slow in recognizing the danger of the virus spread. On 30 January 2020, it declared the outbreak to be a Public Health Emergency of International Concern, a PHEIC, but many lives could have been saved if the WHO had issued an earlier statement than the one on 11 March that raised the outbreaks to the level of pandemic. But surely the most deluded nation's government was China's. Even when the Chinese released the decoded genetic blueprint of the virus to the world on 11 January, they refused to admit there was human to human transmission and the WHO echoed this statement on 12 January. Had the Chinese not deluded themselves as to the potency of the virus, and not fiercely suppressed those who were outspoken in saying otherwise, millions and millions of people would not have travelled for New Year by land and air to spread the virus. Politicians around the world certainly underestimated this new virus, Covid-19, and deluded themselves into thinking a virus originating in some remote part of China could not possibly have any effect on their own nations. Horton points out that the global financial crisis of 2007–8 had resulted in massive spending cuts with a particular effect on health and social spending.[27] We certainly experienced such in the UK. Forward thinking in the event of a pandemic of any kind seemed to have been utterly lacking and put the governments of most nations on the back foot, mostly just "following the science" as if science had all the answers: it does not, even as I write. So, deluded thinking led to shortage of personal protective equipment, challenges to capacity intake in hospitals, and grossly insufficient testing and tracing of infected people. Even as I write, my consultant anaesthetist neighbour has *failed* to get a test for Covid, and can only have one if she has symptoms. If she is an asymptomatic carrier then that is just too bad for the patients with whom she comes into contact daily.

Delusion gets really to the core of government stupidity in this following statement of Horton's:

> The story of COVID-19 in the US is one of the strangest paradoxes of the whole pandemic. No other country in the world has the concentration of scientific skill, technical knowledge and productive capacity possessed by the US. It is the world's scientific superpower bar none. And yet this colossus of science utterly failed to bring its expertise successfully to bear on the policy and politics of the nation's response. More people died in the US from COVID-19 in three months than during the entire Vietnam War (there were 58,318 US soldiers killed in action in Vietnam between 1955 and 1975; deaths from COVID-19 exceeded that figure on 28 April 2020).[28]

President Trump has a lot of deaths to account for as a result of his delusional thinking. On 25 February one of his incessant tweets announced: "The coronavirus is very much under control in the USA. Stock market starting to look very good to me!" The stock market was not good and fell globally within days. The stupidity of Trump's statements to the American people about the "new hoax", as Trump called the pandemic in January, is quite incredible. Horton has gathered these: "By 30 January he was describing the epidemic as 'pretty much under control'. By 2 February, his administration had 'pretty much shut it down.' By 27 February, 'it will disappear.' On 4 March, he claimed there were 'very small numbers in the US'. 10 March: 'It's really working out.' 12 March: 'It's going to go away.'" It was not until 17 March that Trump admitted it was a pandemic.[29] Millions of people travelled from Europe to the US in February and March because there seemed to be no danger while deaths mounted. Black and Latino people in the Bronx died at twice the rate of white people elsewhere and loads of un-refrigerated rental trucks were needed to hold the bodies of the deceased: if the President knew of this, he showed no evidence that he did. Conversely, when Democrat Joe Biden faced the American nation early in October 2020 while Trump was in hospital recovering from Covid, he reminded the nation that 7.3 million Americans had been infected with Covid, 200,000 had died, and 30 million were economically impacted. But when Donald Trump emerged from hospital, he played down the virus as something bordering on being mild and certainly "nothing to be afraid of" – a "blessing from God" he called it!

New York, in particular, should have gone into lockdown much earlier, and in the UK, too, lockdown was late, with the government thoroughly delusional about the nature of the virus and its deadly nature. The Cheltenham Gold Cup racing event was allowed to proceed, as was the football game between Italy and England on 27 March at Wembley stadium in London *with scientific advice*! A quarter of Covid deaths in the UK were of residents in care homes, yet the government was adamant that residents in care homes were comparatively at low risk. As for herd immunity, the UK government was totally delusional about the way that would work and the lives it would cost. Here, its scientific advisors, Graham Medley and Sir Patrick Vallance were keen to see infections throughout the country to create such herd immunity. As we saw in Chapter 2, there is no guarantee that this virus does not re-infect.

What causes such delusional behaviour? In some cases I think it is greed for power or a refusal to accept and rationalize the views of others (as in the case of Donald Trump). Whether at a personal level related to what we regard as our own selves or at a corporate level of political power, I have much sympathy with Quick's words here: "We humans are fantastically arrogant. When we can't believe the evidence before our eyes, we dodge into all kinds of coping behaviors that support our personal worldviews. We choose to believe – or at least to pretend – that a problem staring us in the face either isn't happening or will never happen here or to us."[30] I am sure the average reader will perhaps think that he or she is not culpable in any way of being part of such stupidity, and that Quick's words about choosing to ignore such large scale problems is irrelevant to most of us. But let us think again. In a remarkable article entitled "Meat is Murder" in the *Radio Times* in the UK, that great conservationist, David Attenborough, had this to say:

> Today, nearly 80 percent of farmland worldwide is used for meat and dairy production – four billion of our five billion farmland hectares, an area that would cover both North and South America. Surprisingly, much of this space has no livestock in it at all. It is dedicated to crops like soy, often grown in a different country exclusively as feed for cattle, chickens and pigs. Those living in wealthier nations may order meat raised in their country, but some of the feed for those animals will probably have come from tropical nations that are destroying their forests and grasslands to grow feed crops for those

animals. It is largely in these tropical nations that the expansion of farmland is still happening, and the world's growing appetite for meat is a leading cause.[31]

So are we being delusional and fundamentally stupid and thoughtless about our behaviour in terms of our greed for meat? Yes we are! I think as long as we can go to the supermarket and buy our meat – even if locally produced – we are mainly ignorant of what has to happen to the planet for us to eat it. Thus, delusion filters all the way down to each individual. Given the fact that the average American eats more than 120kg of meat each year, that results in a huge amount of unsustainable harm to the planet. For the Buddha, the destruction of the three poisons brings their opposite, generosity instead of greed, lovingkindness instead of hatred, and wisdom instead of delusion, but each human being has to reflect on his or her life and the ways in which, in particular, greed for food is inimical to our planet. I shall return to the more positive attributes that are opposed to the three poisons in the final chapter. Before closing this chapter, however, it is necessary to deal with the third of the three marks that is a critically important cause of suffering – delusions about the nature of the self.

No-self, *anatta*

The third of the three marks is the doctrine of no-self, *anatta*. It may be a later theory added to the Buddha's first sermon after his enlightenment but given the emphasis on impermanence put forward by the first mark we should really not be surprised that the self is included as an impermanent phenomenon.[32] The word *anatta* is constructed with the negative prefix *an* plus *atta* (cf. Sanskrit *atman*), "one's own person", "self" or "soul". Importantly, it is not the self *per se* that is denied, but any kind of permanent ego or consciousness. The empirical egoistic self is not denied but it has no permanent reality independent of its actions. So there is no "seer" behind seeing, no "thinker" behind thought, no "doer" behind doing; there is only seeing, thinking and doing. The *self* that we consider to be permanent and the agent behind all action of the senses *does not exist*: so there is no lasting individuality, personhood, or autonomous being in any real, ultimate sense.

The empirical self is a *santana*, a "stream" of changing conditions and interconnected causes. Logically, we have a tendency to accept a permanent "I" that is in control of all we do and think, an entity of some kind that unites all experiences, memories, knowledge and sensory perceptions, but Buddhism denies that this entity exists. Nevertheless, since my memories and experiences are different from those of others, the stream of causes that creates me is different from those that create others, so some kind of empirical individuality obtains in each one of us. And, again, it seems logical that the "I" that did gardening this morning is the same "I" that is here writing these words. Because those two activities and others in between have been undertaken by me, it suggests that "I" am the permanent being that links all my activities and makes sense of their continuity in time. What is more, that "I" is believed to be an autonomous being in that had I wished, I could have been writing in the morning and now be out gardening in the afternoon. Such was the thought of the French philosopher René Descartes, who said: "I think therefore I am" suggesting that as long as I can think, I have a real self or soul. But if thinking is a process of consciousness, without consciousness, where is the "I", the self? So Gethin rightly says: "Thus Buddhist thought suggests that as an individual I am a complex flow of physical and mental phenomena, but peel away these phenomena and look behind them and one just does not find a constant self that one can call one's own."[33]

At any one moment we are nothing more than causes that have come together only to disperse and new causes to take their place. Now, those replacing causes will be immediately replaced by others, and those, again, immediately replaced, and so on: each effect may be *very similar*, but cannot be *exactly* the same as the previous causes. Yet I will link all the effects as if they are unchanged instead of a continuous process of becoming and ceasing. We end up somewhat deluded as to the nature of the self and hold on to the delusion of a permanent self that is the agent behind all physical and mental activity. And we can really suffer by trying to create *particular* identities for ourselves, identities that are measured by what we have, what our children have, what kind of house we live in, what kind of car we have and, conversely, what we do not have, what we cannot afford, what it would be like to have a job or economic security. It is easy to see how *tanha*, craving, informs this kind of thinking – all because we have a deluded idea of self.

As we saw above in the discussion of impermanence, *nothing* is permanent in the whole Universe; *everything* is dependent on changing conditions. Thus, to use Malalasekera's succinct words: "What appears to be real is a temporary existence, an instant in a conditional sequence, the effect of two or more conditions combined."[34] So the question can be asked: How can we have *ownership* of that which is not real and not permanent? And to return to *tanha*, craving, the cause of suffering, this is exactly what the Buddha taught: trying to take ownership and say "this is mine", or "I have these wonderful personality traits" is a distorted and deluded way to live life. It is only possible to love and to hate when the objects of both are believed to be pleasurable or objectionable *to the self*. Self and ownership go hand in hand so belief in a self leads to craving that leads to suffering. Again, the Buddha's Five Aggregates – matter, sensations and feelings, perceptions, mental formations and consciousness – are important here. None of these is the self but, rather, they combine together in all sorts of collocations from one moment to the next to give the impression of a self. Many will believe the body to be the self when combined with mental impressions about it. To think, "this is *my* body" would not offend anyone's common sense approach to reality. Similarly, I have *my* thoughts and am conscious of *my* body and *my* feelings and thoughts. But do any of these constitute the self? The Buddha would have replied that they do not, that is to say, there is no unchanging *real* self. The self we think we have is the egoistic self which generates the *me*, *my*, and *mine*, but it is not permanent and not real. The Buddha said: "Give up what does not belong to you! Such giving-up will long conduce to your well-being and happiness". And when asked what it is that does not belong to one, he said: "Materiality, feelings, perception, mental formations and consciousness – these do not belong to you and these you should give up. Such giving-up will long conduce you to well-being and happiness."[35]

So what did the Buddha mean when he said the Five Aggregates do not belong to us? He meant that each is impermanent. The Five Aggregates are each subject to multiple causes and effects that come together momentarily only to disappear as quickly and be replaced by the next rapid rise of causes, coming into being and disappearing like the waves on the sea. As an individual steps into a river, that same individual can never step into the same river again even if he or she does so in rapid succession: the man and the river have changed from one moment to the next. And yet, it would not be true to say that if I do A, then "I" will not be the person who achieves the result of A as B. Yes, the Five Aggregates rise and fall and are impermanent, as are the causes that produce them, but, *continuity* in terms of similar causes from one moment to the next allows the chimera of permanence. Events flow in a process of continual change and flux so while there is continuity, there is no firm *identity*: such is the empirical self and all elements of it.

Many might argue here that memory is the means by which a self can be identified as real. But is memory in an individual reliable? One of the reasons why the self is believed by most to exist is because "something" has to be the connective factor of past and present to make the continuity of the "I". That "I" remembers what it did last week, last year and many of the experiences that accumulate to formulate the "I". Memory is what gives us our identities. But consider David Eagleman's words here: "Rather than memory being an accurate video recording of a moment in your life, it is a fragile brain state from a bygone time that must be resurrected for you to remember."[36] Such recall by *episodic* memory, memory of some event in the past, is different from the memory we have of facts. Episodic memory remembers events in terms of context, time and content, and to do this the neurons of the brain have to reassemble in the same sort of configurations present in the remembered event, with a concomitant memory of the self in that event. This is something that takes place in reciprocal association between the hippocampus and the neocortex in the brain. The problem is that the recreation of a past event is different: *all* the sensations of the time are unlikely to be recalled, causing Julian Jaynes to say: "Memory is the medium of the must-have-been."[37] Moreover, the brain does not store up unchanging neural patterns as it evolves: neurons are reconfiguring all the time to process new information so it is impossible for exactly the same neurons to reassemble to present accurate past events. In fact, brilliant as the brain is in its complexity, memory and recall are not that good: as Jaynes says: "What you can consciously recall is a thimbleful to the huge oceans of your actual knowledge."[38] Memories have to fade because the neurons used for an initial event are re-used in later events. Thus memory cannot be relied on for self-identification because it cannot be completely accurate: that leaves us prone to inventing some aspects. Memories are distorted by subsequent histories, the views of others, exaggerations of events, or what we wanted things to be. And not much of brain activity reaches the conscious level: the bulk affects the subconscious so limiting complete memory recall. Our working memories can only store about seven concepts or memory items at any one time: it is a short-term memory relevant only to the immediate need, so remembering events of the past perfectly is impossible.

Most religions of the West teach belief in a soul that is in some way the true self that, at death, leaves the body and exists post mortem. Eastern religions have a similar concept of a soul that is linked in some way with the divine with whom the soul will be united totally, partially or separately after death, or after a long process of reincarnation to purify the self and rid it of its egocentricity. The doctrine of no-self in Buddhism denies any soul of this kind. In support of this theory, we never have any perception of a soul within and if all sensory perception – ability to touch, see, smell, hear, feel and think – is taken away, what is there? The answer must surely be "nothing". If there is a soul apart from sensory feelings, where is it? There can be nothing that is permanent because all is subject to change, so Buddhism rules out entirely the possibility of an eternal soul that is an unchanging substance of any kind. We cannot make a permanent "I" out of any of the Five Aggregates nor all of them together.

With no "I", no self, there cannot be any ownership, so in terms of suffering there cannot be a sufferer, just as there is no doer only doing and no seer only seeing. But if the self is thought of as *my* self, then *my* action and *my* suffering will follow. There is no real individual, no real personhood, because a person is nothing but a collection of aggregates that rise and fall in every moment. That there are *patterns* of changing causes and effects to make a human being is not denied, patterns that link the baby, child and adult, but there is no *self* that is the linking factor. Gethin explains this neatly: "The 'person' that is me thus subsists not in some entity remaining constant for thirty-five years but merely in the fact that certain clusters of physical and mental events are linked causally."[39] Yet Gethin makes a very pertinent point here when he writes that "the 'I' who exists today only exists by virtue of its dependence upon the 'I' that existed yesterday; there is a definite causal connection."[40] Thus, causal connectivity would make me responsible for my actions yesterday, in the past, and perhaps even in a past life. If this were not so, there could be no possible pathway out of suffering. Each of us is a coming together of appropriate causes, and those causes make us who we are *in each moment* and nothing more. We do not *own* anything here: we do not own our feelings for if we did we could make ourselves happy for the remainder of our lives. Similarly, we do not own suffering. Feelings cannot last because the causes that make them cannot last and, again similarly, suffering cannot last because the causes that bring it about cannot last. Nevertheless, it is still possible to change the way we think and act in order to create better causes for what is ahead.

The self that we think we have then is a delusion. There is no autonomous self that controls actions, sensations and feelings, perceptions, thoughts, and consciousness. There is no self that can control any of these causal factors. In the penultimate chapter we shall see just how difficult it is to control our minds, our thoughts, and what can be done to remedy that because if our consciousness is conditioned by constantly changing causes that we do not recognise, we have little control over it. I think Malalasekera explained consciousness particularly well when he wrote that it "is the experience of the unity between concept and object; it is not something that *is*, but something that *becomes*. It is not an object of knowing, but knowing itself, an ever-repeated new becoming, new upspringing out of its antecedent conditions",[41] So it can be said with some degree of confidence that "I" is not consciousness. Consciousness is totally dependent on the body, sense organs and perceptions arising from impermanent conditions that come and go.

How then does understanding of the three marks, the three poisons or evils and the Five Aggregates help in overcoming suffering? First, the fact that all these theories point to the impermanence of *every single thing* in the Universe, including what we call a self, means that it is really impossible to have ownership of anything other than temporarily. So suffering cannot be owned, cannot belong to a person. Then, if ownership is relinquished what is the point of desiring and craving? It will be control of the mind here that will develop such perspectives as we shall see in chapter 7. Mind is simply a functioning tool not some static entity and if it can be trained to reject the concept of a permanent self then maybe selfishness could stand a chance of being eradicated, the kind of selfishness that makes individuals gain from injury to others. What is there to gratify if the self is denied? The goal is reduction of the ego, that self-centred and selfish aspect of the so-called self. Nyanatiloka Mahathera believed that without egolessness there could be no Buddhism, and without realizing the truth of that there can be no progress to deliverance from suffering.[42] In the Buddha's words: "Whoso understands and contemplates the mind as egoless, in him the Ego-view disappears. Whoso understands and contemplates as egoless (anatta) the mind-objects . . . mind-consciousness . . . mind-impression . . . and the agreeable and disagreeable and indifferent feeling conditioned through mind-impression, in him the Ego-view disappears."[43]

In getting the mind to forget the self, freedom from care results and a tranquil state is achieved. Malalasekera had some wise words here: "When pleasures vanish of their own accord, they end in keen anguish of mind; when relinquished by one's own will, they produce infinite happiness, proceeding from tranquillity."[44] And Williams writes, too: "Liberation results from letting go that which is seen as not being the Self. When one sees things are sources of unhappiness, out of one's control, and impermanence, one sees that they cannot be any kind of Self. With this one lets them go, for having any involvement with them can only lead to misery."[45] All attachment and craving have to be abandoned in order for suffering to cease. The foundations of suffering are the result of clinging to a delusional self that has to be gratified, that wants this and that and that grasps after pleasures of the senses – what to eat, what to drink, who to love, what to get, what to wear, how to look better, how to look younger, how to achieve, how to be the best

– the list is endless and unless it is decreased, suffering will ensue. Reality is escape from the egoistic self that is responsible for the craving that brings suffering: that was the message of the Buddha, but he did not leave it at that for having found the cause of suffering, he proceeded to outline the cure.

5

The Third Noble Truth of the Cessation of Suffering

The third of the Buddha's Noble Truths is concerned with the cure for suffering. The process of the Buddha's enlightenment, his awakening to ultimate Truth, took place during the watches of the night, and in the last watch he realized that *nibbana* was the cure to all suffering. He knew that he had come to the end of his countless journeys through endless lives and would never be born again. The cessation, *nirodha*, of all suffering means the cessation of craving, of desires, the removal of the causes so that the effects cannot come into being. *Nibbana* is the cure, something that can only be *realized* not developed. Cessation here is a letting go, an abandonment of the craving that leads to suffering. No reason or logic can bring this about only meditative practice to experience it deep within – a depth of understanding that dawns on one from some dormant core. In this chapter, there is much that is crucial to the Buddha's teaching and to the reasons why there is suffering in the world. Thus, in the main, I have set aside Covid – though not exclusively so – in order to do justice to three major Buddhist concepts that underpin the theory of *dukkha*, suffering, and that provide answers to how and why individuals suffer.

Nibbana

I dealt with *nibbana* briefly at the beginning of Chapter 3 for it was the goal that the Buddha presented to the monks of his day as a cure, though it was not a result of anything so it was not even the result of the abandonment of craving. It was not even a "state", cannot be "entered into", and really cannot be compared to anything. In rather profound words, Paul Williams writes: "The discovery was absolutely – enlighteningly – liberating. From this sheer wonder of the Buddha at uncovering the inner turnings of the universe, and the overwhelming freedom of stopping their incessant roll, flows the whole history of

Buddhist thought."[1] There is no cause and effect here, for *nibbana* is the Infinite Reality beyond causality and beyond all the impermanence and conditioned nature of the Universe. In fact, the Buddha said: "There is, monks, an unborn, unoriginated, unmade and unconditioned. Were there not the unborn, unoriginated, unmade and unconditioned, there would be no escape from the born, originated, made and conditioned."[2] None of those reading this is likely to experience "the inner turnings of the Universe". They were words aimed at the monks, the *arahats* who assembled around the Buddha. For those who also realized enlightenment, there was freedom, happiness, non-attachment, absence of ego, calmness of mind, speech and action, equanimity, and freedom from suffering, grief, and the fears brought about by desires and craving. It is unlikely that we shall achieve such states in our lifetime!

While not losing sight of the ultimate goal of *nibbana*, it is perhaps possible to gain some measure of equanimity through more proximate goals, and through understanding the causes that underpin the opposite of *nibbana* in the incessant rounds of birth, death and rebirth as a result of *kammic* causes. So my purpose here is to explore three major concepts – the conditioned nature of everything in the Universe through the Buddha's teaching of Dependent Origination, *kamma*, and rebirth – these three being the causes of life and all in the Universe. At the very least, understanding the way in which *kamma* operates means that choices can be amended, maybe not to the extent of transcending all *kamma*, good and bad, as with the enlightened, but just to bring the mind to a better place, to reduce the desires and craving in life that can bring so much anxiety and suffering, and to be less egocentric. The Buddha would have said these more proximate goals would include the destruction of the three evils of greed, hatred and delusion, and lessening the existence of the Five Aggregates (matter, sensations/feelings, perceptions, mental formations, consciousness) – in short, cessation of as much as possible of what gives us a distorted view of reality. So while few will even aspire to the ultimate of *nibbana*, the present chains of events can be modified with thought and a positive aim to act, speak and think in the right way. The Buddha was a pragmatic man and his own experience of trying to find the answers to life by extreme luxury and then extreme asceticism did not work: the Middle Way is the sensible path, a way of moderation, a way that is a little more dispassionate rather than passionate, especially concerning the Five Aggregates.

Dependent Origination

The Buddha's words on cause and effect were quite distinct from other Indian perspectives. While it seems logical to assume that a cause produces an effect, the Buddha awakened to the fact that any cause was multiple in character, as was any effect. Thus, many, many factors contribute to the process of cause and effect. An important point is made here by Joanna Macy: "No effect arises without cause, yet no effect is predetermined, for its causes are multiple and mutually affecting. Hence there can be novelty as well as order."[3] Thus it is by no means a hard and fast rule that causes will create effects with certainty, though the two are likely to be relational so ensuring that we cannot have a sycamore tree coming from an acorn. Then, too, nuances of factors of cause give the arising and ceasing of effects a dynamic character. This dependency of effects on the arising of multiple factors as causes brings us the theory of Dependent Origination (Pali *paticca samuppada*), which claims that all things without exception arise and cease dependent on the presence of multiple factors as causes in processes that inform not only moment to moment but life to life. Dependent Origination (sometimes termed Dependent Co-origination, Dependent or Conditioned Genesis, Conditioned or Dependent Arising, or Causal Conditioning) is, in short, a law of the conditional nature of all reality, all phenomena, knowledge, thought, consciousness and existence. This is a critical part of the Buddha's *Dhamma*. It is not a theory that the Buddha invented but a natural and impersonal law to which he awakened at his enlightenment. It was not actually part of the Four Noble Truths but, nevertheless, the theory of it remained at the heart of the Buddha's teaching and he dealt with it many times. Important to note is that the theory of Dependent Origination avoids giving any permanence to the self, or to any phenomena, and accounts for all things without reference to a creator or a supernatural being of any kind. "Dependence" means that nothing at all in the Universe is independent: everything is dependent on prior causes.

Dependent Origination is not to be seen as being isolated from the Four Noble Truths or the three marks for it is a scheme set out in its standard form in twelve interdependent and relational facets of the human being that result in the suffering that stood at the heart of the Buddha's view of the world and formed the central thought of the Four Noble Truths. It has twelve factors, each impermanent, each fluid, and each dependent because it is conditioned by the others, as it in turn conditions them. Dependent Origination cleverly explains life as interconnected and impermanent, and was crucial in the Buddha's mission to end suffering. Understanding the twelve, as we shall see, provides a means to the wisdom that can break the cycle of life after life – the worst kind of suffering. I am starting the list below with "ignorance" but "ignorance" should not be seen as the beginning of the twelve given the dependent and interrelational character of each, but rather as a wheel that has no beginning point. Each of the following is the conditional cause of the next in mutual reciprocity, and many of the twelve resonate with the components of the Five Aggregates I mentioned above, and that we met in detail in Chapter 3.

- **Ignorance** is not the beginning of the process but it is representative of a root cause of the suffering in life and so is crucial in ridding the causes of suffering. Although we might think that at birth, aside from genetic influences, we have a blank canvas on which to foster the development of the young, the Buddha believed that ignorance from past lives is there at the moment of conception. The ignorance here is of the Four Noble Truths, of *Dhamma* as knowledge, and of the true nature of things as dependently caused. Ignorance is misconception, an absence of truth, and is the root that pertains mainly to past lives where the causes of it have been accumulated. Nothing beyond individual life creates such ignorance: its worst form occurs when each individual creates false notions of "I", "this is mine", "I am this", "this is my ego" or, simply, "I am." This ignorance is delusion, stupidity, the third of the three evils or poisons that we met in the last chapter, as opposed to knowledge, specifically of the Four Noble Truths. So ignorance is not non-knowledge of facts; it is confusion and general bewilderment about life that results in disharmony and suffering. While, as I said, no one of the twelve begins the process, ignorance is a key factor for, as Alfonso Verdu put it, ignorance "pervades with its presence the whole journey of existence and underlies each one of its milestones".[4]
- **Volitions/formations** are also present at conception as an inheritance of desires and actions in past lives: they are *kamma* formations created by ignorance. I shall deal with the Buddhist belief in *kamma* and rebirth below, but here, in this context of Dependent Origination, the Buddha taught that each individual is the accumulation of multiple causes from past existences. So mental forces formed from past time are passively accumulated as "potentials", or "seeds", deep within the mental psyche. They will emerge as habits, the things desired, preferences, and deep-seated subconscious drives. They carry the programmed will to live, to fulfil certain needs and avoid others – all results of causes

accumulated in past lives. Yet, there is no sense here of predetermined beings that cannot change, for the vista of future lives lies ahead and can be changed by present causes. Yet, in their present lives, beings are, through their own thoughts and actions, thoroughly responsible for the present and future states of their own minds.

Volitions will inform all behaviour whether of body, speech or mind. They are what Peter Harvey aptly calls "constructing activities" that bring about subsequent actions.[5] And Sue Hamilton comments: "One might say that it is the individualising faculty, in the sense of being the formative principle which distinguishes individual A from individual B."[6] It is a paradox that volitions from past lives are closely linked and causative to the nature of volitions in the present life: we are not really free from our good and bad habits in past lives. So our volitions in the past will tend to get reinforced in the present and become equally reinforced for future existences. The three evils – greed, hatred and delusion – are the causes of predispositions of volitions. Responses to sense stimuli – whether wholesome or unwholesome – in past lives dictate the kinds of volitions that will be formed as potentials in present existence. Volitions, then, are a store of good, bad or neutral creative actions from the past. Thus far, ignorance and volitions have come from past lives and provide the set-up for a being, waiting to be activated. And that which activates volitions is consciousness, which is very much a facet of the present being, and the link between past and present lives.

☐ **Consciousness/discrimination** is the product, the result, of the volitions that have come from past lives, so it is causally produced. In this case, no consciousness stands apart from the other factors in order to create some kind of "self" over and above the mind and body. In short, there is no permanent consciousness: it is conditioned and itself conditions. Just as volitions are recycled as it were from the past, so consciousness, too, remains in potentiality as the accumulated mental *kammic* propensities from past lives that will come to fruition in present and future lives. Consciousness must always be consciousness *of* something and as one of the Five Aggregates it cannot exist without the other four because it is part of a process. Much of it will be the results of wholesome or unwholesome dispositions built up in present and past lives. Bhikkhu Bodhi incisively reduces consciousness to its true nature: "Consciousness occurs by way of process. It is not an ongoing subject but a series of transitory acts of cognition arising and passing away through conditions. Each act is particular and discrete – an occasion of eye-consciousness, ear-consciousness, nose-consciousness, tongue-consciousness, body-consciousness, or mind-consciousness. Based on its sense faculty it performs its function of cognizing the object, then gives way to the next act of consciousness, which arises in immediate succession."[7]

Thus, consciousness cannot exist apart from the five senses and mind on which it depends: nor can it exist without a body. It is subject to constant flux and change depending on the causative sense perceptions that feed it: consciousness is always changing, always flowing, with successions of causes that rise and fall. In a Buddhist text, the *Questions of Milinda*, it says that "the elements of being join one another in serial succession: one element perishes, another arises, succeeding each other as it were instantaneously. Therefore, neither as the same nor as a different person do you arrive at your latest aggregation of consciousness."[8] A refined consciousness was part of the Buddha's pathway to liberation for monks and nuns and it was achieved through careful stages of meditation in which higher states of wisdom and right perceptions into reality were gained.

☐ **Name and form; mind and body; mind and matter** depict the mental/material being on the one hand and the multiple phenomena that constitute existence on the other. The nature of the mind and body will be dependent on the *kammic* consciousness, so consciousness and name and form are inextricably linked. Name and form, mind and body, will be conditioned by previous impermanent causes but will seem as an "I", an ego. Name and form constitute the world, and consciousness is that which reacts to it resulting in more *kamma* and hence rebirth. "If you do not cling to name and form", says the *Dhammapada*, "Possessing nothing, sorrows cannot attack you."[9] We make sense of the world because we name – and so conceptualize and describe – what we experience in it, but all that we name is, ultimately, insubstantial and traps us into desires.

☐ **The six senses** build up a view of reality, a view of the world around and thoughts about it. The mind as the sixth sense is the synthesizer of all that the senses relay to it. The senses will be linked to *kammic* formations in the way in which they operate. We need the senses to provide us with knowledge of the world and of others, described rather well by Hamilton when she says the senses are "doors through which the individual subjectively interacts with the objective world",[10] but those "doors" open and

close like lightning, constantly being renewed by the next successive moment.
- ☐ **Sense contact/impressions/stimulation** is the point at which everything is set up for reaction, the real meeting point of mind with the visual world: the senses are engaged, and the nature of reaction to that engagement will be causative for the future. Here, as Macy says, "consciousness is colored by that on which it feeds, subject and object are interdependent . . . Sensory experience shapes us and we in turn shape it. The conditioning is mutual."[11]
- ☐ **Feeling/sensation** as a result of sense contact is pleasant, unpleasant or neutral and is a succession of changing states, but the temptation to link feelings with a self is overriding for almost every individual. In short, responses to the sense stimuli of the world make up *kammic* natures. The sense contact is, as Hamilton says, "the *conscious* coming together of sense organ and corresponding object. In other words, it is a conscious sensory event".[12] Such a process is what makes feeling possible. Since feeling is dependent on one of the senses, the sense organ *and* Hamilton's "conscious sensory event", this suggests that feeling is not confined merely to the physicality of the body. Indeed, it may also be completely mind-orientated in order to represent abstract thought. Much of such feeling will already be dictated by the volitions, ignorance and *kamma* of past lives. This has considerable implications for suffering. If we think for a moment of any aspect of suffering, it is twofold – the cause of the suffering *and* our mental reaction to it. If we could overcome the second inner reaction we would probably cope with the initial suffering much better.
- ☐ **Craving/thirst/desire** is the active response to how we feel and is closely linked – as are many of the twelve factors here – with the Five Aggregates and also with the second of the Four Noble Truths. When we are just conscious of something and do not react we are still at the stage of merely recognizing a sense object as pleasant, unpleasant or neutral. But human nature does not leave it there and we *react*. That reaction is what leads to desire, attachment, longing, clinging, the need to make decisions, the desire to possess, avarice, fear, dislike, hatred – all the myriad reactions we have in daily life that result in *kamma*. And that brings us back to the second of the Four Noble Truths, craving, *tanha*. While feeling is natural and unavoidable, what is done about it is dependent on choice. The monk tried to restrain reactions here and replace craving with mindfulness. In Bhikkhu Bodhi's words: "It is at that brief moment when the present

resultant phase has come to a culmination in feeling, but the present causal phase has not yet begun, that the issue of bondage and liberation is decided."[13] Identification with what is craved for makes it a belonging, and a need for the "me" that is created to own it. And as we saw in Chapter 4, craving is not only related to desire for pleasant things, for status, for fame, beauty, success, and happy experiences; it is also craving to avoid what is unpleasant. At this point in the Dependent Origination scheme of things, the *kammic future* is being formed from responses to sense stimuli in the present – all that follows for future lives begins here.

- **Grasping/clinging/attachment** represent the whole world of response to desires. Attachment to all aspects of life, physical and mental, feeds the ego and the idea of a permanent self. Included in the Buddha's teaching about clinging, apart from sense desires, were attachment to false views, and to external practices such as rites and rituals, but the most prolific and delusional attachment was to an egoistic "self", or eternal "soul".
- **Becoming/existence** is dependent on, and caused by, all the *kamma* built up from the grasping and attachment of previous lives and makes rebirth inevitable, though the quality of it is dependent on the nature of the *kamma* and dispositions built up through responses to feeling via the senses. When existence occurs at conception, the ignorance present in past lives joins with the new being with volition formations, consciousness, the nature of the mind and body, as well as senses – all present as results of past interrelated causes. Francis Story pointed out that "becoming" never ceases, it "never reaches the point of completion in *being*. This in itself is suffering."[14] Each person is the result of repetitions of trillions of his or her thoughts and actions that get repeated habitually life after life. Again, each individual does not appear at birth with a clean slate but with a dye cast from all those causes in the past, causes he and she have made for themselves. All life is a flowing process of becoming and transformation that never really becomes. In the words of Thera Piyadassi: "Life is not an identity, it is a becoming. It is a flux of psychological and physiological changes: a conflux of mind and body."[15] In ceaseless becoming there is not a single permanent cause, only dymamic processes of multiple antecedent causes that make everything in the Universe, and everything that comes into being becomes a momentary part of the interconnected causes of something else.
- **Birth** is the result of the "becoming" of the *kammic* causes of the

present and previous lives. It brings about despondency and despair – in short, suffering. Birth points to the future and the blueprint of that future for the being even at conception – the temperament, physicality, life events, nature of death, and the like. In the early Buddhist understanding of birth, it is the rebirth of the Five Aggregates in the womb – albeit in differing and changing collocations – the resetting of the vitalizing mind flux in fresh conditions, as Piyadassi described it.[16] He wrote: "As in the universe no energy can ever be lost, so also in the individual nothing can be lost of the resilient force accumulated by desire. This resilient energy is always transmuted into fresh life and we live eternally through our lust to live."[17]

- ☐ **Ageing and death** also point to the future and are the inevitable results of birth that can never be avoided. Rebirth in Buddhism is the fate of most and is caused by all the misconceptions about reality; the *kammic* build-up of interrelated causes that make related effects necessary. All this comes to fruition at the moment of death, though the last thoughts of a dying being are generally believed to have a marked influence on the state of the next rebirth, "self-reiteration events of the future", as described by Verdu, and "successive reiteration" of all the components of Dependent Origination.[18] Take, for example, individuals that become very attached to their illnesses. They take ownership of them and attach them to a self. They refer to *my* such-and-such, and recount the details of their illnesses whenever they find a polite ear. But this is *attachment* to their own suffering, attachment that is building up causes for the same illnesses in future lives.

Each of the twelve is primarily conditioned by its predecessor and conditions its successor – a "closed circuit of mutually conditioning factors"[19] – an important point since nothing beyond the components is causative. As Verdu said, "each one of the links is the cause and at the same time effects of all the others".[20] Dependent Origination was the way early Buddhism viewed reality, a reality that was not static but an arising and ceasing of moments, each moment providing the multiple causes for the next one, and so on. So there cannot be *one* cause related to *one* effect, only a multiplicity and totality of dynamic antecedent conditions, "point-instants", as Theodore Stcherbatsky termed them,[21] which bring about a moment in time. On this theory, the whole of existence is dynamically and efficiently *causing* in any one moment. Each "point instant" is a collection of impermanent causes informed by multiple facets producing equally impermanent multi-component effects. In the same way, suffering is conditioned by impermanent causes, suggestive that as a result, an effect, it is also impermanent and so curable if the causes of it are removed or changed.

The "dependent" aspect of Dependent Origination is the nub of the cause–effect processes, for all twelve are mutually dependent co-simultaneous and co-originating. And because they are conditioned and mutually dependent, understood *in reverse* they can be used as conditioned causes to ameliorate suffering, acquire wisdom, understand the *Dhamma*, and be on the pathway to *nibbana*. Understanding Dependent Origination as the way reality is becomes a means to end suffering. While as I said there is no one of the twelve that starts the process, a few of the twelve stand out as keys in the pathway to liberation from suffering. Clearly, the dispelling of ignorance is crucial, as is dispelling craving in response to sense stimuli. If just these two aspects were to be changed, then the *kamma* acquired that informs volition and consciousness, would be positive and evolutionary. The bottom line of Dependent Origination is that since all is impermanent it is futile to crave for anything: realization of this means that changes in response to such impermanent structures *can* be made and alter the effects for the future. The first two *kammic* formations, ignorance and volition, clearly relate to past lives: they make up present consciousness and all the other factors with the exception of the last two. These last ones, birth, and ageing and death, project into the future. But ignorance is the key in having its roots in the past, while craving creates the roots for the future. Nevertheless, even if we divide up the twelve to suggest past, present and future influence, all twelve operate in *one* present existence to inform every aspect of life.

Understanding Dependent Origination is the understanding of the wisdom of the Buddha's *Dhamma*, the true nature of reality. Moreover, every aspect of the phenomenal world is composed of *dhammas*, impermanent combinations that come together fleetingly and then disappear, only to be replaced by the next combination of *dhammas*. This is all there is to reality, and that reality includes all physical phenomena, all mental formations, minds and consciousnesses. Nothing in reality is permanent; there is no eternal self beyond the *dhammas*. Everything is part of the flux of processes of change. To understand the nature of Dependent Origination is to understand how suffering arises – when there is "this", there is "that", and when "this" arises, "that" arises – as stated in the first two of the Four Noble Truths. Conversely, reversing the process of Dependent Origination gets rid of suffering – where "this" is not, "that" is not, and when "this" ceases, "that" ceases. In short, all suffering and the whole cycle of rebirths are dependent on the arising of the twelve conditions and will cease if the twelve are controlled. The *dhammas* condition reality as the natural, impersonal way that things are, so suffering is the result not of haphazard chance or of determinism: again, the Buddha presented a Middle Way between these two. But an important point is raised by Bhikkhu Bodhi when he says that "dependent arising, as a teaching of specific conditionality, deals primarily with structures. It treats phenomena, not in terms of their isolated connections, but in terms of their patterns – recurrent patterns that exhibit the invariableness of law."[22] His point is that whatever arises – the "that" from the "this" – does so specifically in relation to myriad patterns of conditions that supply equally myriad specific structures. In relation to the self, actions, thoughts and speech are not owned by a "self", but are the results of multiple natural and impersonal causes.

The twelve facets of Dependent Origination presented here are not to be viewed in a linear and progressive manner. To demonstrate this, the twelve are sometimes portrayed in the form of a wheel to illustrate the interdependency of the components, though the symbol was a later development in the *Abhidhamma* texts. Thus, there is no real beginning to suffering nor, importantly, to its cessation. Macy's simile here is a sound one: "Like a house of cards, the constellation of factors that condition our existence can be disrupted and collapsed at any point."[23] For later Buddhism, the wheel became a prominent feature of iconography and the "wheel of the law" an important idiom. There are, indeed, a number of variations of the twelve and the Buddha himself spoke of the twelve from different starting points, depending on what he wished to teach, and this was the case, too, in the reverse order that he used to show the cessation of suffering. Some of the factors of the twelve may be omitted, or the order of the twelve changed or added to. I have given the standard twelve, but it should be remembered that such variations occurred frequently. Similarly, the twelve may be sectioned in different ways, for example in order to represent past, present and future, as I have hinted at above. However they are interpreted, they always remain mutually interdependent on each other, interrelated, necessarily conditional, continually arising and ceasing and informing each moment of life. Prayadh Payutto reiterates this point: "The continuum of cause and effect which enables all things to exist as they do can only operate because such things are transient, ephemeral, constantly arising and ceasing and having no intrinsic entity of their own."[24] Without such a nature, phenomena such as the Five Aggregates would not be able to be understood as the chimera they are and there could be no release from the bound and suffering condition of the self.

So a "cause" in the light of Dependent Origination is a combination of a number of interacting *dhammas*, and an "effect" is, equally so, a conglomerate of interacting conditions. There is never a situation in which *a* cause, a *single* cause, produces *an* effect, a single effect. Dependent Origination makes all cause multi-faceted as is any effect; a "harmony of causes" as David Kalupahana described cause.[25] And if the factors combine differently in the cause, then a slightly different effect with the same different components of the cause will result. Networks of conditions as cause produce an effect with networks of components. Williams describes reality as a "torrent of cause and effect with no stability within it",[26] an apt description of reality that is in constant flux from moment to moment. There is, too, a momentariness about reality, tiniest fractions of moments succeeding each other just as a single point on the rim of a rotating wheel touches the ground just once only to be replaced by the next point, and the next, and so on – Stcherbatsky's "point instants" that we met above. The life moments of an individual, including consciousness, are so similar, arising and ceasing in perpetual flux, and yet there is continuity though not identity of moment to moment because of the similarity in the coming together of the components of cause. However, the same components of causes in one moment are never likely to be exactly the same in the next moment but their similarity enables the patterns and order of reality.

Conditions come together to create effects, making reality a process, a process that is no less true of the cosmos than it is of each individual, of death and rebirth, of arising and ceasing of all things. There is no static *ultimate* reality in the sense of an eternal force beyond Dependent Origination. Dependent Origination *is* the ultimate Truth of the impermanence of reality and the ultimate teaching of the Buddha. As to ordinary reality, ordinary existence, the Buddha accepted it as *conventional* reality, a reality that gives names and forms to all things and sees permanence where it is really absent. Even the Universe both evolves and involves,[27] and is impermanent in the Buddhist view so there is absolutely no sense of a creation in time, just a Universe that, like everything else, is conditionally and dependently changing and impermanent. In this way, the Buddha deconstructed the concept of "Universe" in much the same way as he did "soul".

Such was the Buddha's teaching on cause and effect presented in the *Suttas*. The Buddha centred on the problem of suffering, old age, death and birth and sought to provide a means by which they could be overcome, a means that overthrew conceptions of "I", "me" and "mine". Bhikkhu Bodhi summed this up nicely when he wrote: "The challenge is to see that whatever happens in the course of existence is merely a conditioned event happening through conditions in a continuum of dependently arisen phenomena. It is not happening *to* anyone. There is no agent behind the actions, no knower behind the knowing, no transmigrating self passing through the round. What binds the factors of experience together, at any given moment and from moment to moment, is the principle of dependent origination itself."[28] The cessation of suffering is also a natural process that dispels the conditional causes that produce it, reversing the factors that cause things to be – "this" not arising, "that" cannot arise – getting rid of the causal factors that are at the root of all suffering.

Kamma (Skt: *karma*)

Many individuals in the West are now familiar with the eastern concept of *karma*, the powerful law that is described rather well in the Sanskrit *Dharmapada*:

> Not in the sky nor in the ocean's middle,
> Nor if you were to hide in cracks in the mountains,
> Can there be found on this wide earth a corner
> Where karma does not catch up with the culprit.[29]

Karma is not without its adherents outside India where it originated. Since the Four Noble Truths on which this book is based are grounded in early Buddhist and subsequent conservative Buddhist belief, I am going to retain the Pali term in which the early scriptures were first written and use *kamma*. *Kamma* is the law of causes that will result in effects, that also to which the Buddha awakened. But it is not simply a cause resulting in an effect. As we saw with Dependent Origination, multiple conditions create cause and multiple factors are present in effect. Buddhist *kamma* is a natural law that exists independently of any divine being and has no inherent purpose: it simply operates in relation to the microcosmic and macrocosmic factors that inform it. Intentional actions, speech and thoughts leave residual traces, and when these are positive, the traces will be positive: if negative, negative traces will be left. The effects of *kamma* have nothing to do with rewards and punishments; they are simply effects that come to be as a result of prior causes, and effects – good or evil – are totally dependent on the *kammic* causes.

Nevertheless, *kamma* has an overriding moral dimension in that since like causes produce like effects, good produces good, and evil, evil. Coming from the root *kar*, "to do", "to act", *kamma* means quite simply "action" and that would be action of body, mind or speech, but it is also action *with intent*, desire, action undertaken to bring about a result, so *kamma* is also equated with volition, will. It is important to note here that *kamma* is *only* action, not the effect of action, for which another term, *vipaka*, "maturation", is used. So it is not bad *kamma* if you trip over a stone, just clumsiness! *Kamma* as causative can be weighty if seriously bad, or highly meritorious when positive acts have been committed. It is built up through persistent habits to produce an abundance of like causes. Some *kamma* may be due to ripen subsequently, or may not ripen due to the right conditions not coming together. This last suggests that when there are insufficient traces of *kamma* of a particular nature, it can be changed – an important point for the ending of suffering.

All *kamma* is completely impersonal and its effects – good or evil – are totally dependent on the antecedent causes that arise from that *kamma*. That said, *kamma* becomes personal in that its effects, the *vipaka*, accrue uniquely to one individual – the individual that put the actions in place in the past. So *vipaka* for each individual is predetermined by that individual's past *kamma*, as long as it is sufficient enough to come to fruition. It is impossible to have the *vipaka* without *kamma*, the interconnected causative actions in the first place, because all effects must have causes. And in our everyday lives we function by actions that are intimately connected with *desires*: most of what we do is done through volition and mostly for a desired result. Many of our volitional activities are not actually known to us because, "in every human consciousness there is a complex of hidden motivations. They are hidden", according to Francis Story, "because we do not wish to acknowledge them. In every human being there is a built-in defence mechanism which prevents him from seeing himself too clearly."[30] Added to such motivations are the tendencies we have to act in a certain way because of the build-up of *kammic* habits from the past. Then there is the overwhelming desire *to live*, and the instincts – conscious and subconscious – to preserve the self in life that are equally overwhelming examples of *tanha*, craving. We must view *kamma*, then, as *volitional* actions of body, mind/thought, and speech. So if I *intend* to kill someone, the resulting effects are much worse than if I accidentally kill someone. And that *intention*, that *volition*, constitutes an act of craving, *tanha*, equating with causative *kamma*.

The moral weight of volition here is clear: if an activity involves morally good purpose, good intention, the *kamma-vipaka* will also be good and the converse is true for the morally evil. Non-volitional actions will produce no future effects at all. So *kamma* may be of good, wholesome, "skilled", "profitable", *kusala*, causes, or of unwholesome "unskilled", "unprofitable", *akusala*, actions. The range of possibilities for unwholesome *kamma* is accounted for within the three evils of greed, hatred and delusion – inauspicious causes that are the roots of evil and are morally faulty. The opposites of the three evils in non-attachment, friendliness and loving-kindness, and wisdom produce wholesome *karma* – auspicious causes. Nyanatiloka Mahathera advised that: "If we practise unselfishness and liberality, greed and avarice will become less. If we practise love and kindness, anger and hatred will vanish. If we develop wisdom and knowledge, ignorance and delusion will gradually disappear."[31]

The idea that one has to be "skilful" in thought, word, and deed suggests that elements of discernment and wisdom are necessary in living. Nevertheless, though early Buddhism clearly saw good actions as yielding good effects and the converse for evil actions, overall effects were considered more heterogeneous: that is to say, eventual effects could turn out not to resemble their original causes.[32] There was certainly a moral causality in the animate world, but this could not be applied to inorganic matter. Here, it was accepted that causes and their effects were uniform and homogeneous – like producing like in rapid succession from moment to moment, to give an idea of permanence, even though impermanence was at the core of such natural succession between causes and effects. As to the organic world, natural causal laws produced the same kinds of changes from causes to effects; the kinds of changes that permitted one kind of seed to ripen to its appropriate effect and no other.

I shall deal explicitly with rebirth below but, here, it is important to note that no self exists to which *kamma* accrues, so the answer to what passes through the multiple experiences of endless existences is simply logical effects that come about because of certain combinations of causes. The so-called self is of the nature of the Five Aggregates produced by causal conditions in a previous existence(s). *Kamma* blends the Aggregates into a body with a "personality" and is the link that connects the present form and personality with all those Aggregates of past lives. And as long as the individual travels through life after life in ignorance, *kamma* will go on building a new form for another existence. But its expression in each life is complicated by all the multiple causes of the past. An evil act by one person will not produce the same effects as exactly the same evil act of another. Both individuals will have other complex counteracting causes that make *kamma* different, particularly with *intention* behind the actions. Thus, the same causes by different individuals will by no means produce the same effects.

The important factor about *kamma* is that it is dynamic and changeable: there is nothing that is deterministic about it. If this were not so, then the Buddha's message that suffering can be overcome would have no meaning. Whether an action is good or evil does not mean an appropriate effect *has* to take place. The initial action may, in fact, be strengthened by other *kamma*, weakened by *kamma* that counteracts it, or even totally annulled by other *kamma*. These are points that reinforce the concept of *multiple* causes being necessary for an effect to occur. So he or she who appears to be a very good individual may not be able to prevent adverse evil effects, just as it is possible for a particularly evil person in the present life to reap wholesome results: thus are the inequalities in life explained, it simply depends on the multiple ways in which *kamma* has been built up. And *kamma* is not only determining causes of present experiences. K. N. Jayatilleke believed that other factors – physiology, genetic inheritance, and social and environmental influences could also have effect on the present situation.[33] Certainly, present actions are able to modify existent *kamma* to some extent. Any adverse *kamma* can be offset by wholesome actions: choice is always possible and choosing to have the right views about life will offset much previous negative *kamma*.

But let us suppose or, in the light of the adverse circumstances in which we currently live with Covid-19, that we are suffering. The impersonal law of *kamma* suggests that it is impossible to lighten the burden of that, but consider these words of Leonard Bullen who says, "in general, even if you have no choice of external action, at least it's possible to regulate your mental and moral responses to a situation, even to a slight extent. Thus, under a difficult set of conditions that you are unable to alter, you can at least exercise patience and tolerance, facing the situation without allowing it completely to overwhelm you."[34] These are wise words and I fully understand how difficult it is for those suffering the physical and mental strains of living with, or with the threat of, the coronavirus to put them into practice, but as Bullen goes on to say, "you're at least building up within your mental structure new progressive reaction-forces, thus using the situation to its best advantage".[35] The Buddha would have said that Covid *cannot* be permanent because *all* is impermanent. If suffering through Covid is a result of unwholesome past *kamma*, then those who can summon great positive courage and will-power, and remain generous and compassionate to others are changing their future lives. Just acting and speaking kindly or being generous and giving are ways of building up good causes, good, wholesome *kamma*. But the *kamma-vipaka* we have now as suffering cannot be avoided – only changed for the future.

Each individual is reaping what he or she has sown in the past, but can sow new wholesome seeds in the present for the future, particularly if they become habitual.

But any effect from past causes has to have a certain amount of accumulated *force* coming from past actions that were responses, choices made innumerable times in the past. This is an accumulating trend, a *kammic* force that is habitually strengthened and that remains until the right kinds of conditions and circumstances occur in the present for it to come into effect. Bullen likens this process to a water tank that has been filled up sufficiently for a particular *kammic* force to have effect. Such effects are drained from the "tank" until exhausted, unless replenished by the same kind of *kammic* causes.[36] Thus, the results of *kamma* in *kamma-vipaka*, say in happiness or suffering, will eventually be used up, for the fruits of *kamma*, whatever they are, will always be impermanent: suffering also has to be impermanent. So we certainly have free will and choice in the way we live our lives, even if results of past actions determine to some extent what we reap in our lives. To be a Buddhist is to make the right choices in the present, choices that might alleviate any adverse *kamma*. We are thoroughly responsible for how we act, think, or speak in our present existences, but only if we do so with *intention*. Events that happen *now* may well be determined by past *kamma* but how we react to them will shape the future.

So what about so-called "collective" *kamma*, situations such as our present one in which we are all vulnerable to possible severe illness or death? Francis Story's answer to this was to suggest that "collective" *kamma* has to be constructed from individual *kammas* that are all similar. He said: "No man necessarily shares the Karma of others of his national or other group simply by reason of being one of that group. He is responsible only for his own particular share in its deeds. If he does not share them, his own Karma will be quite different."[37] In Story's view, wide-scale suffering is still the result of individual *kamma*: it is just that the conditions of the time are collectively ripe for many to experience the effects of their actions. The Buddha was, however, never explicit on such a point.

Dependent Origination, conditionality, determines the nature of an individual in the next life in a purely impersonal way. A multiplicity of interrelated causes will come together to form a new body, a new personality, to reap the results of the past. Nothing outside one's own self makes these causes: all that an individual is in one life is just as relevant as actions in determining his or her nature in the next one, and counteracting factors will also be relevant. It is a causal process that is naturally systematic and orderly but fluid and flexible. The systematic and orderly nature of *kamma* stems from past causes but, even though an individual's personality is shaped by those past causes and his or her world view is the result of them – not exactly a clean slate with which to start – *kammic* causes in the present life are changeable and flexible, leaving an individual open to making the right choices for the future. And whatever befalls a being in life, that being's *responses* to such experiences – negatively or positively – are part of the building blocks of present causes that change the future. Differences in *kammic* make-up account for individuality and all the inequalities among human beings, but we must remember to keep Dependent Origination in mind with its concept that causal conditions arise then vanish only for other causes to replace them. Thus, the causal constituents of *kamma* also arise and perish throughout an individual's existence.

Death

I am not old enough to have lived in any part of World War II, the last time the number of deaths ran into the tens of thousands. In the late spring of 2020, all of us witnessed an unprecedented period of time when millions were being infected globally by the hidden enemy, the coronavirus, and tens of thousands were dying of it. Now, in the autumn of the same year, the virus is rising again, not that it ever really went away. As I write this, here in the United Kingdom almost 50,000 people have died from the virus. I am fortunate to be able to say that none of my own friends and family is amongst the dead, and yet I am grieving because of the recent death of my mother – not from Covid, but from old age: it is not an easy time, and I understand and empathize fully with those who have suffered loss of a loved one through the virus.

Whatever our beliefs about death and our ideas of the fate we await beyond it, it is surely something that most of us fear. Even if we believe we have one life and nothing more, there may be that nagging doubt expressed rather well by William Shakespeare's Hamlet: "In that sleep of death what dreams may come?" Belief in God and an afterlife in Heaven is a massive comfort to so many, even if it is unclear what exact form that will take. Would we still fear death if there were no thought of an afterlife? We probably would, it seems to me, particularly as the years close in. But whatever one's belief concerning death, when it occurs for someone close, it is immensely hard. The gay Reverend Richard Coles, whose great and warm character has lent itself to being a member of the rock group The

Commodores, as well as many appearances on British Broadcasting Corporation radio and television, lost his partner David, last year. And he has this to say about his loss: "No matter how fervent your faith, how abundant the spring, how brilliant the dawn, death is still death."[38] And, so realistically, he writes: "Watching someone you love die has a finality unlike anything else, and when death subtracts them so bluntly from your life, they leave an absence where the future used to be. You literally cannot imagine tomorrow, let alone a future in which all loss is restored and all hope is fulfilled; so easy sentiment or glib pieties are unbearable."[39]

Not only do we have to face the trauma of chronic illness and death of loved ones in this incredibly strange, weird world of a pandemic, but even to say goodbye, to have closure after a life is lost, has become almost impossible. Whatever life-cycle rites we have in our lives, death rites are common to us all. And in many religious cultures, death rites are elaborately performed to assist the departure of the dead to whatever is to come after life, and to give comfort and closure to those left behind. Indeed, we have a tendency to positivize death in quite elaborate funeral arrangements. Is that because we disguise death as something less grim than it is? This often means much expense – an expensive container in which to place the body, lavish flowers, extensive rituals and eulogies. In the Buddha's day, it was far less formal; for the average peasant it just meant leaving the body to decay in a forest.[40] My mother's death should have been followed by the funeral she would have wanted, but lockdown interceded. We were fortunate in some ways that my mother died of old age and not of the coronavirus or we may not have been able to have any kind of death rite at all – just her ashes to scatter. In the end, because of lockdown our farewell officially came down to a hurried placing of my mother's casket in the grave and our being told we were allowed just ten minutes to say goodbye at the graveside. I had asked the vicar of my mother's church how long he would take to say the relevant words at the graveside. His reply was: "About ten minutes, ashes to ashes and dust to dust *and all that stuff."* I thought I could do better than *"all that stuff"* and gave him the sack. So four of us stood at my mother's grave reading things we thought she would like to hear and reading gentle poems with words we thought she might like to say to us. The cemetery was quiet and there was no one to follow us, so we were granted a good half hour for our final goodbye with very carefully chosen words that gave us much-needed closure. For so many, however, closure is difficult if not impossible, and it is concerning that the scars of such departures from life are going to remain a long time etched into the hearts of so many.

So what of the Buddhist perspective? A "Middle Way" was always in the thoughts of the Buddha, so he would have advised a compromise between preoccupation with death and a total disregard of any thought about it whatsoever. For Buddhism, death is the disappearance of life's vital faculty, of the physicality and psyche of a being: it is a purely natural process. If death is feared, then the fear can create more unhappiness and suffering than death itself. In the Buddha's teaching, the body ceases at death but the mental force fuelled by *kamma* continues. This *impersonal* mental force that flows between one life and another, is not a soul, but *kammic* energy, the next life having similarity to the previous one because of similar *kamma* but in no way having identity. Any survival from the past is but energy impulses of accumulated *kamma* that, like consciousness, is never permanent but is constantly changing and fluid. We can say that this is a re-becoming consciousness, a last moment of consciousness in life flowing to the next consciousness that is in a new life but the two are similar consciousnesses. In a way, death takes place in every moment as one consciousness arises and ceases to be replaced by another: life to death to rebirth is exactly the same. Death is but a moment and Bhikkhu Khantipalo rather sensitively wrote here: "Really, instead of an ogre who lies in wait for all who have set their feet to the trail of life, death is just a rather greater manifestation of impermanence than we experience normally within the stream of mind and body."[41]

It is probably the belief in a permanent self or soul, a personhood, that makes death more difficult to bear. But the Buddhist view of impermanence attempts to overcome that sense of "I" especially with its emphasis on the Five Aggregates that are the sole constantly changing constituents of any being. Walpola Rahula wrote here: "Will, volition, desire, thirst to exist, to continue, to become more and more, is a tremendous force that moves whole lives, whole existences, that even moves the whole world. This is the greatest force, the greatest energy in the world. According to Buddhism, this force does not stop with the non-functioning of the body, which is death; but it continues manifesting itself in another form, producing re-existence which is called rebirth."[42] So the Buddha said: "Whosoever has no clear idea about death, and does not know that death consists in the dissolution of the five groups [the Five Aggregates] . . . he thinks that it is a person or being that dies and transmigrates to a new body."[43] In each moment, the Five Aggregates come into being and pass away incessantly, so that it could be said that we actually die *in each moment* and are reborn again in the next, and all without a permanent self or soul. The force of craving, of *tanha*, is that which creates the mental energy force for continuation and, of course, results in suffering. Detachment in life is the key to approaching death; that is to say, working to reduce craving, reduce desires, along with non-delusion about reality and its impermanence. From the Buddhist viewpoint, it is important to understand that the moments that compose life are perishable. I rather like the words of William Gilbert here, who wrote: "There is in truth no death though every form must die. We cannot permanently possess the life that flows through us any more than the electric bulb can own the current that gave it light. Life alone is continuous ever seeking self expression in new forms."[44]

So there is no ongoing soul, just an ever-changing life-current that passes through death. And at the very last moment of life, the nature of the arising consciousness will influence the consciousness at conception. So instead of reflecting on our sins at death, Buddhism regards it important to remember the good that we have done and think calmly about the life that has been led. In other words, the *kamma* that is there at the moment of death will cause a wholesome or unwholesome effect after death. The Buddha said that death is the demise of the former consciousness, and birth is the arising of future consciousness – one moment to another.

Rebirth

In early Buddhism, "rebirth" rather than "reincarnation" was the preferred term for the passage from one life to the next since the latter tended to suggest a reincarnating "soul" or "spirit" that was alien to Buddhist thinking. Further, "rebirth" was a term used more for rebirth in a human existence as opposed to elsewhere. A far better term is "re-becoming", reflecting part of the Dependent Origination links and the *stream* of consciousness and becoming from one life to the next. In fact, rebirth in human form is important and precious – a result of very good *kamma*, for it was believed that only in human form could enlightenment, *nibbana*, be realized. Most however, use the term "rebirth", and it is the term I shall retain here. Rebirth was a "re-becoming", a continuity, with new causes coming together to inform new life. Nevertheless, the problem of any such belief was rooted in the nature of what exactly was reborn, and hints of a continuing self of some kind clung to the concept of rebirth. When the Buddha became enlightened, he gained knowledge of all his past lives in animal, human and divine forms – rebirths attested to in the *Jatakas*, "Birth Stories", that are part of the Pali canon. Monks, too, had experiences of their past lives. The continuity of identity of the Buddha in the *Jatakas* almost suggests that there is a more permanent self that transmigrates from life to life. But "transmigration" of any kind is rejected by Buddhism because, again, it suggests that a "self" or "soul" passes from one life to the next.

The tension between such a continuity of identity and the total absence of any self through the arising and ceasing causes in line with Dependent Origination is, I think, one that is never really solved throughout Buddhism. But the Buddha's view of some Middle Way between a self eternally existing and a self that is annihilated at death should always be borne in mind. In the *Visuddhi-Magga* he said: "It is only elements of being possessing a dependence that arrive at a new existence: none transmigrated from the last existence, nor are they in the new existence without causes contained in the old."[45] What *is* eternal is the beginningless and endless aeons of time in which beings pass from life to life. The self exists because of the impermanent factors of Dependent Origination, so on the one hand the self cannot be eternal, and on the other, it cannot be annihilated if Dependent Origination maintains it. So there is no self as such that transfers from one body to another: indeed, personal evolution would be even slower if identity, particularly ego-identity, were to occur between each life. Only the *kammic* elements built up in past lives are the potentials for a new existence; they are, as Verdu described them, "the 'dormant' seeds of fructification in a future existence whose worldly status and circumstantial set-up will be determined by such fruition or re-germination".[46] So in the next existence, the being is more a *reflection* of the past life, a reflection built up by *kammic* causes in the past life.

Nothing from the past *really* passes from one existence to the next in exactly the same form, just as a flame from one candle is similar but not identical to the flame taken from it with another candle. A new individual is not the same as in a previous existence, but he or she is similar, the product of a past life, the heir of patterns of effects from patterns of causes. The idea that continuity obtains between one life and the next one is embedded in the theory of Dependent Origination. Whether or not early Buddhism accepted a kind of in-between state between each life remains uncertain, but the Theravada tradition based on early Buddhism eschewed the idea. Nevertheless, the craving characteristic of almost all beings is thought to continue after death when whatever it is that continues craves a new life in a new body. And the same rising and ceasing of causes is believed to continue whether or not an intermediary state exists between lives. As well as all phenomena being *dhammas*, both the physical and mental aspects of a being are informed by *dhammas*, physical "things" and mental thoughts.

The coming together of *dhammas* to create such effects is part of the impersonal natural law of causal continuity and causal connectedness. There is no break in this process but, rather, a continuum, and the empirical self that exists in one life is causally and uniquely connected to that which existed in the last life and to lives before that, in an uninterrupted succession, just as there is a causal continuum between a baby and that baby in old age – again, like the flame that passes from one candle to the next that is the same but different. *Kamma*, as we have seen, is the main key that links one life and the next, producing the physical and mental effects of causes that create a new being. The ways in which an individual thought, spoke and acted in a past life leave *kammic* traces and residues that causally inform who he or she is and how behaviour is in the present life. Individuals are put together in a way that reflects the complex causes made in past lives, but they always have the choice of what causes are made for the future. What individuals are is entirely of their own making: and they continue to construct their own future time, space and identity.

There is no way in which the consciousness that passes from one life to the next is unchanged. Again, Dependent Origination ensures that consciousness is *always* informed by continuous arising and disappearing of *dhammas*. As I said above, *kamma* is dependent on *intention, volition*: the Buddha, in fact, was the first to equate *kamma* with intention – action of thought, word and deed that is intentionally done. Such linking of *kamma* with intention was a departure from Hindu and Indian understanding of the concept. Richard Gombrich describes this as "an audacious use of language" that "ethicised the universe".[47] Intention behind act, thought or speech introduced a profoundly moral perspective, every experiential action constructing an empirical self from individual *kamma* that fed into the physical and psychological being with all its dispositions and inclinations, likes and dislikes, in the next existence. Maria Heim says of *kamma*: "Karma is a matter of creative world making and entails agency in this important sense: intentional action is the active construing and construction of experience. But this is a process that is also highly conditioned – shaped (though not definitively determined) by past experience, by deep-seated motivations and dispositions, by the demands of custom and normative social life, and by intricate entanglements with others."[48]

An action, then, has no causal consequences if it is unintentional: we have to *will* to do, think or say something and be conscious of that volition for *kammic* residues to be left. Those residues, if sufficient, will combine to cause a future life in whatever realm, whatever body, whatever mental state has been designed in previous lives. Intention, will, involves coordinating many factors. As Heim says: "It is operative whenever there is energetic activity of putting the factors of mind to work on their objects. It is a dynamic activity of collecting and animating rather than a state, decision, choice or inclination."[49] So the complicated processes involved in intentional activity become the equally complicated causative factors for future effects. What is important here is that *kamma* according to the Buddha becomes an *internal*, mental force, suggestive that if the mental state can be changed and intentions modified, the effects of *kamma* can be altered or changed into positive effects.

While the being in the next life has no permanent self, it is, nevertheless, a unique being since it is the result of its own causes and not of anything beyond itself. Each being will have a unique temperament with a unique blend of elements and unique physicality. Thus, an individual is in some ways the same as he or she was in past lives, but is also different and new. In every life, an individual is still composed of impersonal *dhammas* making up the changing Five Aggregates and existing through the rising and ceasing of these *dhammas*, but continuity of life to life does not mean any permanence. A key component of constructing a future personality is thought, *chitta*. Peter Harvey translates the word as "train of thought", "mind-set" or "heart" and says: "In the latter two meanings, it represents the dynamic, fluctuating focus of personality. Conditioned by mind-and-body, particularly by volition, it becomes the co-ordinating, guiding, creative focus of mind, marshalling and integrating other aspects of mind, including volition itself, in an ongoing process of mutual interaction and change."[50] As an "ongoing process", the *chitta*, the mind-set, is continuously discerning this and that, building personality in the present life and setting in place the causes for a future life or lives in the process. Since accumulated causes in one life will be mainly similar to those in the next life – and perhaps the next and the next – personality is not the result of haphazard chance but the logical outcome of processes of combinations of conditions. These combinations form in patterns and so beings build themselves from moment to moment, reproducing similar patterns within one life and from life to life. As Rupert Gethin puts it, "death is then not an interruption in the causal flow of phenomena, it is simply the reconfiguring of events into a new pattern in dependence upon the old".[51] Thus, the *formations* in the twelve links of Dependent Origination are the causal patterns that inform not only present life from the past one but are those that create the causal patterns for the next lives.

Personality in life, then, is a continuation of the flow of causes from past lives constructing the flow of consciousness from moment to moment, while that consciousness constructs good, bad or neutral dispositions for the future in a never-ending process. Such dispositions are likely to be as much subconscious as conscious and they shape and mould the character traits, habits and desires and aversions of an individual, constructing the fluid formation of the Five Aggregates in continuous flow. A unique reality is created from dispositions – a theory that chimes well with present-day theories of neuroscience. And because it is a *process*, Buddhism makes mind dispositions continuous through death to another life. Macy describes this superbly when she says: "The mind is a changing dynamic of shifting factors, not a static enduring collection of states. Change is a matter of previous conditions constructing present experience, which in turn is an active process of creating the future."[52] How much freedom of action and choice does the Buddhist have then? It would seem not that much and I think Payutto is to the point when he says that nothing is really our own: "We would find instead inherited behaviour patterns, learned from schooling, religious upbringing, social conditioning and the like. Individual actions are simply chosen from within the bounds of these criteria, and although there may be some adaptations made, these will again be at the direction of other influences."[53] Even if rebirth is disregarded, genetic inheritance, environmental influence, familial and social influences all impede the freedom of who a person can claim to be.

So the flow of consciousness from one minute to the next and from life to life depends on the predispositions that inform personality, dispositions that will determine responses to sense stimuli and create the experiences that make up life. Such experiences will cultivate and deepen the *same kinds* of dispositions for the next life. All such dispositions are causally created, providing the formations that are one aspect of the mutually combined Five Aggregates. Early Buddhism generally believed rebirth to be instantaneous following death, so that the continuum of consciousness was not broken between death and conception in a new existence. In Bhikkhu Bodhi's words, "generated by a kammically formative consciousness of the previous life, it brings with it into the new life the whole stock of dispositions, character tendencies, and kamma accumulations impressed upon the continuum".[54] Again, what is reborn is neither the same nor different from the previous existence(s) and, similarly, the last act of consciousness is neither the same nor different from the descending of consciousness into the womb at conception in conjunction with the physical being. And nothing here is permanent. Harvey uses the terms "person process" to describe such continuity and "segments" of a "process stream", which serve to describe the flux of the continuity moments of existence rather well.[55]

The accounts of the Buddha's multiplicity of past lives in all kinds of forms are suggestive of a being passing through every possible aspect of cosmic experience. The interconnection of microcosmic beings and macrocosmic worlds is a delicate one; all worlds in the cosmos seem to be traversed in the endless pathway of continuous rebirths. And still we have to ask "what is the relation between a being at one point of that pathway and one aeons further along it"? Is the answer still partly the same and partly different? The Buddha's experience of aeons of past lives at enlightenment suggests, it seems to me, a strong connective identity. Gethin says that the Buddhist cosmos, the macrocosm, incorporates all conceivable experience. "In short", he says, "what we experience from day to day is a microcosm of the cosmos at large."[56] Even more suggestive of the relation of the being to the cosmos, the microcosm to the macrocosm, is his statement that "in many respects the workings of the vast cosmos are nothing other than the workings of our minds writ large".[57] So if we have to traverse all the experiences within the cosmos, what is it that passes through all these experiences? The answer to such a question is still not some permanent self but *kammic* residues that pass from one life to the next.

An oft-raised query about Buddhist rebirth is that if everyone is continually reborn – albeit in different form from one life to the next – why is the world not completely overrun with beings? Buddhism answers this query by positing different planes of existence for re-becoming as well as different states of existence. There are three planes of becoming – the gross material world in which we live, a subtle material plane, and an immaterial plane. The greater the wholesome *kamma* from a life, the greater the likelihood of re-becoming in one of the less gross realms. Then there are five states of existence other than human – the lower state of the hells; the unhappy spirit state that is the realms of ghosts; the animal state; the higher spirit/godlike state; and highly spiritual and immaterial divine worlds. In fact, there are thirty-one planes of existence in which it is possible to re-become. And yet, re-becoming in every plane and state is impermanent and temporary until the *kamma* by which a being arrived there is used up.

So re-becoming is like being on a wheel that has no beginning, just an endless round of birth-death-birth for which there is no first cause and no end without enlightenment: such is the ultimate suffering for Buddhists. And each being that is reborn has caused itself to be from the multiple choices of its past life or lives; a current of multiple causes. Those causes cluster together to form similar patterns. Gethin comments here: "From this perspective a 'person' is a series of clusters of events (physical and mental) occurring in a 'human' pattern, as opposed to, say, the canine pattern of a 'dog'. Furthermore, causal connectiveness is such that the patterns in which events occur tend to reproduce themselves and so are relatively stable over a period of time."[58] Nothing is constant and permanent here but the important point related to re-becoming is that death is, as Gethin says, "simply the breaking up of a particular configuration of those events".[59] But it is also the immediate building of new ones to create a new birth, crucially, from *mental* events that have formed patterns from *kammic* activity. Also crucially, as Gethin says: "And just as this causal connectedness is the basis of continuity within a particular life, so it is the basis of continuity between lives. Just as no substantial self endures during a lifetime, so no substantial self endures from death to rebirth."[60] The succession of consciousness moments simply carries on making continuity of the stream of consciousness but not identity between existences. And those Five Aggregates about which so much has been said will reconfigure in a new way from moment to moment at death and continue from moment to moment in a new existence without any break at all. Then, too, the craving for survival after death is a strong contributory mental factor in reinforcing re-becoming, added to all the volitional desires and aversions throughout a life. These factors compose the energy of mental forces that ensures re-becoming, a passing over of impulses, rather like a strong and powerful electric current, to use an analogy offered by M. Walshe.[61]

Re-becoming is a means for moral and spiritual evolution. Get things right in one life and the next will be improved. So it means that moral endeavour is essential and I shall have much to say on that when we look at the fourth of the Noble Truths in the Eightfold Path in the next chapter. So according to Buddhism we are born with a predisposed energy force, though genetic inheritance is not eschewed, and neither are environmental influences. But an embryo, when formed, carries such inherited causes alongside *kammic* energy from the past life or lives, though it is the *kammic* energy alone that provides the link between two lives – something of a quantum leap. Some of that *kammic* energy may be sufficient for effects to materialize in the next existence, but some may be left until the right circumstances and conditions occur for those results to happen in later lives. But all the potentialities for the fruit of past *kamma* will be there in the new existence. At a purely scientific level, no energy is ever lost, or if it is used it must be replaced. That in itself suggests that the energy of action, thought and speech does not disappear, but can be stored: maybe the subconscious and unconscious holds much of this energy. And if negative events come your way, the exercising of kindness, tolerance, forbearance, patience and wholesome actions will at least store away good *kamma* for the future.

Existences tumble on one after another, fired by a stream of consciousness that never stops until, that is, *nibbana* is experienced. Then, no being exists because there is no *kammic* consciousness to create it. The aim of the third of the Noble Truths is to dispel the illusion of a permanent self and to see the so-called self for what it is; a vision that dispels, too, the need to feed the ego that moves the individual away from any path to enlightenment. With insight, suffering is seen, as everything in life, to be impermanent: it cannot possibly last but is simply a process, like everything else, including every being. Everything in the Buddha's *Dhamma* comes together in a remarkable whole: the Five Aggregates, Dependent Origination and the Four Noble Truths interweave the same truths about the way reality is and the way in which human beings are caused and composed.

Unless an individual takes charge of his or her own life, he or she will simply aimlessly drift on this planet without ever finding or even searching for the answers to life. And this would hold true whether or not one believes in *kamma*, rebirth or even Buddhism. In rather profound words, Nyanaponika Thera wrote: "Hence *kamma* is the true creator of the world, and this includes ourselves. *Kamma* is the womb from which we all have sprung. And through our *kammic* actions in deeds, words and thoughts we are unceasingly engaged in building and re-building this world and worlds beyond."[62] It may well be that many readers will strongly object to the ideas of *kamma* and rebirth. But, aside from rebirth, *kamma* is a pretty good and practical belief for living life. Cultivating good wholesome actions is surely a way to improve one's own life, but especially the lives of others. The same can be said for trying not to speak unkindly of or to someone. It is *thought*, however, that is more difficult to guard and where greater effort is needed. I shall have much to say about this in the next chapter. Attempting to change towards the good must surely reap some good in life.

6

The Fourth Noble Truth
The Noble Eightfold Path

We come now to the fourth of the Buddha's Four Noble Truths, the Eightfold Path as the means to end suffering or, at the very least in terms of contemporary living, to improve one's life and lessen suffering. Our materially-based lives are bombarded with sense stimuli in every dimension in a worldly existence that leaves little or no time at all for the spiritual. And by spiritual I do not necessarily mean religious, for the term also has secular meanings in the sense of "refined", "sensitive" and, in contradistinction to what I have just written, *not* concerned with the material.[1] I have defined spirituality elsewhere as that experienced when an individual is moved to heights or depths of his or her being in positive and meaningful ways, and as a moment or moments of inarticulate sense experience that transcends the mundane, lending a certain "wholeness" to the experience.[2] Such spirituality barely touches the individual in the post-modern world. Depth in valuable experiences of goodness, love, kindness, empathy, and equanimity will not come from material gains. The Buddha's teachings are very much about these kinds of more spiritual inner experiences in the lives of ordinary beings as well as in those of the monastic setting of his day. Today, we are technology led, and our smart phones we can barely put down. Our smart televisions enable multiple programme viewing and even our home gadgets as well as our televisions can be set to work from a distance: they are indeed "smart". I did not have a television for over twenty years and when I eventually succumbed, was utterly astonished at the amount of graphic sex scenes, swearing and violence that appeared on the screen before me in quite general programmes. The Buddha's Eightfold Path is asking us to *think* about such things and the ways in which we live our lives, so bringing about a better balance in how we think and act.

The Noble Eightfold Path

There are eight aspects to the Path that cover all aspects of life and all dimensions of the human being. The eight are:

- ☐ Right understanding or view
- ☐ Right thought or intentions
- ☐ Right speech
- ☐ Right action
- ☐ Right livelihood
- ☐ Right effort
- ☐ Right mindfulness
- ☐ Right concentration

The Path, Pali *Magga*, contains almost everything taught by the Buddha. The term "right" that prefixes each aspect of the Path is important because it signifies something complete, fully comprehensible and in contradistinction to what is wrong. As a brilliant teacher, the Buddha adapted what he taught to suit the level of understanding of his listeners and in many ways that is how we should approach the Eightfold Path. Since we are not monastic monks, *bhikkhus*, and since we are separated from them in time by hundreds of years, we have to adapt the Buddha's words to contemporary living without taking away the true essence of their meaning. The Eightfold Path is not really a "path" at all, for it is not undertaken stage by stage but each part is practised simultaneously. Neither is it an austere Path: the Buddha, we should remember, steered a "Middle Way" between sensual indulgence and extreme asceticism: he saw both as harmful to spiritual evolution of the human being. As such, the Path is relevant to all and excludes none. And a Middle Way means there is no duality of body and soul in the Buddha's teaching: the body needs to be cared for in order to enable the strengthening of the mind.

The Eightfold Path is not permanently retained by the one who attains *nibbana*. To use the simile of the Buddha's from a previous chapter; it is like a raft one uses to cross a river and abandons when one is on the other side. The culmination of the Path, when one crosses from the shore of this world to the other and leaves the raft behind is full knowledge of the way the Universe is and understanding of the whole *Dhamma* of the Buddha. But while some aspects of the Path are more difficult than others it always has to be borne in mind that all of them are complementary and thoroughly interdependent and supportive to each other, even when we are on the lower slopes of exploring them. Progress in the Eightfold Path, however, is always gradual and dependent on motivation and effort, whether one is attempting to change the way the mind works, the actions and speech of daily life, or the concentration on meditational praxis. But it is so important to remember the first three of the Noble Truths, for without those in mind the Buddha's message will have little impact and the aim of full and right knowledge will be continually elusive. Rupert Gethin puts this well when he writes: "Without some initial trust in the fact that there is a way out of suffering, without some seed of understanding of the nature of suffering and its cessation, we would never begin to look for the path and we would have no hope of finding it."[3] I am well aware of the immense suffering that is pervading this world while the present pandemic causes sickness, death, separation from those we love, and I do not have the answers myself to such trauma and sadness. But I hope the Buddha's teachings will provide some comfort. In very sensitive words Bhikkhu Bodhi wrote:

> The search for a spiritual path is born out of suffering. It does not start with lights and ecstasy, but with the hard tacks of pain, disappointment, and confusion. However, for suffering to give birth to a genuine spiritual search, it must amount to more than something passively received from without. It has to trigger an inner realization, a perception which digs beneath the facile complacency of our usual encounter with the world to glimpse the insecurity perpetually gaping underfoot. When this insight dawns, even if only momentarily, it can precipitate a profound personal crisis. It overturns accustomed goals and values, mocks our routine preoccupations, leaves old enjoyments stubbornly unsatisfying.[4]

To tread the Eightfold Path, then, we must re-evaluate our normal goals and values, give thought to how we live, and be prepared to make changes.

While the Buddha's teaching was primarily for monks and nuns, he also wandered widely and taught those who wanted to listen, adjusting his teaching – as every good teacher does – for his audience. His teachings have remained universal, for the good of the many, for their happiness, and out of compassion for the world. The Eightfold Path is also *practical*, not a philosophical treatise but a pragmatic programme for changing one's life, for creating a better way of life, and for a good way of life that has nothing to do with intellectual or academic ability. And it is a Path for every individual regardless of gender, race, religion or culture. No one extraneous to the Path itself directs an individual on the journey: *individual* effort is the key. So Thera Piyadassi wrote: "Now this deliverance from mental taints, this freedom from ill, lies absolutely and entirely in a man's own hands, in those of no one else, human or divine. Not even a Supreme Buddha can redeem a man from the fetters of existence except by showing him the path."[5] The pragmatic Path does not ask one to deny the body in any way making oneself thoroughly miserable as if on a perpetual slimming diet, but to make alterations in life that transform the inner being to make the outward life more satisfactory. The Path is for ordinary non-Buddhist individuals as much as the dedicated Buddhist. The former need only adapt their lives with some effort remembering that the precepts of the Path are not commandments but guides. Again, Piyadassi said: "Conduct builds character. No one can bestow the gift of a good character on another. Each one has to build it up by thought, reflection, care, effort, mindfulness and concentrated activity."[6] And yet, one needs to travel the Path free from doubt, because doubt is generally inimical to progress in anything that is done in life. Gethin offers some sound advice here for the ordinary man who "cannot, as it were, simply open the door and set out on the noble eightfold path, first he must negotiate the jungle of his views, behaviour, and emotions in order to find the eight qualities".[7]

In earlier chapters I have dealt with the three evils – desire/greed, hatred, and delusion/stupidity – that bedevil humankind and cause so much suffering. The Path is designed to bring out their opposites, and I shall have a good deal to say about those opposites – non-attachment linked to loving-kindness, compassion, and wisdom in the final chapter. Guidance for getting rid of the three evils or poisons comes in the form of precepts and we will find most of these embodied in the Eightfold Path: abstaining from taking the life of anything that breathes; abstaining from taking what is not given; abstaining from indulging in sexual misconduct; abstaining from speaking falsehood; and abstaining from intoxicating liquor are the basic Five Precepts. Buddhists would, at the very least, observe these Five. There are others – the Eight Precepts, the Ten Precepts and the Ten Good Paths of Action – but the Eightfold Path really deals with most aspects. The notable exception is the abstaining from taking intoxicants, which the Buddha believed dull the mind and prevent clarity. As the Buddhist saying goes, "First a man takes a drink, then the drink takes a drink, then the drink takes the man." The important point about the precepts, of whatever number, is that they embody the Buddha's *Dhamma*. They are ethical principles for right living, the adopting of which help us to do our very best in the way in which we live. In the Eightfold Path there are three divisions:

- **morality** or ethical conduct, *sila*, includes *right speech*, *right action* and *right livelihood*
- **mindfulness**, *samadhi*, includes *right effort*, *right mindfulness* and *right concentration*
- **wisdom**, *panna*, includes *right view/understanding*, and *right thought/intentions*

My route in dealing with these aspects of the Path is to take them in the order I have them at the outset of the chapter, dealing with the wisdom group first, followed by the morality group. I shall close the chapter with the first of the mindfulness group, *right effort*, leaving space to develop the other aspects of mindfulness and concentration in the following chapter. So we begin with right view/understanding.

Right view/understanding

Right understanding or view is the first of the Eightfold Path and belongs to the wisdom group. It is, wrote Bhikkhu Bodhi, "the forerunner of the entire path, the guide for all the other factors, enabling us to understand our starting point, our destination, and the successive landmarks to pass as practice advances".[8] Thus, this first aspect of the Path is immensely important. Previous chapters of this book have dealt with the three prior Noble Truths and right view means understanding what they said about the nature of suffering, its cause and cessation. More than that, right view means an understanding of existence, of life itself, of reality, of the conditioned nature of all things, of cause and effect, and a clear understanding of the nature of the self as impermanent. This last I have dealt with a number of times in the context of the Five Aggregates (matter; sensations/feelings; perceptions; mental formations; consciousness) as impermanent, constantly-changing components of the so-called self. The Five have to be understood in order to progress on the Path. So right understanding gets to the heart of the Buddha's *Dhamma*, which shows suffering to be a much wider, deeper and inimical force than external pain, mental strain or psychological imbalance. The correct view is to know what is "wholesome" as opposed to "unwholesome", terms that occur throughout the Eightfold Path as we shall see. So all that was dealt with in the previous three chapters is encapsulated in this directive of right view.

Right view also includes knowledge of *kamma* and how it operates in the cause–effect processes of life. Each individual is the owner of his or her *kamma*: no other being, mortal or divine, can affect that, so the

Path is a pointer to the ways in which an individual can change his or her attitudes in order to reap wholesome *kamma* for the future. On this the Buddha said: "All beings are the owners of their *kammas*, heirs to their *kamma*, born of their *kammas*, related to their *kammas*, abide supported by their *kammas*; whatever *kamma* they shall do, whether good or evil, of that they will be heirs."[9] At death nothing gained in life can accompany the deceased *except* the imprint of energy as *kamma* created and caused by that being and so must reap its effects for that being in the future. So nothing owned can be a permanent possession, only *kamma*. Thus, the three evils, poisons or "fires" as the Buddha called them – greed/desire, hatred/aversion, delusion/stupidity – need to be eradicated or, at the very least diminished, in order to gain freedom from suffering. *Reactions* to sense pleasures that reach consciousness through the eye, the ear, the nose, the tongue, the body and the mind, are the key to overcoming the three evils. I am writing this at the time the world is reacting to the murder of George Floyd in Minneapolis in the United States of America. Delusion here was at the heart of the crime; delusion in thinking that people of certain race, classes or religions can be objects of hatred, and then the expression of that hatred in anger and violence. Our views inform the ways in which we act and wrong views will result in suffering in one way or another. *Kamma*, action, starts in the mind, in the intentions developing there that find their outlet in speech and bodily actions. Wholesome thoughts will have good outcomes and unwholesome thoughts bad ones. The three evils that produce unwholesome *kamma* are countered by their opposites, non-greed is expressed in being detached from sensual craving and being generous; hatred or aversion is countered by showing loving-kindness, sympathy and gentleness; and getting rid of delusion and stupidity results in wisdom.

There are two kinds of right understanding, the mundane kind and the supra-mundane kind. For ordinary mortals as you and me we can understand much of the Buddha's teaching and with effort we can adopt a good deal of it to change our attitudes: some are thinking deeply about that in the case of George Floyd, for example. But we are unlikely to reach the second level, the supra-mundane, when the depths of the Buddha's teaching are penetrated to the extent of the understanding gained by a Buddhist monk who has been long on the Path. Both mundane and supra-mundane levels promote moral and spiritual progress in life, but they are deeper in the supra-mundane level. The mundane view does not lead to *nibbana*, whereas the supra-mundane view leads to intuitive knowledge and, importantly, *insight* into the Four Noble Truths at a level close to enlightenment. Concentrated meditative processes provide the means here and we shall look at this higher level in the next chapter. At the higher level *all* misconceptions about reality, *all* wrong views are eliminated. These are important distinctions so that the aims for the ordinary being are realistic on the Eightfold Path, the journey gradual, and any failures do not prevent and inhibit trying again. The Buddha was realistic and pragmatic about life and did not expect the ordinary human being to experience *nibbana* in one lifetime or even many, many lifetimes. Nevertheless, both ordinary mortal and dedicated monk follow the same Eightfold Path and both undertake self-examination, particularly relating to the Five Aggregates, but it is at the supra-mundane level that the Five Aggregates are truly understood through insight meditation and true wisdom. The mundane level involves *learning* with systematic attention, not with superiority over others but with a measure of humility and openness. One of the Buddha's sayings is that one may conquer in battle a thousand times a thousand men, yet he is the best of conquerors who conquers himself. Right view means the understanding of the true nature of the impermanent self and an inner battle to get that right perspective.

Wrong views and misunderstanding see permanence in the world where there is really impermanence; finds things satisfactory when they are really unsatisfactory; sees a permanent self and soul when there is no such thing; believes that actions – even mental activity – do not have consequences. Holding a wrong view means that somewhere the consequences of it will bring suffering: with wisdom, such misunderstandings and sufferings can be overcome. The right view that starts at the beginning of the Eightfold Path is also the conclusion of it in ultimate wisdom. Although the conclusion may be far in the future, even in distant future lives, the beginning is the *now* that asks for a change of mind, a change of heart in the ways in which life is lived. I rather like the words of Nyanaponika Thera here when he wrote: "And all what is required for the therapy is again found in a human's body-and-mind. The therapy proper which aims at the root of the illness, starts with rightly understanding the true nature of Kamma and, thereby, man's situation in the world. . . . Therefore, he who wishes for the greatest benefit from his good actions and thoughts may always dedicate the fruits thereof to the final liberation from all kammic bondage, for oneself and all sentient beings."[10]

Right thought/intention

The second of the Eightfold Path, right thought or right intention, is also concerned with wisdom. From previous chapters we learned that *intention* behind action was what produced fruitive *kamma*. Good, wholesome intentions lead to good actions and good *kamma*. These are thoughts and intentions that are devoid of greed, hatred and delusion, the three evils or poisons, and avoiding these will put one on a spiritual pathway. Right thought is a product of the first of the Eightfold Path, right understanding, seeing things from the correct perspective. Whatever our actions in life, they are generated by mind functioning: on the whole, I think about doing something and then suit the action to the thought. If the mind is right, the actions and speech that follow will also be right. So what is right thought? If we think of the first of the three evils, greed, it is manifested in desire, wanting, a must have attitude in life. Contemporary society is very much consumer driven; advertisements for the latest this or that, a new car, new clothes, new appliances are constantly fed to us. Given the effects of lockdown, I wondered how many people found it difficult not to shop for, say, fashionable clothing items, especially when they could not go anywhere: is there any point to a new article of clothing in lockdown? When nations got back to some kind of "new" normality, did people think of what they did not need in lockdown and temper their desires for things accordingly? Does lockdown help people to be more reflective about what they really need and what they hardly need at all? Renunciation of the desire to have so many things, is one important way of changing the mind according to Buddhism. Many nations are currently in a recession, and if they ever see the end of Covid will be in an even deeper recession until the economy recovers and the massive expense of coping with the pandemic is balanced. During that process there will be economic hardship for many, and the "I want" state of mind will need to be tempered for some time. Training the mind to cope with less, to need less, is going to be an exigent task for the post-pandemic individual. But in the here and now, there is time for practice in the effort to curb desires. But most crucial is right thought *for the planet*: we are killing it. Our selfish behaviour is massively destructive. We cannot win the battle against viruses and we will invite more such killers if we go on warming up the planet, destroying forests, eating meat, herding animals together in mass production plants: we cannot win. Humanity is already the virus of the planet and if there is no right thought about what is happening to the planet, viruses will increase and, possibly, destroy the lot of us.

Then there is the second of the three evils, aversion or hatred, the former being slightly less toxic than the latter. If aversion towards another being arises in the mind, whether because that being did something or is something that is believed to be distasteful, then resulting actions will be equally distasteful. Here is where racism, homophobia, xenophobia, nationalism have their roots. The opposites to cultivate in the mind here are kindness, friendliness and compassion that will not lead to aggression against, or harm to, others. And delusion in life, the third of the three evils means a radical change of the mind that incorporates, in particular, the acceptance of the impermanence of all life including the self that is composed only of the ever-changing Five Aggregates.

So right thought is all about the restructuring of the mind. Habits of thought and responses to stimuli build up in patterns in the brain. As was seen in the last chapter, we are not actually in control of our minds for our brain neurons have been programmed into configurations formed by our responses to sense stimuli throughout our lives, coloured too by environmental, societal and cultural factors to make up a unique personality. The electrical charges of the brain that have been configured throughout life will be slightly ahead of our conscious thought and actions. So to dislike someone repeatedly will mean the brain is configured to match that dislike *before* the thought of disliking that person comes into the conscious mind. Now, *habitually* changing the way the mind works, say by being kind or thinking warmly of someone disliked, will cause changes in the neurological configurations in the brain to change a bad habit into a good one.[11] In short, right thought means restructuring the values we hold in life. Bhikkhu Bodhi's words here are very wise: "The cause for the endless competition, conflict, injustice, and oppression does not lie outside the mind. These are all just manifestations of intentions, outcroppings of thoughts driven by greed, by hatred, by delusion."[12] In the mind are the beliefs, the goals, the likes, the dislikes configured into neural patterns uniquely built up by each one of us. Whether or not one would want to accept the concept of *kamma* that causes now reap effects in future lives, it remains a valuable goal to change thought patterns in the here and now: the result will be a better life and better relations with others. Being generous instead of grabbing, kind instead of harming, and compassionate instead of aggressive are the goals for right thought.

Changing the mind is no easy task and is only done by determination and gradual practice. Just one simple change in attitude to life may be the first step. The footballer, Gianluca Vialli, who played for Chelsea in the UK and for a number of Italian teams, is currently suffering from pancreatic cancer. He loves mantras and one that he has included in his latest book is simple: "In a world where you can be anything, be kind."[13] We can be kind with a smile, a compliment, or by giving a little of our time. And another of his mantras is "Perfection is not attainable but if we choose perfection we will catch excellence."[14] Beginnings are usually hard and beginning to change the mind is a high hurdle to master. We need to analyse what we think, how we think, and why we think in that way in order to change the way in which we think. We should remember that such wholesome sentiments of mind come within the group of wisdom on the Path. It is wise to reflect on who we are and how we think and adjust mind and thought for the better. Again, in Bhikkhu Bodhi's words of wisdom: "The direction we take always comes back to ourselves, to the intentions we generate moment by moment in the course of our lives."[15]

Moral and ethical conduct

To live by a deep ethical integrity is the result of an inwardly spiritual character. Since we are all probably among the "mundane" rather than supra-mundane individuals in life who strive for enlightenment, the precepts of the Eightfold Path are ethical principles that we may want to adopt to help us lead better lives, to reduce suffering for ourselves and others, and enable us to reach out with integrity to other beings. Moral living is cultivating the good in actions in conjunction with right thoughts from where actions spring. The "Golden Rule" of do to others only what you would want done to yourself is strengthened in Buddhism to the premise that since *all beings seek happiness and wish to avoid suffering*, never do anything to anyone you would not like done to yourself.

Morality in Buddhism is Pali *sila*, which means something like "virtue" or even moral training, but whereas morality and ethical standards can vary from culture to culture and can be subject to changing social conventions, the Buddhist concept is a wide one that encompasses the *means* to an inner purity that is a prerequisite for meditation and concentration, the last two of the Eightfold Path. So *sila* may mean moral actions in life; the principle and precepts of moral actions; qualities of moral character; formal ethical training; harmony; even coordination.[16] So when *sila* becomes embedded in the mind and activated in speech and actions, it promotes harmony in the self, in the family, in interpersonal relationships, in society, and leads to a more contemplative state. *Sila*, then, is a foundation for the other limbs of the Eightfold Path but especially for the higher levels of meditation.

There are three constituents of right ethical and moral conduct – right speech, right action and right livelihood, and we need now to examine each of them in turn. Importantly, they are not goals, ends in themselves: as I said above, they are *means* to higher levels of spirituality but, from the mundane point of view of the ordinary man and woman, they are sound means for living a good life, and for promoting love, kindness, charity, gentleness, compassion, modesty, tolerance, and joy in the happiness of others. The Buddha did not lay down such precepts as *always* right, rigidifying them into commandments always to be obeyed in any circumstances: things are right or wrong depending on their contextual situations and it would depend on the outcome for a person or persons on whether an action were moral or not. So to break one of the precepts is not to have sinned, it is simply to have erred in a particular context from which it is important to begin again. Another of Vialli's mantras is: "Start where you are. Use what you have. Do what you can."[17] To do something that is not right means putting it right if possible and starting again, but it does not mean carrying the burden of a sin around the neck for the remainder of life. Each individual is responsible for his or her own actions so unless the wrong action is a crime, there is no one other than the doer of the action to suffer the *kammic* consequences of it.

Right speech

We are unique in the animal kingdom in being able to speak and articulate our thoughts, our ideas, our wishes, likes and dislikes. But control over what we say is immensely difficult. The configurations of neurons in our brains probably dictate to a great extent the spontaneity of speech in moments when we feel we've had little control over our tongues – hasty moments, cross moments, defensive moments, unkind moments. None of us has complete control over what we say. You can probably see here how important right view and right thought are in informing the spontaneity of our speech, since if they are good and right, the tendency to say something wrong is lessened: indeed, what is speech other than the vocalization of our thoughts and intentions? I am sure we would all want our words to be accurate, thoughtful, gentle and sincere. Whatever is in our minds has the outlet in both action and especially speech: indeed, speech itself is an activity, something overt that has consequences dependent on its nature. Right speech is concerned with four areas:

- ☐ restraining from false speech
- ☐ restraining from bearing tales
- ☐ restraining from speaking harshly
- ☐ restraining from useless chatter

False speech is that which is simply untrue but it may also be speaking truth in such a way that it seems untrue. It also extends to saying we know something when in fact we do not. If individuals are known for speaking the truth and are comfortable in admitting they do not know something then they are respected along with their opinions. This also means not embellishing or exaggerating facts or putting emphasis on some words in order to convey a different meaning. And yet, once again it is *intention* or right thought behind the speech that makes it false. *Intending* to say something false is unwholesome, whereas if something is said that is wrong without intention, it is simply a mistake. We can see again how right thought informs right speech. In contemporary societies around the world we now have to deal with *fake news* and deliberate misinformation and disinformation in visual or written form. The written word is still speech and can be sufficiently vitriolic to destroy lives. We hear much about free speech and the freedom of the press to report what it considers is in the public interest, but we all know that the paparazzi, in particular, will stop at nothing for a "story", however cruel the outcome may be for an innocent person, or an innocent person until he or she is proved to be guilty. There is no wisdom or kindness here. And now the speed at which news travels on the internet has vastly increased the possibilities for harmful lies for trial by public reading as opposed to in the courts, as well as the endemic harm of trolls who threaten public figures, and the young people who taunt and bully their peers with online abuse.

I think we would have to say that the world is rather replete with false speech, particularly in the written form. There are many in the news media who engender fear in their readers because overemphasis of illness, suffering and deaths *sells papers*: no wonder many now feel that they have had enough of the negativity of the news. And where does the truth lie between what we are told by governments as opposed to scientists in this time of fear and danger? We have to know who to trust in taking precautions against the silent killer amongst us. If trust is there, societies will understand and behave accordingly: if trust is lost then behaviour will become sporadically inappropriate. And in terms of truth, much cover-up took place in China when the coronavirus broke out there in Wuhan. Amidst the fear and death toll of Covid we even find deliberate disinformation about cures. Then, too, there is irresponsible misinformation for example that on 24 April 2020 by the President of the United States who suggested swallowing disinfectant or being injected with it as a possible cure. All kinds of treatments from Vitamin C to cocaine have been put out globally through such incorrect information. The World Health Organization, the WHO, has now coined the term "infodemic" as a criticism of the misinformation that is globally endemic. One example of such misinformation is the rumoured theory that 5G wireless technology is damaging the immune systems of people so contributing to severe Covid. In India, Hindu nationalists argued that Muslims were deliberately spreading the virus amongst Hindus.[18] With the ability to tweet in a few seconds, or use other social media for misinformation, such delusional ideas are out there in cyber space as the fastest means of spreading incorrect information. Disinformation, on the other hand, is more deliberate and sinister especially with the intention of discrediting governments, and amounts to deliberate lying. A liar is anti-social and if that liar is a politician, a national leader, or member of government, he or she undermines the whole of society.

Intentionally *concealing* truth is also regarded as false speech and there are times when the truth has been forcibly concealed as, for example, in the case of the very brave medics in China who spoke out about the human to human Covid infections in the early days of the virus there. The Chinese government is habitually intolerant of anyone who may have evidence that would embarrass it. Dissidents who tell the truth can be put in prison, brutalized or placed under house arrest and harshly encouraged to change their viewpoint.[19] Since China is so often the source of new viruses, without honesty from its government it is difficult to see how pandemics similar to Covid can be avoided in the future. But in a similar, though less harsh situation, Richard Horton was given this piece of information by a National Health Service worker in the UK: "Colleagues have to attend disciplinary meetings for speaking out... I never thought I lived in a country where freedom of speech is discouraged." The statement obviously implies that any complaints of NHS staff during the initial stages of the pandemic when they were short of protective equipment were quashed, and Horton adds many more such testimonies.[20] Horton also points out the failure of the UK Prime Minister, Boris Johnson, to tell the truth about the pandemic. Johnson's view was that the UK was well-prepared and he was still arguing that as late as March 3. Consider his words of 5 March cited by Horton: "Perhaps you could take it on the chin, take it all in one go and allow the disease, as it were, to move through the population without really taking as many draconian measures. I think we need to strike a balance." And it took Johnson some time to stop regularly shaking hands with people and bragging about it.[21] This was clearly a policy of herd immunity that the UK government later refuted ever having: that was a lie. And then there are President Trump's antics in the face of the pandemic. Again and again he concealed or, rather, avoided the truth about Covid. So often he did this by simply dismissing anything he did not want to hear. He blamed staff in hospitals for shortages of personal protective equipment (especially those in Democrat states) and he criticized governors of Democrat states like New York, downplaying the numbers of infections and deaths there as fake news.

Tale bearing or slander involves the detriment of a character such as telling tales on a person about one of his or her friends so that dissension between them results. This is malicious speech that *intends* to bring discord and disunity between people. Taking someone's words out of context – a feature of much tabloid newspaper reporting – is intentionally misleading and harmful not just to the individual involved, but also to the public who are encouraged in the wrong views presented to them. There seems to be a perverse delight amongst some less scrupulous reporters to do their utmost to denigrate an individual in order to get the scoop they so desire and to win praise for it. In ordinary life the Buddha would ask that we take great care that we bear no slanderous tales. Telling someone something nasty another has said about him or her is mean spirited. Conversely, it is a lovely thing to pass on a compliment someone has said about an individual: it makes their day brighter.

Harsh words are often impulsive, are words spoken in anger, and are abusive, insinuating, scolding, insulting, sarcastic, unkind and rough. Harsh words hurt, create unhappiness and are likely to lead to reprisal, a row, an argument, because they diminish a person by taking away any dignity. And facial expressions here speak volumes – the eyebrow arched with disdain, the crooked smile, or the nasty gesture. And, of course, bad language is the epitome of harshness and a long way from gentle speech. Admittedly, there is a certain degree of stress release in the use of bad language in the classic case of the hammer hitting the thumb instead of the nail, or if a situation gets exasperatingly out of control. But even here the Buddha asked for restraint, a gentle response which, after all is said and done, would do much to de-escalate an aggressive situation. Patience and tolerance are the hallmarks of the wise person even to the extent of enduring abuse without being overcome by the need to retaliate. These are difficult virtues to inculcate when television, film, video games, novels, and newspapers contain an immense amount of violence and bad language that are really thoroughly harsh: no wonder such language has become part of everyday speech. Years ago, it used to be a popular and accepted form of academic writing to lay into the argument of another scholar but this, too, is harsh speech in written form. Disagreement, and the reasons for it, can be put gently without harsh language and certainly without adopting a wholly fundamental critical style of writing.

The fourth area is the avoidance of useless and frivolous chatter and this also extends to novels and films that have no hint of good conduct in them. Thirty-two types of vulgar talk are included under this rubric, which, if adopted, would rule out almost all of everyday speech, but we should remember that the Buddha was, in the main, addressing the monastic traditions when idle chatter was decried. But one area of chatter is gossip, even of the "I'm not saying anything but . . ." kind, accompanied by the disparaging facial expression. And then there is the person who talks *a lot*, hardly stopping for breath, just going on and on without ever stopping to ask a question of another person. "One does not become a wise man by talking a lot" the Buddha said in the *Dhammapada*. It is unlikely that we would ever reach the Buddha's standard of our words always being at just the right time, in accordance with the facts, useful, a treasure to the listener, said at the right moment, accompanied by reason, moderate and full of sense. We cannot always speak with purpose and depth but we can at least be aware of the influence of the continuous media stream of information and sort out the needless from the informative. After many discussions with my students during lectures on ethics, I came to realize how media-led our ethical and moral standards are. We need to think carefully what our *own* standards are not adjust them to suit current social media norms.

Right action

For the monk of the Buddha's day and those who wish to undertake the path of spiritual purification leading to *nibbana*, right action means the total renunciation of unwholesome actions in a very profound way. Here, right actions are spontaneously good and there is no egoistic involvement in that action. But right action for the more mundane of us, and for lay Buddhists in the days of the Buddha and subsequently, is a more measured path. The ordinary individual is involved in everyday life, has a family and has to work, and that means adapting the Buddha's precept of right action to a more pragmatic life. But a pragmatic life does not mean it is less spiritual and right action is the outcome of a sound mind with sound understanding of life. Consider Piyadassi's words here: "Conduct builds character. No one can bestow the gift of a good character on another. Each one has to build it up by thought, reflection, care, effort, mindfulness and concentrated activity."[22] To live life well is to live life in the best possible way, with the best possible outcomes for oneself and for others, outcomes that avoid suffering and create happiness. This is what Buddhism terms "skilful action", *kusala*, ethical living. And with right action, the end *never* justifies the means: all action should be ethical and skilful. The kinds of wholesome, good, and skilful actions here are presented in the Buddhist texts as giving; moral conduct; developing the mind; reverence; being helpful; dedicating good acts to others, listening to the *Dhamma* and teaching it; and inculcating right views. Many of these characteristics are just as relevant to contemporary living, but there is an underlying theme that is essential, and that is *selflessness*. If individuals are self-centred and self-regarding then their actions become unwholesome, *akusala*. Self-centred actions are usually greedy ones, ones that are undertaken to satisfy craving, or to make the perpetrators of those actions superior to others. We meet these individuals in their selfish actions in the work place, in schools, and in their self-praise when they speak of themselves.

Apart from such general conceptions of right and wrong actions, the Buddha had three specific categories of right actions

- abstaining from taking life
- abstaining from taking what is not given
- abstaining from sexual misconduct

These are the first three of the well-known Five Precepts of Buddhism that even lay Buddhists are asked to abide by at times. The remaining two are abstention from lying, which right speech incorporates, and abstinence from taking intoxicants.

Abstaining from taking life

The basic premise of abstaining from taking life is not to intentionally kill any living creature, be that human, animal, bird, insect or whatever is living. I use the word *intentionally* here because it is crucially important for *kammic* results. If, for example, I accidentally run over a rabbit in my car and could not avoid doing that, then that does not break the rule of no killing and will not accrue negative *kamma*. The *intention* has to be there and the victim has to die for the precept to be broken. Even if a death occurs as a result of negligence, that is not as wrong as intentional killing. Buddhism is founded on the *compassion* of the Buddha and that compassion is to all living creatures, everything that breathes. Whatever the living being, the living creature, *nothing* wants to die so wherever life is, it is precious to that creature, human or otherwise. If life is the greatest good, then taking it is the greatest harm and evil. We find in one Buddhist text the words:

> All fear punishment
> Life is dear to all;
> Comparing one with others
> Kill not nor cause to perish.
>
> As I am so are they
> As they are so am I;
> Comparing one with others
> Neither slay nor cause to kill.[23]

Piyadassi's words here are stark: "Thus it is incumbent on all men of understanding to stop hurting and harming others and to cultivate a boundless heart full of pity and benevolence. Killing is killing whether done for sport, or food or – as in the case of insects – for health. It is useless to try to defend oneself by saying 'I did it for this good reason or that'. It is better to call a spade a spade. If we kill we must be frank enough to admit it and regard it as something unwholesome."[24] Most of us are probably sufficiently removed from killing not to even think about it – albeit that we may swat the occasional wasp or fly without any thought. But killing anything is an expression of the mental state of a being. I kill wasps because I am afraid my dogs snap at them and if they are stung in the mouth or throat could die. So 'I did it for this good reason' applies to me and is just as wrong. Suicide, too, is regarded as violating life and, needless to say, torture or the intentional harming of someone without death occurring is obviously also a completely unwholesome action. Even if one does not perpetrate the killing but gets someone else to, the act is unwholesome. The important issue is the *relationship* we have with other beings and creatures, and the *interrelation* of all things on the planet. Implications of not taking life are wide in the contemporary world – vegetarianism as opposed to partaking of meat, poultry, fish or insects; anti-abortion; opposition to nuclear weapons, and the manufacture of armaments, are some examples.

Buddhists at the time of the Buddha and in contemporary Buddhism are not necessarily vegetarian. There is nothing in the early Buddhist texts to prohibit meat eating. Monks of the Buddha's day and even today among conservative, Theravada, Buddhists leave their monastic settings before midday and travel through the villages and towns with a begging bowl. They are not allowed to ask directly for food but are dependent on ordinary folk to place food in their bowls so that they can return to the monastery and eat. Whatever is in that bowl – be it animal flesh, fish, poultry, or just cooked rice – the monks eat it. Nevertheless, this precept prevents your having meat if you know that an animal has been slaughtered especially for you. Fertilized eggs are also excluded for consumption. So it is really up to the individual to think carefully about this particular precept.

We are killing our planet with the greed for meat – a point I took up in Chapter 3 in the context of greed. The incredible suffering of creatures in the live animal markets in China where viruses including Covid have jumped from creature to human is stark evidence that we are harming ourselves in the long run, and that we are causative to our own suffering as a result. China has a lot to answer for in its use of creatures in Chinese medicines and in allowing illegal animal trading of creatures to support such medical praxis. International trade of animals for exotic pets, for agriculture, for scientific experimentation are multibillion dollar industries, says Dorothy Crawford, all of which can carry viruses ready to take up home in human cells. Crawford gives examples of a haemorrhagic fever from African green monkeys, monkeypox from giant rats, and a dangerous worm in farmed crocodiles in Papua New Guinea that could threaten humans.[25] Then, there are the immensely lucrative animal factory farms where animals are kept in appalling conditions for the benefit of all of those who want to eat meat. Is it any wonder that we have a pandemic of Covid?

In today's world killing is done for us, so we do not have to be faced with the issue. We can detach ourselves from the suffering of the lambs taken from their mother ewes, herded together in great stress and headed for the abattoir because the lamb we buy from the butcher or the supermarket looks entirely different from the original living creature. We had a Buddhist neighbour many years ago, a lay Soto Zen Buddhist. He thought nothing of *choosing* which lamb he wanted slaughtered in the farmer's field behind his house for his freezer content. I suppose it has to be asked are we any better buying the cuts of lamb from the supermarket? There is a popular phase of veganism in society at the moment that might stem from those who sympathize with the animal that is killed for consumption but more evidently, for healthy eating in order to avoid the chemicals on which cattle and sheep feed. And then there is the killing of creatures for scientific medical research. Here again is an aspect of deliberate causing of harm to animals in order to produce medicines for human diseases. We are in the midst of a pandemic, hoping for a vaccine against Covid-19, with little thought for the millions of creatures on which experimental drugs are used before they can proceed to human trials. We need to know that millions of small animals, and regularly macaque monkeys, suffer and die in the processes of finding a vaccine for you and me. How do we balance such creature suffering with the need to prevent human deaths from this incredible viral killer? Most of us probably do not even think about it and just hope that a vaccine will be available soon whatever the cost. Here, then, the end would justify the means in the minds of many, but not according to the Buddhist precept where, again, the end never justifies the means.

But even if we endorse the use of animals for drug manufacture it is at least encouraging that the cosmetic industry has moved away from testing their products on animals, though not entirely. I was drawn to the work of Jane Goodall after seeing a television interview she did recently. Her books, I am afraid to say, I cannot read fully because as an animal lover I find it difficult and upsetting to see, to hear of, or to read of distressing harm done to animals or even to see one animal killing another. But her book written with Marc Bekoff has a list of ten trusts that rather embody many principles that would by no means be outside Buddhist thinking here. They are:

- ☐ Rejoice that we are part of the animal kingdom.
- ☐ Respect all life.
- ☐ Open our minds, in humility, to animals and learn from them.
- ☐ Teach our children to respect and love nature.
- ☐ Be wise stewards of life on Earth.
- ☐ Value and help preserve the sounds of nature. Here this "concerns the immense damage we have already inflicted on the complex web of life on Earth. So many beautiful animal voices have been silenced in so many places. We cannot bring back creatures who have become extinct, but we can work much harder to reduce pollution, to be less destructive, to save all the beauty that is left."[26]
- ☐ Refrain from harming life in order to learn about it. The authors endorse peaceful protests against companies with bad environmental and humanitarian practices; the boycott of entertainment involving the exploitation of animals; the creation of personal good footprints by adjusting our lives for the better future of our planet.
- ☐ Have the courage of our convictions. Thinking about the products we use and whether they have been manufactured from cruel practices is part of the remit here. If consumers make ethical choices and refuse to buy products such as cosmetics and household goods tested on animals, manufacturers will have to make policy changes.
- ☐ Praise and help those who work for animals and the natural world.
- ☐ Act knowing we are not alone and live with hope. Every little action we take to make the world a better place is important.[27]

The Ten Trusts was published by these authors in 2003. One of the accounts in the book concerned the use of Premarin, a drug widely used for the amelioration of menopausal symptoms. The *pre* stands for "pregnant", the *mar* for "mare" and the *in* for "urine", in other words Premarin is manufactured from the urine of pregnant mares. I thought the gap of seventeen years since Goodall and Bekoff brought the abuse of mares to make this drug into the public domain would mean that it is discontinued. I checked on the internet and was horrified and upset to find that the horrendous conditions in which this drug is manufactured still obtains to the present day. I shall leave it to the reader to find out more if he or she is interested: the cruelty is too stark to reproduce here.

Finally, the following words are full of Buddhist sentiment:

> Do we really want to live in harmony with nature? Are we truly the people we think we are? These are simple yet extremely challenging questions. If we answer yes to either or both, which not only is politically correct but also ethically and ecologically correct, we are compelled to move forward with grace, humility, respect, compassion, and love. We will need to replace "mindlessness" with "mindfulness" about our interactions with animals and the Earth. Nothing will be lost and much will be gained. We can never be too generous or too kind.[28]

In the human realm, early Buddhism believed that a new life post-death began at conception, when sperm and ovum are fertilized. This is the moment when *kammic* energy passes between lives. Taking life, therefore, begins there at conception and so abortion is not acceptable. With life being a continuum from one life to the next there is really no beginning and no end to that life continuum between lives. That said, Japanese Buddhists now accept abortion, but soften it with a memorial service for the aborted foetus.[29]

Abstaining from taking what is not given

At first sight, abstaining from taking what is not given seems a simple case of a precept that one should not steal, but the Buddhist idea is wider. If you want to take what is not given to you, clearly there is a *desire*, a craving, for something, and we know from the second of the Four Noble Truths that craving and desire lead to suffering. Consideration of the fraud endemic in society, not just of criminal scams, but the appropriation of commodities in the workplace, "perks of the job" – even just a pencil or pen – is an act of taking what is not given. Employers who do not pay adequate wages are taking the work and energy of their employees, while lazy employees who do less than their fair share of work are taking from their employers. Not paying a debt is also offending this precept for it is withholding something that is not one's own. Taking what is not given springs from covetousness and if not clandestine is overtly violent in trying to take from someone something he or she does not want to give. In today's hectic world one thing that people value so much is their time. So to take someone's time by endless self-centred chatter on the phone, or by visiting someone uninvited when he or she is busy is thoughtlessly taking the energy and time of a person. Sangharakshita called such people who drain the energy of others "human vampires".[30] So this precept goes beyond what we normally understand as robbery, fraudulence, and overt theft. Dishonest dealings in the trade and sale of such things as cars, houses, and many commodities are again an infringement of this precept. Again, the severity of the unwholesome act is dependent on the intention behind it, the wrong thought.

Abstaining from sexual misconduct

While monks of the Buddha's time were expected to be celibate, lay followers were not expected to divorce themselves from sense pleasures such as sex. But the Buddha had advice on the kinds of sexual conduct that were unwholesome. We are what we are in our minds, products of our thoughts. If we allow those thoughts to indulge in covetous sexual relations then we are in danger of actualizing them. So the Buddhist texts list sexual misconduct as that with persons who are still in the care and protection of their parents or other relatives, and with married or engaged women. Sexual misconduct also includes that with close female relatives. For women also, a married man and close relative are excluded. In cases of rape, the violator is always the guilty party, not the victim. In all these cases the underlying rationale is not to cause suffering and harm to anyone so, providing that lack of hurt to anyone is upheld, sexual relations between unmarried couples is not offending the precept. In an ideal world, it would be good if gender could at times be transcended, just as it would be with class or race. At a spiritual level a human being is just that, whereas male and female are more usually regarded as a dualism, polarized beings that are essentially different in every possible way. Sexual attraction is based on this duality and can blur the kind of respect necessary from one human being to another. It is sad that in the situation of lockdown the abuse, control and harm of women has escalated phenomenally and the number of women seeking help from an abusive partner has increased dramatically: this is one of the harsh evils of lockdown.

Not included in the Eightfold Path are two other precepts against intoxicants and gambling, the former because they cloud the mind, distorting right view and right thought, and the latter, as we well know, often causes harm to the gambler and to his or her family. And these prohibitions do not mean "in moderation" either. Ledi Sayadaw refers in an interesting little account to a lecturer on Buddhism talking to a Buddhist Society about the Five Precepts. When it came to intoxicants he brought up the Buddha's middle way in things: so that means not getting drunk and not abstaining, just drinking in moderation. I rather like Sayadaw's comment here: "The lecturer does not seem to have reflected that the same standards if applied to the other precepts will be astonishing indeed! Not wholesale murder, not total abstention from killing, but just killing in moderation!"[31] The message of right action is to think carefully before acting and to get the mind in a good state so that the actions that spring from it are good and wholesome.

Right livelihood

The last of the morality group is right livelihood, which dealt with occupations in the time of the Buddha that were unacceptable for Buddhists. It was unacceptable to deal in weapons; to be involved in the slaughter of animals or human beings; the making and selling of intoxicants; and making poisons. These were the five prohibited types of work in the fifth century BCE. Transferred to contemporary times, a more up-to-date and extended vocabulary for such precepts would be abstaining from dealing with arms and nuclear weapons; involvement in the alcoholic drink industry; work that involves any slaughter or vivisection of animals – livelihoods that involve harming animals such as work in an abattoir or even as a butcher. So such unwise occupations in contemporary society would include work in the pharmaceutical or biochemical industries with their prolific testing on animals: even experimentation on fruit flies would be against the Buddhist principle. The countless mice, other rodents and macaque monkeys used to find a vaccine for Covid, with all the deliberate suffering and deaths accrued by the creatures, would not be noble Buddhist practice. Then, too, advertising industries that present dishonest and deceptive claims about products; tradesmen who deliberately and dishonestly overcharge customers, or harass people to spend their money unwisely are contemporaneously relevant. The Buddha would not have endorsed warfare where it is necessary to kill other human beings and would certainly have found the armed forces the wrong kind of livelihood for a Buddhist. Here, however, I must point out that at the height of the first phase of the UK Covid pandemic, members of the army were employed at the frontline and were invaluable in conducting testing for the virus. The Buddha also had a distaste for soothsayers, astrologists, palmistry and the like, whom he regarded as treacherous and deceitful. In short, money needs to be earned in a peaceful and ethical way without causing any harm or violence to any creature or human being. It should never be based on wrong conduct, improper means, deception or poor knowledge.

The Buddha's call to abstain from livelihood that harms human beings was aimed at slavery and prostitution. Today, we have seen remarkable protests about city benefactors of the past who gained their wealth through the slave trade. As a result of the *I can't breathe* protests following the death of George Floyd in May 2020 in Minneapolis, a group of protesters pulled down a statue of Edward Colston in Bristol in the United Kingdom and hauled and rolled it into the river. Colston was a great benefactor to the city of Bristol and so streets and municipal buildings were named after him. But his wealth was gained through the slave trade of Africans that were herded up and sold abroad. People – both black and white – find this obscene and, as a result, similar statues around the world are now being taken down: wealth acquired through the sale of human beings is totally unacceptable. But we have a new slave labour phenomenon in our times, certainly in Britain, when people from eastern bloc countries are coaxed to leave their homes and find better-paid employment in the United Kingdom, only to find that they are barely paid and fed, live in squalid conditions, and are unable to leave and return to their homes. Women are also deceitfully promised a better life and find themselves trafficked to work as prostitutes. Then there are the sweat shops, as they are called, in countries far from the West where people have to work long, long hours in order to make products, especially in the clothing industry, for those in more affluent societies. The motivation here is the greed of the three evils.

Despite what has been said, the Buddha was not against wealth *per se*. For the individual who worked hard and honestly, it was right that some wealth could be accumulated in order to support a family. The Buddha was sufficiently pragmatic to know that without a certain degree of economic security and without the stress of finding sufficient to feed oneself and one's family, spiritual progress would not be possible. People's minds can never be at rest if they are struggling to pay bills. The Buddha endorsed ownership of a home, economic security gained by lawful means and right conduct, the enjoyment of wealth, and the comfort of not being in debt to anyone, providing one was blameless in securing such assets. Many today would find those basic necessities hard to come by. The Buddha was always aware of the struggles of the poor, understanding their economic and social needs remarkably well in the political milieu of his day. His message then is no less relevant than it is today with the loss of jobs, redundancies, post-furloughing problems, and the incredible level of insecurity of jobs in the future whenever we emerge from this pandemic.

But let us turn to right livelihood in our present times. Long before the pandemic, people were clamouring for an end to immigration and there was little warmth extended to those who came here to work from Romania, Bulgaria, Poland and even as far afield as the Philippines and Fiji. Where would we be without these individuals who came here as nurses, doctors, care workers, hospital cleaners, porters and cooks? The "clap for carers" each Thursday evening at eight in the UK was a massive thank you to these people who have cared for Covid patients, putting their own lives at risk: many lost their lives from the virus. Now those who were not wanted are very valued and it is hoped that when all this is over and life is back to normal – if ever that can be – the contribution of these individuals will not be forgotten. So, we need to be careful in saying who we do not want in our country – whatever country that may be – for the ones we ban could be the very ones destined to save our lives.

Right effort

The next of the Eightfold Path, right effort, takes us out of the morality group and into one aspect of the meditation and mindfulness group. That said it is intimately relevant to all the other factors of the Path, calling for effort in every aspect. I am dealing with it here as the bridge between the wisdom and morality groups that lead to the more introspective, meditative facets of the Path. Despite the energy effort suggests, it is a spiritual energy not a physical energy that is required. It is concerned with wholesome and unwholesome states of mind, and is directed to four areas in the journey of the Path. The first of these four is preventive effort to avoid and stop unwholesome thoughts from arising in the first place. Secondly, there are results that have already arisen or are about to happen from past unwholesome choices. Sometimes we can do nothing about such effects except get through them with as much equanimity as possible. This second aspect of effort is the relinquishing and abandoning of these unwholesome states as they arise by non-attachment to them, by disallowing attraction and craving that would result by reaction to them. I am reminded of another of Gianluca Vialli's favoured mantras: "Remember that our life is made of 10% by what happens to us and 90% by the way we react to it; if we change the way we look at things, things begin to change."[32] And again: "Between stimulus and response is our greater power: the freedom to choose."[33] When consciousness is stimulated we get attachment, desire for, aversion to, or just neutrality to the stimulus. That is the point at which greed can step in, the ego come into play, and unhappiness follow the results of the choices we make. So the second part of effort is the abandonment of unwholesome states of mind that have already arisen.

The third of the four aspects is effort in creating and developing good states of mind before they arise, bringing them into the mind so that they will aid future wholesome evolution in the right directions. The fourth is the effort to hold, maintain, and not lose these wholesome states of thought that have been brought into the mind, especially in meditation and concentration, where effort is a prerequisite. This is why right effort belongs with the last two of the Eightfold Path, right mindfulness and right concentration, which I shall examine in the next chapter. We move here from moral restraints to inner mental training and a calm mind, as we shall see. Effort, then, is the energy to create a wholesome mind with wholesome states of consciousness, at the same time maintaining the other factors of the Path. This is aimed at keeping the three evils of greed, hatred/aversion, and delusion in check.

Our world today is one that involves a high measure of stress and tension, heightened now by the fear of the coronavirus. In the first three months of the pandemic, I only ventured out once and remember on that occasion the sheer terror in a woman's eyes as I entered a cycling shop when she was on her way out. It is probably right to be cautious and careful, but not terrified. Our normal lives are governed by limited time in which to do a lot and it was not difficult to find strain and stress on the faces of many we passed by in the street or shop long before we had ever heard of Covid-19. We seem to have got used to a life of stress and perhaps that has informed the increased mental problems many now experience through sudden cessation of normal routine and the strange world of more isolation and less to do. If we are now free from the rush and strenuous lives we usually live, then we have time to take stock of our lives and think how we can move forwards in positive ways. According to the Buddha, we do not really understand life; we are ignorant of its real nature. Are we really happy despite the post-modern consumer culture that we have? Do we ever think carefully what happiness is? Do we think if I do this, change that, or have this or that I shall be happy, only to find what we wanted was not the answer? Are we secure in life or insecure? We cannot help our bodies through illness if the mind is agitated, and resistance to illness and to the coronavirus may have a lot to do with the mental state of each of us. Meditation may help to create a calmer state of mind, a state of mind that can weather the horror of the virus, and the next chapter will deal with that. But I want to end this chapter with some very wise words of the Greek philosopher Plotinus who wrote so long ago:

> Withdraw into yourself and look. And if you do not find yourself beautiful as yet, do as does the creator of a statue that is to be made beautiful; he cuts away here, he smooths there, he makes this line lighter, this other purer, until he has shown a beautiful face upon the statue. So do you also; cut away all that is excessive; straighten all that is crooked, bring light to all that is shadowed, labour to make all glow with beauty, and do not cease chiselling your statue until there shall shine out on you the splendour of virtue, until you shall see the final goodness surely established in the stainless shrine.[34]

7
The Noble Eightfold Path
Mindfulness and Concentration

The Eightfold Path divides well into the three areas of morality, mindfulness, and wisdom. In the previous chapter, I used right effort, which is actually in the wisdom group, as the bridge between the other groups and the seventh and eighth of the Path as the wisdom of right mindfulness and right concentration. Mindfulness is meditation and we have to bear in mind that it was through deep meditation that the Buddha came to enlightenment. Meditation was not new at the time of the Buddha but it was mainly based on *yogic* praxis that focused on destroying the egoistic self by very austere practices; denying the body in every way possible in order to break free of the cycle of births and deaths. In contrast, the Buddha adopted a more reasonable approach in his Middle Way, a life not wholly luxurious and affluent, nor totally austere. He had tried both and neither gave him any answers. Thus, the Buddha's meditation methods are generous to mind and body: there is no necessity for painful experience in it, but neither should the meditator seem as if he or she is having a nap.

Mind and body

The very image of the Buddha sitting comfortably with legs crossed and hands joined in his lap is the epitome of comfortable meditation. In examining meditation, then, I think we have to take a pragmatic approach. Again, we are in the realm of either a mundane pathway or a supra-mundane one, the latter being for the more advanced monk and nun whose lives are dedicated to practices in secluded living beyond the milieu of ordinary mortals. This is not to say that the Buddha had two separate ways for each type of person. No, the Eightfold Path is exactly the same for monastic or lay individual, or even for Buddhist and non-Buddhist. It is just that the Buddha knew that many would not be able to adopt fully the entire Path.

Nevertheless, for all on the Path, the journey is a spiritual one rather than an intellectual one. The spiritual experience of the Path is one of the whole being – mind and body – and the expression of that spirituality in engagement with life. And that is a personal journey for each individual. Ajahn Sumedho's words here are wise: "No-one's enlightenment is going to enlighten any of the rest of us. So this is a movement inwards: not looking outwards for somebody who is enlightened to make you enlightened."[1] What is required is *effort* from within: nothing beyond the self is going to prod or encourage development in meditation/mindfulness, or any aspect of the Path.

The key that unlocks any part of the Eightfold Path is the mind. According to the Buddha: "Well, monk, the world is led by mind (thought); by mind the world is drawn along; all have gone under the sway of mind, the one *dhamma*."[2] So how does the mind of "the world" appear in these weird times? When England allowed retailers selling non-essential goods to reopen, I was surprised to see that people queued extensively outside a well-known retailer from the early hours of the morning. The shop sells clothing – just clothes! With all the time during lockdown to think and reflect on life, clearly for so many people being able to buy clothes was a primary importance. This must surely suggest that we are locked into a world of craving and greed. That is something of a subjective comment but note Sumedho here concerning the consumer society in which we live when he writes about advertisements: "The materialistic society tries to arouse greed so you will spend your money, and yet never be contented with what you have. There is always something better, something newer, something more delicious than what was the most delicious yesterday . . . it goes on and on, pulling you out into objects of the senses like that."[3] Will such materialism bring happiness? We want happiness, but it is difficult to pin down what exactly happiness is when our bodies and minds are torn this way and that by the countless things to have, to do, to buy, to achieve.

I do not think the Buddha would have claimed that all suffering is the result of past *kamma*, but a good deal of the way in which we live our lives is out of our control. Covid-19 may well be put down to past *kamma* for some, but the Buddha certainly recognized that adventitious suffering was, and is, part of the backdrop of existence – like the asteroid that wiped out the dinosaurs. But it is worth reiterating that we are subject to a good deal of conditioning in life that entraps our minds into patterns of thought about which we scarcely think. Without waking up to reality, our families, peers, cultures, class, gender, race, nationality all have a bearing on how our minds develop. Experiencing lockdown has brought out aspects of personality that surprise many individuals. Many enjoyed the time and space to "catch up" with things, or to undertake and explore new things. And yet, probably few enjoyed the opportunity for quiet space. I live in the Welsh countryside in a beautiful and quiet area. I do not normally see anyone living here, so to begin with having to self-isolate was no problem. But after two and a half months I began to have nightmares and this outcome, it seems, became quite common for people in lockdown. Even though I have open fields around me, a quiet forest just along the road, *something* was disturbing me or happening in my mind to cause the frequent nightmares. After we had been in lockdown for three and a half months, the nightmares were still there. As to *monotony*, even with a book to write the daily chores were always the same and became more prominent in the mind than before. What of those isolated in flats and tenement blocks with no expanse of green around them? The suffering here must have been, and probably still is considerable, and with a further wave of Covid and new restrictions, is going to become more so: a new lockdown is now present in England. I came to the conclusion that however reclusive and busy one is, *other people* are essential to well-being. Persistent lockdown is inimical to the mental health of individuals and has brought its own dimensions of suffering. I was reading recently an article by a well-known television presenter, Jeremy Paxman, who was commenting on lockdown. He made the point that: "This bloody virus has shown what social animals we are" and I think this gets to the heart of the depressing attitudes that accompany lockdown. Paxman said it hurt not being able to enjoy the seasons. We were just into spring when lockdown began and were almost in autumn when restrictions were lifted a little. Now, as autumn turns to winter, in the UK local and national lockdowns are becoming again the "new normal" for many people. As Paxman says about the spring and summer months of lockdown: "This unseasonable hibernation has reminded us how much, despite generations of urban living, we still live by natural rhythms."[4]

But silence is good: it is the medium in which great things happen. Thera Piyadassi believed, "it is in and through solitude that the human mind gains in strength and power. The greatest creative energy works in silence, but people seem to like noise better than silence. The vast majority are so burdened with everyday affairs, so engrossed in things seemingly very important, that they overlook the importance of silent contemplation." Have we then missed the opportunity in lockdown for contemplative solitude and silence? I think the majority of individuals may not have given much thought to the possibility of precious quiet. Will we look back on lockdown as a time wasted because we could not go out, or will we have gleaned from it something to take with us in the remainder of our lives? Again, Piyadassi continued: "When we withdraw into the silence, we are absolutely alone to see ourselves as we really are; we stand face to face with actuality, and then we can learn to overcome the weaknesses and limitations of ordinary experience."[5] The whole point here is of *being mindful*, trying to see one-self as different from the conditioned selves we have become; selves driven by habits that form our personalities. Meditation/mindfulness aims at dislodging ordinary thoughts and shifting the mind to a more reflective mode in order to experience a different reality. As we explore mindfulness now, it should be remembered that any serious meditation is accompanied by *effort* – not the effort of straining the mind but the effort of being prepared to undertake it regularly, daily, and at fixed times, whether for the ordinary individual or for the more practised monk or nun in a monastic setting. Meditation/ mindfulness is a retraining of the mind from its normative conditioning to a calm, inner peacefulness: that is not something achieved overnight.

Meditation/mindfulness

For many people meditation and mindfulness are different: meditation is understood as sitting in a certain posture for a considerable length of time and concentrating on something. Mindfulness, on the other hand, seems as if it is just being mindful of something in a more ordinary setting. However, in early Buddhism and much Buddhism in general, these two terms are synonymous simply because meditation is focusing the mind and being mindful of what comes into the mind. With any distinction between the two eroded, there is no reason why meditation has to be confined to a special place, position and time: in the sense of mindfulness, it can be practised anywhere. So I am going to use the terms interchangeably in this chapter. Meditation can be done in a quiescent situation or in activity and much Buddhist meditation may be specifically walking meditation: either way, it is central to Buddhist thought and practice. Meditation is *bhavana*, a term that Rupert Gethin translates as "bringing into being" with the following apposite explanation that "it refers to mental or spiritual exercises aimed at developing and cultivating wholesome mental states that conduce to the realization of the Buddhist path".[6] The synonymy with mindfulness is clear from Gethin's definition here. And I think Damien Keown is to the point when he writes that *bhavana* as meditation "is the principal strategy for making oneself what one wishes to be".[7] We should see meditation, then, as the means to overcome suffering and sadness especially since it is not separate from daily living but can be applied to all aspects of life as mindfulness of the individual in all actions. Now this is particularly so in that meditation is frequently medically advised for decreasing high blood pressure, reducing stress, and the like. As Edward Conze put it: "However diverse in nature the numerous exercises which come under the heading of mindfulness may seem to be, they all have in common this one purpose, that of guarding the incipient and growing calm in one's heart."[8] So whatever sect of Buddhism one meets, meditation, mindfulness, will lie at the heart of practice. The aim of meditation is to rid the mind of wrong thoughts – especially of those linked to the three evils of greed, hatred/aversion and delusion/stupidity – and to cultivate good thoughts, thoughts that aid and benefit the individual in living life for the better.

There are two kinds of meditation, *samatha*, which is calmness, serenity, and *vipassana*, which is insight. They are certainly not distinct from each other but overlap and complement each other. In *samatha* meditation the mind concentrates on an object such as breathing and allows the attention to focus on it in such a way that the mind becomes calm. *Vipassana* is insight meditation in which there is no object of focus but, instead, a focus on watching and observing one's own thoughts in a highly concentrated, detached and objective way. The aim here is to gain a deep understanding of the nature of reality, so *vipassana* is a much deeper concentration than *samatha*, though it includes, too, the calmness of *samatha*.

In any form of meditation there is the aim of coming to know the conditioning that has informed the self that we know; a clearer perspective of who we are and what makes us as we are. When negative perspectives arise here, they are bypassed for more positive ones, so harmful thoughts are replaced by beneficial ones. Take for example a difficult person with whom there is regular contact; a person who flies off the handle and becomes irate at the slightest thing; a person who will never listen to reason, is always right and always accuses others. Thinking of this person's *good* qualities and the common human nature he or she shares with the rest of humanity may help to alleviate the overwhelming tendency in oneself to argue, forcefully disagree, or even cower in such a person's presence. What gets in the way here is *emotion*, and calming emotional responses is part of the purpose of meditation through understanding the feelings that come into the mind. That is a hard call, but Buddhist meditation asks for this kind of inner change of anger/aversion to a positive, calmer inner self to cope with our irate person. In normal life, the difficult person becomes a stimulus to the mind for habitual reaction of distaste or anger, and it is just that point between stimulus and reaction that needs to be arrested. Changing reaction should change the way the person is viewed. That said, lockdown has brought about an alarming increase in the number of women who are physically and mentally abused by their partners at home. They are not just locked down, they are locked in. There is no point whatsoever in expecting a change here through meditation, so the answer surely has to be *get out* and *now*. But, if anything, mindfulness may encourage the strength to do that.

Meditation seeks to alter the state of mind, to alter consciousness through controlling the thoughts that come into the mind, and to develop the mind and bring it into a better state of being. With mindfulness an individual keeps control of his or her mind so that thoughts, words and actions are totally under control. According to the Buddha: "Mindfulness, O monks, I declare, is essential in all things everywhere",[9] so it is not divorced from ordinary existence by any means, and is not the sole prerogative of the monastic setting or even Buddhist allegiance. Mindfulness is *paying attention* to thought, speech and action, especially in all those other aspects of the Eightfold Path, so developing the powers of observation in what we do, and getting rid of mental negativities. These, again, are not easy things to accomplish, which is why *right effort* is part of the wisdom group. To be beneficial, meditation involves a good deal of sustained practice in order to train the mind: it is not practised to make one withdrawn and immobilized, but alert. Bhikkhu Bodhi said of the mind here: "The mind is deliberately kept at the level of bare attention, a detached observation of what is happening within us and around us in the present moment. Mindfulness is 'choiceless awareness', awareness that observes what is happening without 'picking and choosing', without becoming entangled in the net of discriminating thoughts."[10] And he went on to say: "To practise mindfulness is thus a matter not so much of doing but of undoing: not thinking, not imagining, not wishing. All these 'doings' of ours are modes of interference, ways the mind manipulates experience and tries to establish its dominance. Mindfulness undoes the knots and tangles of these doings by simply noting."[11] In mindfulness there is awareness of the body, of sensations, of the stimuli that enter the mind but *no reaction*. Such a state of non-reaction and yet awareness is not as alien as it may seem at first. The psychologist Mihalyi Csikszentmihalyi's work on "flow" experiences is an exploration of "optimal experiences" that I think we all encounter from time to time – in music, in nature, in sex, the view from the top of a mountain, a sunset, holding a newly born baby – when normal consciousness seems to be transcended and attention is not diverted into the multiple but is confined to a kind of one-pointedness.[12] In the same way, meditative practice focuses attention away from peripheral sense stimuli.

We do not have to withdraw into solitude to practise meditation: we all experience things that are disagreeable and annoying in life, things that lead us to dwell on negativity, unkindness, anger, conflict. Developed mindfulness should be able to restrain the mind so that reaction to such things in life is improved, lessened or even overcome. If we can change ourselves through our own mind control, we should be able to change others. And while effort is necessary to control the mind, that does not mean a massive inner battle is necessary: in meditation, exercises are a natural means, a quiet means of control. Wrong thoughts create stress and need to be brushed to one side, pushed away: it is a simple thing to do if every time a negative thought enters the mind it is simply brushed aside. That is one way how meditation can be adopted in daily living and is one means of restraining the senses. We fill our minds with all sorts of rubbish, all sorts of anxieties and worries, all kinds of must-do-this and must-do-that, things to do tomorrow or next week, hopes or fears that this or that will happen. Our senses are keen to do such things, latching on to the things outside the moment. We would be a whole lot more relaxed if we could just concentrate on the task in hand, the moment in time. How we walk and talk reflects our minds: if we are angry, the body, facial expression and speech will soon show it, and we will speed up when walking. These are the noticeable changes that take place on the exterior but the changes in inner metabolic processes are the hidden harmful ones that take place within our bodies. Changing external *reactions* to stimuli in terms of bodily reactions is also a facet of mindfulness. With mindfulness, the body and the mind can be under control. So important is mindfulness that one *Sutta* devoted to it, the *Satipatthana-sutta*, is regularly recited by monastic and lay Buddhist alike to this day. What is important about this *Sutta* is its relation to ordinary life, ordinary living and its ups and downs, its joys and sadnesses. The beauty of the *Sutta* is reflected in its words that wish for the happiness and security of all beings: "Whatever living beings there may be – feeble or strong, tall, stout, or medium, short, small, or large, seen or unseen, those dwelling far or near, those who are born and those who are yet to be born – may all beings, without exception, be happy-minded!"[13]

The calm mind

The surface of the mind is a crowded place of competing thoughts, ideas, plans, preparation for actions, behaviour in interaction with people, work and leisure. It demands multiple adaptations and, really, multiple expressions of "self", depending on the context in which a person is. Conze wrote of a still, calm and quiet centre at the bottom of the mind beyond both consciousness and unconsciousness. This is a still point beyond the surface turmoil, but it is only the latter that is normally experienced. He said: "The depth is, however, usually overlaid to such an extent that people remain incredulous when told of a submerged spot of stillness in their inmost hearts. In most cases the surface is so turbulent that the calm of the depth can be realized only in rare intervals."[14] Meditation searches out this inner depth. We may perhaps think of it as "spirituality", that encompasses a deep and positive sensitivity to reality. This may be experienced in quietude – what we usually think of in terms of meditation – but it may also occur in activity. I have argued elsewhere that such experience is a biological facet of what it is to be human and that it is qualitative but by no means quantitative.[15] This is partially what calming meditation is all about. Those who attend meditation or yoga classes will perhaps be aware of the feeling of floating and calm that meditation supports.

Such calming meditation is beneficial for those at the mundane, ordinary level of life and experience, leaving the supra-mundane level for the more experienced and those in the monastic setting, but even here calming the mind remains part of the practice as preparation for knowledge and insight. For the more mundane among us, and those who suffer from surface turmoil of the mind, calming meditation is the easier path that, with a little effort, can be adopted into daily life. When overwhelmed by anxiety and worries life becomes distorted, reality becomes confused, tensions lead to lack of good sleep, measured responses in daily life are lost, and interaction with others can be fractious. In contrast, meditation increases attentiveness and the ability to focus the mind even in difficult circumstances. The "I" of the self is not quite so forcefully present and becomes less identified with the turmoil of the surface mind.

The beginner in meditation is usually given something on which to focus, perhaps the breathing process, or an object, so that the restlessness of the mind is reduced, thoughts are slowed down and a more relaxed feeling pervades the body. In the sense of mindfulness, just concentrating on the activity of the moment stills the multiple stimulating thoughts. Cleaning one's teeth, peeling potatoes, gardening, can all be done with concentration on the task in hand as opposed to thinking of the next task, and the next, and so on, or thinking of persistent worries. Again, it is a matter of brushing away any other intruding thoughts from the mindfulness of the moment. So meditation in its early stages is not endless sitting still and contemplating one's navel, it can be activity of the body coupled with quiet focus of the mind. That said, having a quiet place in which to sit for a while and meditate is the kind of peaceful situation to enjoy. And contrary to what might be expected, kindness to oneself is one of the first steps in Buddhist meditation, with thoughts on being free from enmity, ill-will and distress, and being happy: Buddhist meditation does not set out to make an individual miserable. A mind devoid of its turbulent thoughts is naturally calm so early stages of meditation block the disturbances that flood into the mind by encouraging focused mindfulness. Just half an hour's practice a day will reap all kinds of positive benefits. Mindfulness is centred on four areas – the body; sensations or feelings; the mind's activities; and mind objects in terms of thoughts and ideas.

Mindfulness of the body

The most natural observable aspect of the body is its breathing and this, indeed, is the way in which many begin meditation. Being mindful of the regular breathing in and out trains the mind to let go of other things and concentrate on the action of breathing. Our normal breathing is spontaneous and natural, not something we notice, but for meditation purposes here there is concentration on every moment of the inhalation and exhalation, not tensely and forced, and not controlled but relaxed. Later, higher stages of meditation on breathing will be adopted for those advanced on the Path, but mindfulness on breathing is a good process for beginners. Mindfulness on breathing is simply awareness, awareness of a process in the moment. Note Bhikkhu Bodhi's words here: "The awareness of breath cuts through the complexities of discursive thinking, rescues us from pointless wandering in the labyrinth of vain imaginings, and grounds us solidly in the present. For whenever we become aware of breathing, really aware of it, we can be aware of it only in the present, never in the past or future."[16]

To be really comfortable and get the best from such meditation, posture is important – sitting with the legs crossed with a straight back is best, so that the spine is straight and the head not drooping forward but the neck keeping the same line as the spine. Early Buddhist texts actually stipulated this posture for meditation on breathing. These days, sitting on a straight-backed chair is acceptable. Eyes can be closed or just open and looking at the tip of the nose. It is no good thinking that the mind will immediately become calm while meditating on breathing: it will not, and thoughts will enter simply because the mind so loves to wander off on its own. Again, the gentle brushing away of the thought and the equally gentle pulling of the mind back to being mindful of breathing is all that is needed. Eventually, the breathing should become slower, calmer, more even and effortless. It will not come right straight away because it needs practice and diligence, but for the individual who is faced with stress and anxiety, breathing meditation should reap great benefits. Walpola Rahula warned how difficult the practice is at first: "At the beginning you will find it extremely difficult to bring your mind to concentrate on your breathing. You will be astonished how your mind runs away. It does not stay. You begin to think of various things. You hear sounds outside. Your mind is disturbed and distracted. You may be dismayed and disappointed. But if you continue to practise this exercise twice daily, morning and evening, for about five or ten minutes at a time, you will gradually, by and by, begin to concentrate your mind on your breathing."[17] But, said Rahula, results are immediate, with greater relaxation, better sleep and physical health.[18]

Movement or postures of the body are also aids in meditation. So whether walking, standing, sitting, lying down, the mind is brought to be mindful of the particular posture. The key here is awareness of the postures and the impersonal nature of the body, which is dependent on volition for its movements. The use of a mantra is widespread in all forms of Buddhist meditation and said quietly at the back of the mind as in transcendental meditation, or chanted vocally as in Nichiren Daishonin Buddhism it is a useful tool to focus the mind. Of course discursive thoughts intrude but they are brushed aside or, in the case of Nichiren Daishonin Buddhism a positive thought or need is superimposed over the mantra. For Theravada Buddhism, which descended from early Buddhism, the mantra *Buddho* is sometimes used alongside breathing – *Bud* for the inhalation and *dho* for the exhalation. It is always important to be aware of the discursive thoughts that come into the mind – aware, but that is all. To know the mind and be skilful in controlling it is to understand how it operates, how it entices the ego, and how it can be mastered if thoughts are just noticed but not responded to.

Whatever the mode of meditation, the mind should be at peace. Meditation is not a task or a burden or something that must be done as a chore: it should be relaxing, something to which one can look forward, a bit of peace in the day. Telling oneself that there is nothing else to do, nothing to worry about will aid relaxation. And in daily living, being rooted in the present, in the activity or even non-activity of the moment, focusing the mind on the here-and-now moment is controlling the mind. Many of us eat our food at speed or "on the hoof" and we would be a whole lot healthier if we slowed down and were mindful of the process of eating. Despite what has just been said, it is important to lose the "I" in meditation. If there is too much emphasis on *I* am doing this and now *I* am doing that, the *me* aspect of the self is to the fore. It is better to lose oneself in an action, forget the self and be absorbed in what one is doing. As Rahula commented: "All great work – artistic, poetic, intellectual or spiritual – is produced at those moments when its creators are lost completely in their actions, when they forget themselves altogether, and are free from self-consciousness."[19]

Mindfulness of feelings

Mindfulness of feelings is exactly that, being mindful of the feelings and sensations one experiences both outwardly and inwardly but not responding to them by any reaction. So feelings and sensations, whether pleasant, unpleasant or neutral, are simply noted with a detached attitude. The aim is to see them as fleeting and impermanent and nothing to do with any kind of permanent self. Feelings here are not emotions; they are just fleeting moments of consciousness that appear because of contact with something by way of one or more of the senses. The problem with feelings is that they stimulate the three evils/poisons of desire/attachment, aversion, or delusion. Mindfulness of a particular feeling as a fleeting arising of what is pleasant, unpleasant or neutral and nothing more means there is a possibility of breaking the moment of response. Bhikhu Bodhi clarified the process rather well when he wrote: "By turning it into an object of observation, mindfulness defuses the feeling so that it cannot provoke an unskilful response. Then, instead of relating to the feeling by way of habit through attachment, repulsion, or apathy, we relate by way of contemplation, using the feeling as a springboard for understanding the nature of experience."[20] So a feeling is just noted for what it is and then brushed away, for feelings themselves are impermanent, as we know from their being one of the Five Aggregates that have featured so much in earlier chapters. Mindfulness on feelings reinforces one of the central messages of Buddhism that *all* is impermanent.

Meditation on feelings aims to assist *detachment* from the feeling, almost as if observing it as someone else's. Probably all of us at some time or another have those sleepless nights where thoughts tumble over each other to the extent that we cannot sleep. Then comes anxiety because we cannot sleep, while the mind throws up more of the anxieties or excitements that stopped us sleeping in the first place. No doubt, concerns about Covid-19 have led to many such sleepless nights, to worries about health, finance, work, redundancy, the fears of having to shield or self-isolate, and these are feelings that lead to considerable unhappiness. But note Rahula's words here: "First of all, you should learn not to be unhappy about your unhappy feeling, not to be worried about your worries. But try to see clearly why there is a sensation or a feeling of unhappiness, or worry, or sorrow. Try to examine how it arises, its cause, how it disappears, its cessation. Try to examine it as if you are observing it from the outside, without any subjective reaction, as a scientist observes some object. Here, too, you should not look at it as 'my feeling' or 'my sensation' subjectively, but only look at it as 'a feeling' or 'a sensation' objectively."[21] In other words there is an effort not to get lost in one's own thoughts but observe them in a detached way, "regarding them like clouds passing across a clear blue sky, or bubbles floating to the top of a glass", to use Keown's similes.[22]

Mindfulness of the mind

Contemplating the mind itself means assessing objectively how far the mind is engaged with desire, aversion and delusion with the aim of controlling it. In addition, understanding the mind leads to the knowledge that it is not "me", it is not a "self"; it consists merely of a constant stream of changing impressions. Rather like watching a stream of images on a screen, the meditator "watches" the processes of thought until, with practice, skill allows the meditator to push aside, brush away, thoughts that are irrelevant, emotional, imaginative, so that the mind becomes restful, quieter, calmer. Again, Rahula offered wise words that "here is no attitude of criticizing or judging, or discriminating between right and wrong, or good and bad. It is simply observing, watching, examining. . . . When you observe your mind, and see its true nature clearly, you become dispassionate with regard to its emotions, sentiments and states."[23] What Rahula pointed out is that it is important to be kind to oneself in the process and not "own" the aspects thrown onto the screen of the mind. If unhappy, just observe it without ownership; similarly with anger or other states of mind. In the *Dhammapada* it says: "The mind is hard to restrain, light, flying where it will. Control of it is good. Mind controlled brings happiness."[24]

The five hindrances

Meditation, mindfulness, is rarely going to bring satisfaction at the first attempt. The Buddha was wise enough to know that there would be a number of factors inimical to mindfulness. Five are to be found in the texts – desire; aversion; dullness; restlessness and doubt. After a very short time for the beginner the mind starts to wander. **Desire** runs through all minds as something attractive that is wanted and it may be as simple as what one wants to eat and how hungry one is. In the here and now with our present constraints it may be the desire to go somewhere that the government forbids; the desire to see a loved one who is shielding; the desire to plan a funeral that cannot happen; the desire to go to a church service; to re-join one's choir, gym, art class, piano lessons; or attend a sporting function: the list for us all is long. These are desires that will seem so much more important to have in the mind than mindfulness. Even the desire to be better at meditation and not fail at it will turn up frequently. But with practice, if meditation is to be valuable, such desires need to be recognized as such and brushed aside. If nothing else, the ability to do this would lessen the stress of governmental and "new normal" constraints on society. Desire leads to clinging, the second of the Four Noble Truths that the Buddha put forward as the cause of suffering. It is to be expected, then, that mindfulness of its influence will be an important part of meditation practices. **Aversion** usually surfaces as those little things that annoy us about someone, the things that niggle that we have to do but do not want to, and aversion, too, for pain and illness. We may find it difficult to meditate because someone else is making a noise nearby or next door; a dog is barking or the clock seems to be ticking too loudly. Such things cause irritability and anger. These aspects of the mind also have to be recognized for what they are and brushed aside.

Dullness is a frequent experience when beginning meditation. It is expressed in drowsiness, tiredness, sleepiness, lethargy, or just "I can't be bothered to meditate this morning". These are moods that need to be noted not reacted to with aversion or the desire to get rid of them. In many senses they are inner mental expressions rather than bodily ones but all such feelings of dullness are to be brushed aside. The opposite of dullness is **restlessness** expressing itself with fidgeting, anxiety, worry, tension, wanting to get up and go, the very opposite of being still and calm. And many of the aspects of restlessness here are those given as the reason for beginning meditation in the first place so when experienced there may well be dissatisfaction with one's progress as not working. On the other hand, when meditation is going very well it can promote excitement that also creates restlessness. Again, observing the restlessness as an attitude in the mind and nothing more, and letting it go is the way forward. Understandably, beginning meditation practices of whatever kind will rarely be satisfactory at the first attempts so the mind will start to **doubt** the veracity of it, whether it is being done properly, whether it is having any effect, or what the point of it is. But in fact, you cannot know for certain what the outcome will be and whether it will be successful in changing attitudes to life. So the answer again is to brush the doubt aside and continue.

Sumedho calls the hindrances "teachers" because though hindrances we are able to learn from them: "They can be pretty trivial, petty, foolish, annoying and obsessive. They keep pushing, jabbing, knocking us down all the time until we give them proper attention and understanding, until they are no longer problems. That's why one has to be very patient; we have to have all the patience in the world, and the humility to learn from these five teachers."[25] The five hindrances, then, are not to be blocked and repressed but recognized for what they are, understood and, if possible, brushed aside. Understanding why and how the hindrances occur gives the opportunity to be objectively critical of them and to control them. The hindrances, then, are themselves *objects* of meditation. As meditation advances, there are counteractive mindfulness practices to overcome them. For example, desire can be overcome by unity of mind; aversion by joyful thought, dullness by more applied thought; restlessness by thoughts of happiness; doubt by practising sustained thought.

Mindfulness, therefore, need not be of positive thought but includes an understanding of negative thought. The Five Aggregates, for example are also used as mind objects for meditation in order to free the mind from ideas of permanence, particularly the idea of a permanent self. Subjects of meditation may also involve aspects of the Four Noble Truths and the characteristics of enlightenment such as its joy, tranquillity and equanimity. These are more advanced stages and for a beginner an object may be used on which to focus the mind as a preliminary practice. Such a visual object has the advantage of holding the attention, and when attention strays into the hindrances can more easily be brought back onto the object, though not without effort, practice and skill. With repeated practice benefits of meditation become clearer. There is a certain amount of calm that stems from an inner quiet and less agitation from the things in life that worry and make one agitated. There are clear benefits to the physical well-being of the individual and changes in brain functioning that I shall deal with below. In the stressful times in which we live, witnessing the presence of a silent killer that is out there and everywhere, meditation has a lot to offer.

Concentration, *samadhi*

Moving from mindfulness to concentration is to pass into higher stages of meditation, *samadhi*, which Damien Keown interprets as "a powerful technique for the acceleration of ethical and intellectual development towards their perfection in *nibbana*".[26] *Samadhi* brings a certain unity of being, perhaps something of the Jungian concept of a harmony between the conscious and subconscious. Indeed, the union of opposites in Jung's work is of interest here with its emphasis on the harmonizing and unifying of the disparate elements of the human conscious and subconscious elements that bring about a "whole" person. Perhaps this is what experience of spirituality is all about – a moment of fusion of consciousness and subconscious, a harmony and balance between both. Indeed, one of the common statements about a "peak" or spiritual experience is that the "I", the ego, the self, is momentarily lost. Whatever our level of consciousness, the foremost and most important content of that consciousness is that of our *selves*, the *me*, which lives within and relates to the world. And that self is composed of the tendencies and habits, the fears and aspirations and the multiple experiences that have dropped into the less conscious parts of our mental being. All this disappears with experience of *samadhi*, when the mind and all its functioning is focused on just one thing alone. There is nothing exclusively religious in this experience, and it should be remembered that the Buddha denied any existence to a supernatural divinity. Indeed, *samadhi* may have some similarities with the secular transcendent "peak" or "optimal" experiences researched by Csikszentmihalyi as we saw above. In Buddhist concentration there is absorption of consciousness into the object – physical or in the mind – that stills consciousness into calm equanimity. This is meditative absorption that Piyadassi described as "a state of mental purity where disturbing passions and impulses are subdued and calmed down, so that the mind becomes unified and collected, and enters into a state of clear consciousness and mindfulness".[27] This is, indeed, an excellent description of right concentration, the eighth part of the Noble Eightfold Path.

The rationale for right concentration here is to rid the mind of any defilements and to avoid giving the mind free rein to its natural inclinations. Again, Piyadassi describes right concentration as "the intensified steadiness of the mind comparable to the unflickering flame of a lamp in a windless place. It is concentration that fixes the mind right and causes it to be unmoved and undisturbed. The correct practice of *samadhi* . . . maintains the mind and the mental properties in a state of balance."[28] All that we have seen in earlier chapters comes to bear here in every action of body and mind in integrated absorption where what was known previously by the intellect becomes, instead, intuitively known within. And yet, advanced though such concentration may be, it has a thorough relevance for mental and physical health, especially for the former here. A term that arises frequently in many Buddhist pathways is *shunyata*. It means "emptiness", "voidness" when the emptiness of all phenomena is realized even the emptiness of *shunyata* itself: nothing remains in terms of perceptions. In concentration, stimuli of the senses from the outer world and the inner mind are gradually reduced, withdrawn and renounced to leave the mind calm, "a soft, tranquil and pacified passivity", as Conze described it.[29]

The stages of concentration are called *jhanas* (Sanskrit *dhyanas*), and there are eight of these that progress to higher and higher states of concentration as modes of trance.

1. In the first stage, there are five "limbs" or factors of absorption in the object of concentration. The first limb is concentration as a real application of one's mind to that object. For the second limb, increased examination of the object of concentration brings about a more sustained application of the mind. The third limb brings feelings of joy, rapture, as a result of intensity of concentration on the object and the fourth brings happiness from success. The fifth limb is important as "one-pointedness" of the mind, a unity of the whole mind with the object. These five limbs really need to be in balance at this stage, and each one counteracts a corresponding one of the five hindrances we saw above, which are quelled. So this stage is *absorption* when one becomes one with the object of concentration; subject and object are fused. But this stage is not a lasting one since detachment from thoughts of other phenomena is only short-lived.
2. More intensive concentration at the second stage means the concentration can be accomplished without application of thought. At this stage, any discursive thoughts present at the first level are lost. Increased feelings of rapture and joy occur, and the mind is enlivened.
3. At the third stage of trance rapture gives way to equanimity. Joy is a sensation that is abandoned at this stage because it is a pleasant, attractive sense feeling, and it gives way to happiness until this, too, is abandoned for the same reason.
4. The fourth *jhana* places the meditator beyond equanimity and beyond all pleasure and pain. The mind is now still and calm and in many ways the stages of trance that follow are really refinements of this fourth stage, a stage in which there may be experience of psychic abilities, extra-sensory perception such as clairvoyance and telepathy. The Buddha did not consider such powers important and suggested that instead of wasting time

learning how to walk on water it would be better to hire a boatman!
5. When the fifth *jhana* is experienced we are in the very heights of meditative praxis bringing here experience of infinite space as concentration has become more and more subtle and refined. The whole world of the senses has disappeared. The stages of *jhana* from now on are very deep modes of trance, converging totally to a single point.
6. Infinite consciousness is the characteristic of trance at the sixth stage.
7. Nothingness.
8. Neither perception nor non-perception occurs at this level of trance and the concentration is at such a level that the meditator brushes *nibbana* with the body.

The one-pointedness of *samadhi* is the point at which all the desires, aversions and dullness of the mind are overcome. All the worries and anxieties disappear; the scattered thoughts are no longer there and the mind is opened to true reality in every way. As Bhikkhu Bodhi said "Like a lake unruffled by any breeze, the concentrated mind is a faithful reflector that mirrors whatever is placed before it exactly as it is."[30] When one-pointedness occurs all mind functioning is unified, *wholesome*, pure and rarefied. The world of sense stimuli has been gradually diminished until it is no longer there in the mind. We know from earlier chapters that all is impermanent and that each moment occurs, dies, and is immediately followed by another, and another, and so on. Just the same happens in concentration in meditation, but here the moments, though one after another, are stable and held by the concentrating mind without any fluctuation.

Beyond the realm of meditation, the possibilities of similar transcendent feelings to *samadhi* may be possible. Csikszentmihalyi understands the transcending of normal consciousness as a leaving behind of the ordinary self because attention is not diverted into the multiple but is confined to one-pointedness of mind. This would not do violence to the Buddhist position but Csikszentmihalyi does not deny the existence of a "self" albeit one temporarily suspended. In the kind of transcendent experience of which he writes, the self is forgotten when it is lost in the activity of the moment, and the loss of a sense of self that is different from its surroundings creates a union of the self with the environment. Csikszentmihalyi terms such experiences *optimal experiences*. Importantly for him, however, he points out that loss of self-consciousness does not involve a loss of self, and certainly not a loss *of* consciousness of the self. What slips below the threshold of awareness is the concept of self, the information we use to represent to ourselves who we are. And being able to forget temporarily who we are seems to be very enjoyable. When not preoccupied with our selves, we actually have a chance to expand the concept of who we are. Loss of self-consciousness can lead to self-transcendence, to a feeling that the boundaries of our being have been pushed forward.[31]

Csikszentmihalyi's view is that the energy for such experiences comes from the change in an individual's attention, which is why, of course, the experiences are intensely subjective and yet open up the individual to what Ursula King calls "a larger horizon".[32] Such trans-personal experience is usually accompanied by time seeming very different from normal time. What I want to point out here is that, irrespective of the Buddhist denial of a permanent self, there is good evidence to suggest similar experiences of a "kind of" *samadhi* in special moments of our lives. And for Csikszentmihalyi, the optimal experience is something we can cause to happen[33] perhaps through mastery of a task. He calls this *flow*, "the state in which people are so involved in an activity that nothing else seems to matter; the experience itself is so enjoyable that people will do it even at great cost, for the sheer sake of doing it".[34] Individuals lose themselves in such flow experiences so that the activity becomes naturally spontaneous, almost automatic. And we must remember that the Buddha never advised withdrawing from life but engaging in it. So perhaps Csikszentmihalyi's point is very relevant here to the early Buddhist experience. For him, the ordinary self is transcended, attention is one-pointed and there is a feeling of unity with the activity or the surroundings. It is an experience that can happen in any activity – surgery, music, mountaineering, dancing, swimming, rock climbing, playing chess, art, sex, horse riding; the list is endless. But the moment flow occurs the activity becomes effortless even though it is on-going. Unlike Buddhism, it is a subjective experience, but certainly a human one. This is surely mindfulness in a very full sense.

Meditation: The medical evidence

So how convincing is it that meditation can alleviate mental or physical suffering. There has been much recent neuroscience research into the effects of meditation. While meditation is so often associated with religious praxis, it need not be; indeed, it can be medically advised for decreasing high blood pressure, reducing stress, and the like. The aim of meditation is an enlightened state when the normal flow of conscious thought is interrupted and the senses no longer inform the mind. At its advanced level, dualities give way to unity and subject–object differentiation ceases to exist. The absorption of consciousness into the object of contemplation, the state of stilled consciousness, is also the highest state of *yoga*. Csikszentmihalyi clearly links the *yogic* ability to concentrate with flow experience and considers that "it is not unreasonable to regard Yoga as one of the oldest and most systematic methods of producing flow experience".[35] Daniel Goleman is in agreement, he writes: "A strained concentration – a focus fuelled by worry – produces increased cortical activation. But the zone of flow and optimal performance seems to be an oasis of cortical efficiency, with a bare minimum of mental energy expended."[36] The ancient Chinese belief system of Taoism has the same kind of natural focus of attention that enables one to act without assertion. *Wu-wei*, here, is the ability to act with minimum forced effort by going with the natural flow of things, with *Tao*, the natural Way; this is also *tzu-jan*, naturalness and spontaneity.[37] Such a thought is rather different to Csikszentmihalyi's idea of flow as optimum attentive focus.

The whole point of meditative praxis is to focus attention away from peripheral sense stimuli, and if Csikszentmihalyi is right, then such focus of attention will produce the flow, peak, transcendent or spiritual experience. The important point here is that in meditation it *can* be measured empirically. There have been a number of very interesting studies of changes in the brain during, and as a result of, meditation.[38] Buddhist mindfulness is one aspect of meditation that has been examined in such a way. Such mindfulness focuses on the activity of the moment. If I am peeling potatoes then I focus on that and nothing else at all. I focus on what happens from moment to moment as a means of counteracting attentional imbalances. There is now evidence from magnetic resonance imaging (MRI) and arterial spin-labelling MRI that stress reduction through such meditative practice correlates with structural changes in the amygdala – that part of the brain that has much to do with emotions.[39] Research found that as stress levels decreased, there was a decrease of grey matter density in the right amygdala. The amygdala, especially the right amygdala, relays sensory modalities to other subcortical brain structures and so it is the mediator that promotes stress-related messages to the brain that result in heightened blood pressure, stress-hormone release, and the like. The reduction of grey matter density in the amygdala has prompted researchers to state: "This finding is particularly interesting as it suggests that an active re-learning of emotional responses to stress (such as taught in MBSR [mindfulness-based stress reduction]) can lead to beneficial changes in neural structure and well-being even when there is presumably no change in the person's external environment."[40] A similar study by Sara Lazar, Catherine Kerr *et al.* has revealed increased cortical thickness as a result of meditation experience.[41] These last researchers examined mindfulness in the sense of insight meditation or focused attention to internal experiences. They found that: "Brain regions associated with attention, interoception [stimuli produced within the body, for example visceral] and sensory processing were thicker in meditation participants than matched controls, including the prefrontal cortex and right anterior insula."[42] In other words, meditation is likely to be associated with altering those parts of the brain that are involved with sensory, cognitive and emotional processing. Interesting in this research is the fact that prefrontal cortical thickness was pronounced in older meditators, indicative that meditation may slow down age-related cortical thinning.

In a related, but different, study, Zeidan, Martucci, Kraft *et al.*[43] found that mindfulness meditation reduces pain levels in the body. This research sought to understand how meditation influences sensory experience and concluded that "these data indicate that meditation engages multiple brain mechanisms that alter the construction of the subjectively available pain experience from afferent information." In other words, pain can be self-regulated through mindfulness meditation or focused attention, described by the researchers as "the cognitive practice of sustaining attention on the changing sensations of the breath, monitoring discursive events as they arise, disengaging from those events without affective reaction, and redirecting attention back to the breath."[44] The researchers emphasize that the participants engaged in what they understood to be a secular experiment and needed only four, separate, twenty-minute sessions of meditation over four days to reduce pain intensity. This point is important because it demonstrates that there is a change in brain cognition during meditation as, surely, there must also be in a spiritual or peak experience.[45] Mindfulness, then, encourages concentration on the moment itself, acting by being involved intrinsically with the action and not thinking of extrinsic goals. Another study involving integrative body-mind training (IBMT) has shown that: "Just 11 hours of learning a meditation technique induces positive structural changes in brain connectivity by boosting efficiency in a part of the brain that helps a person regulate behaviour in accordance with their goals."[46] Changes in connections involving the anterior cingulate of the brain, an area that is concerned with regulation of emotions and behaviour, occurred after only six hours of training in meditation. Transcendental meditation, too, is now proved to reduce the brain's response to pain. Here, focus on a mantra increases blood flow in the prefrontal cortex, the control centre, of the brain along with a wide number of other effects on the brain.[47]

Thus can we train the brain with meditation? I think we certainly can if the research into meditation is anything to go by. It seems that a variety of meditation techniques all have the ability to enhance those peak, or transcendent moments and, most importantly in the times of the Covid world, reduce stress and even reduce pain for those ill with the virus. As observation of the movements of the mind without reacting to them meditation is now a technique used in many religious and non-religious cultures. It can have clinical uses for serious or mild medical problems, for psychotherapy, or simply for the improvement of general stress levels and well-being.

The meditative processes of the seventh and eighth parts of the Eightfold Path are not divorced in any way from the other Noble Truths. Indeed, the other parts of the Eightfold Path have to inform meditation. The wisdom of the last two parts must also include good conduct that is directed from the level of wisdom; good conduct and wisdom gained in meditation are complementary not mutually exclusive. Similarly, right understanding and mindfulness and concentration are mutually supportive to each other. Right understanding also reveals the true nature of all *dhammas*, phenomena, as impermanent and ultimately unreal. The Four Noble Truths themselves are objects of meditation and concentration and, at times, even the three evils of desire, aversion and dullness. In today's world there are so many who bang their fists and shout about what is right to do, or give out information that is untested with great gusto as if it is proved and worthy of putting out to everyone. To be calm and measured when life is trying and going wrong in many directions is a difficult task, but the alternative is to heap stress on an already tired and beleaguered self. We probably cannot master the advanced stages of meditation but I included the work of Csikszentmihalyi to show that his "optimal experiences" are possible in a turbulent life if the right attitudes to it are maintained: alongside the earlier phases of meditative praxis, I am sure mindfulness can be an aid to the disturbing times in which we live. I rather like these words of Piyadassi, who wrote: "The man who cultivates calmness of mind rarely gets upset when confronted with the vicissitudes of life. He tries to see things in their proper perspective, how things come into being and pass away. Free from anxiety and restlessness, he will try to see the fragility of the fragile." And he adds words by Robert Louis

Stevenson: "Quiet minds . . . go on, in fortune or misfortune, at their own private pace, like a clock during a thunderstorm."[48]

Insight meditation, *vipassana*

It may seem as if touching *nibbana* with one's body and the higher levels of full concentration in *samadhi* is the end goal; but there is more. The inner experience of *vipassana*, "insight meditation" is a level after the fourth *jhana* at which things are known *as they are*. The mind is expanded to watch everything that occurs so there is no focal point for meditation but a deeper mindfulness of the whole of existence and all phenomena. Sumedho explains it thus: "You no longer concentrate on just one point, but you observe insightfully and reflect on the conditions that come and go, and on the silence of the empty mind. To do this involves letting go of an object; you're not holding on to any particular object, but observing that whatever arises passes away."[49] This is not to say that other thoughts are obliterated from the mind for they do emerge even at this advanced level of mindfulness. But such thoughts – emotions, fears or whatever they may be – will come into the mind probably from the subconscious level and need to be brought into conscious light, into awareness, and objectively examined before they can be passed away and let go of. Importantly, this is not turning from such thoughts with aversion; on the contrary, it is facing them with full awareness, recognizing them for what they are and then letting them go: the aim is detachment, not aversion.

Samadhi in the wider context of Indian religion was, and is, believed to be the ultimate level of meditational experience, but the Buddha inaugurated this addition of *vipassana* to complement and build on the calming meditation that is the preliminary to it. It was a remarkable addition and expansion into the ability for a complete understanding of reality. Just as the lower levels of mindfulness of body, feelings, mind mood, and mind objects is an important stage of meditation, here, with *vipassana*, these are used to analyse every aspect of the self but with bare attention without any reaction to them. The breathing, sense feelings, the mood of the mind with its emotions and the objects thrown into the mind by sense stimuli are noted and left behind. The aim here is to be able to see everything about the so-called self as unstable and impermanent and, as such, unsatisfactory. As an example here, in relation to breathing, Sumedho writes: "The impermanent nature of the breath is not yours, is it? Having been born, the body breathes all on its own. In and out breaths – the one conditions the other. As long as the body is alive, that is the way it will be. You don't control anything, breathing belongs to nature, it doesn't belong to you, it is not-self. When you observe this, you are doing vipassana, insight. It's not something exciting or fascinating or unpleasant. It's natural."[50] The point here is that the mind acquires the wisdom to understand fully the nature of the Four Noble Truths – suffering, its cause, its cessation, and the means to its cessation.

Insight meditation necessitates good conduct in the sense of the right action and livelihood of the Eightfold Path as a preliminary. And skill in calming the mind and consciousness is not separated from *vipassana* but is an essential facet of it. Mindfulness of the conditioned world is still necessary when *vipassana* begins. Focusing on right view, right understanding, gradually gets rid of the sense of a permanent self. Here, meditation on the Five Aggregates as well as the ways in which the senses operate to stimulate the mind's reactions help to break down the concept of a self-substance. Gethin explains this aim: "The purpose here is to impress upon the mind that, when we look at any particular experience, what we find is not a substantial person or being but just mind and body in dependence upon one another. Like two sheaves of grass propped up against each other, if we remove one the other falls."[51] So here, the interdependence of mind and body is understood as the source of all experience, leading to denial of any substantial self. Thus far, the meditator reflects on the insubstantiality of his or her own self but the next stage is to broaden that knowledge to the wider context of all things past, present and future until there is understanding that all things, events, experiences, are subject to the Dependent Origination that we saw in Chapter 5. Further, an understanding that the whole Universe is subject to this law comes as a sudden light in the darkness, a cathartic moment of sheer wisdom and deep inner knowledge, "a matter of direct experience that cannot be denied" as Gethin puts it.[52] Any doubts about the veracity of the *Dhamma* vanish.

In reaching the higher levels of wisdom meditation, and having understood the nature of everything past, present and future as dependently arising, there follows insight into the way in which the Universe is composed of patterns and categories of impermanent phenomena that rise and fall moment to moment. Gethin cites Buddhaghosa's similes here – "like dew drops at sunrise, like a bubble on water, like a line drawn on water, like a mustard-seed placed on the point of an awl, like a flash of lightning; things in themselves lack substance and always elude one's grasp – like a mirage, a conjuring trick, a dream, the circle formed by a whirling firebrand, a fairy city, foam, or the trunk of a banana tree."[53] Such a cathartic experience is not to be grasped at, held in the mind and enjoyed, otherwise desire becomes inimical to anything further: even the good experiences have to be abandoned. But if these can be brushed aside and a more relaxed awareness of the rising and passing away of all things achieved, other discerning knowledge comes to the fore leading to a thorough knowledge of the three characteristics of existence – impermanence, suffering, and no-self. The Four Noble Truths as a whole are understood simultaneously, fully comprehended as the truth of suffering in all existence; the truth of its cause in desire; the cessation of suffering; and the realization of *nibbana*. In a flash of complete understanding and perfect balance of being, there is here a full understanding and penetrative wisdom of the interconnected whole of the *Dhamma*, of Reality, and the Four Noble Truths about that Reality. At the end of the Path, insight, *panna*, wisdom, intuitive knowledge, obliterates all the subconscious, latent tendencies of the so-called self through the intense *vipassana* meditation; nothing of a self remains and the knowledge that is acquired is a deep intuitional "knowing" of Reality.

The outcome of deeper insight through *vipassana* meditation is the ability to be aware of happiness and pain as impermanent: both are insubstantial. Nothing is permanent so neither happiness nor pain can last. As I said above, in Buddhist practice, calming and insight meditations are complementary, the former bringing the mind to a quiet state and the latter bringing wisdom and knowledge into that calm, though the union of the two may have been a later development. Fear of coronavirus is very much out there in the world, in families, communities, societies and nations. If there is anything to be learned from Buddhist meditation, it is that the fear should be allowed to surface even though the mind will want to have an aversion for it and push it deeper. But to do this is to repress it and keep it there, partially locked away. *Meditating* on it, listening to it, observing it, is the way the Buddha would have suggested dealing with it. Fear is a condition of the mind, and an impermanent one at that: it is not a permanent aspect of a permanent self. We need such fears to be expressed at the conscious level in order to deal with them, so ridding the mind of its aversion. Negative thoughts seem to be there before we've ever had time to think about how or why they arose, so once brought into the conscious level they can be analysed in order to see how they began, how they developed and how they ended. Sumedho says of *vipassana*: "This wisdom practice is a very gentle one of even allowing the most horrible thoughts to appear, and let them go. You have an escape hatch, it's like a safety valve where you can let off the steam when there's too much pressure".[54]

Wisdom according to the Buddha is concerned with true Reality, the meaning of life and the conduct of life. No amount of intellectual knowledge and factual learning can have an outcome in true wisdom with its ability to see things clearly and truthfully. And that is a truth that is embodied in the Buddha's *Dhamma*. Wisdom is a quiet strength of mind that comes about first through a certain amount of learning – about the Buddha, the Four Noble Truths and what they tell us about suffering, its cause, cessation and the means for its cessation – then comes discursive reflection in thoughts and meditation about what has been learned and, finally, meditational development itself. The Noble Eightfold Path with its moral discipline, mindfulness and wisdom is the means to assist mature development so that, as Bhikhu Bodhi wrote, "the eye of wisdom opens by itself, penetrating the truths, freeing the mind from bondage".[55]

The Buddha's *Dhamma* is a gentle pathway to freedom. There are no negative prohibitions and laws – you should not do this or that. The *Dhamma* is more an affirmation of what is good and is a positive view of what each being can achieve. The Buddha never suggested that his teachings were only for the spiritually privileged or the monastic environment, but meant them for ordinary folk as a means to overcome the widespread sufferings that he witnessed and understood. As Piyadassi said of meditation: "Meditation should be applied to the daily affairs of life, and the results are obtained here and now. It is not something separated from the work-a-day life. It is part and parcel of our lives. If we ignore it life lacks meaning, purpose and inspiration."[56] And Sumedho wrote of the results of meditation on the mind: "When you are patient, allowing things to cease, then you begin to know cessation – silence, emptiness, clarity – the mind clears, stillness. The mind is still vibrant, it's not oblivious, repressed or asleep, and you can hear the silence of the mind."[57] There is nothing religious in the Buddha's message, though there is a lot that is fundamentally spiritual. His Path leads to ultimate Reality, freedom and happiness. "Following this Path you shall make an end to suffering", the Buddha said in the *Dhammapada*.[58] His parable of the raft that crosses from one shore to the other is meant to convey that his *Dhamma* will make people safe, tranquil, peaceful and happy. For some who undertake to try the Path of the Buddha the journey to the near or other shore will be a slow one. There is an adage that says some individuals will run; some will walk; some will creep along very slowly; but all those who keep going will reach the goal at the end.

8

The *Brahma-vihara*

Love, Compassion, Sympathetic Joy, Equanimity

The culmination of all that we have seen of the Buddha's *Dhamma* is a mind reaching out to all humanity because it is filled with four sublime states called the *Brahma-vihara*. These are:

- *Metta*: love, loving-kindness
- *Karuna*: compassion
- *Mudita*: sympathetic joy
- *Upekkha*: equanimity

Brahma is a divine being that featured widely in Hindu ancient texts. In Buddhism, Brahma is said to be present in the sublime worlds to which those near to enlightenment can exist after their death. But in the sense we have it here, "Brahma" means "divine-like", "sublime", "like the god Brahma". *Vihara* means "abodes", "dwelling places". Put together, *Brahma-vihara* in referring to the mind means states in which the mind rests and is at home. The four are also called *boundless* states of mind because they radiate outward to all beings, are totally inclusive, impartial, non-selective and non-prejudiced. In short, these states of mind are developed in order to reach out wider and wider until they encompass all humanity and all creatures. Their generation comes from concentrated meditation.

Since the *Brahma-vihara* are *jhanas*, meditative states, when fully realized they are accompanied by the wisdom that knows the true state of all phenomena as insubstantial and impermanent. At their fullest extent, the *Brahma-vihara* are accompanied in the mind by total renunciation of desire and craving – the means to freedom from suffering. Such a state of mind comes about by reducing attachment to whatever is desired: the stronger the attachment, the greater the suffering, and the less the attachment, the less the suffering. Thus, a thorough understanding and insight into the Four Noble Truths is what informs the *Brahma-vihara*. Insight through meditation is the complement of the four states with deep absorption of mind.

While what has been said thus far might suggest that the *Brahma-vihara* are rarefied states of mind far removed from any purpose in ordinary life, we should perhaps look at their opposite to see how relevant they could be. Consider the words here of Francis Story when he said, "I believe it to be axiomatic that if all the wealth in the world were to be equally distributed one morning, there would be the rich and poor again by evening".[1] And as Story also pointed out: "The world-stuff is neither good nor bad; it is man's thinking which makes heaven or hell out of it."[2] The *Brahma-vihara* epitomize the very best of thinking in the human mind. They are the complete opposites of the three evils/poisons. The opposite of greed/desire, the first of the evils is its renunciation, detachment rather than attachment, sharing, and generosity of giving and not taking. The second of the evils, hatred/aversion, is overcome by love and loving-kindness, gentleness, friendliness, forgiveness, forbearance, and by the third of the *Brahma-vihara*, sympathetic joy; while equanimity has the wisdom to overcome delusion. But this is not a question of only trying to alter outward actions. No, changes have to come from within if they are to be meaningful and lasting, which is why the *Brahma-vihara* are meditative actions that get through to the way in which the mind thinks. Thus, concentration on each will bring out the gradual wearing away of the unwholesome evils. The mind has difficulty in concentrating on two opposing factors at the same time so if there is a good deal of wholesome thought in it then the unwholesome aspects have less chance of coming to the fore.

All beings seek happiness and the *Brahma-vihara* seek to engender in the mind the wish for happiness for all beings and a wish that they will be well and at peace. This is how we should understand these four mental states. Beginning with the self, the states are then radiated out to others, like ripples of pebbles thrown into a pond, until the outer boundaries of humanity are reached. So while the four states are qualities developed through meditation, qualities developed in order to reach the higher levels of *jhana*, meditation practice will need to be persistent in order to achieve them and to build gradually their boundless nature and extend them to all creatures. But for the ordinary mortal with little will for serious meditation the *Brahma-vihara* are, at the very least, positive subjects for the mind to contemplate, and positive attitudes to adopt in speech and action as well as thought. Life can be difficult, irritating, tense, stressful and problematic. From what was seen in the last chapter on the changes to brain functioning and the benefits of meditation on the mind, any one of the *Brahma-vihara* would be a positive thought to bring in gently to meditative praxis.

Metta: Love, loving-kindness

The first of the *Brahma-vihara* is *metta*, "love". I prefer the translation often given as "loving-kindness" because it lends a different nuance of thought to *metta*. Loving-kindness is different from love in the sense of desire, attraction, personal love, family love, parental love, the love that is wanted, needed, for in the *Brahma-vihara* it is used in the best possible sense of love given selflessly and altruistically. Loving-kindness as *metta* has nothing to do with a self and is not centred on particularities but is natural and is radiated outward to others and, ultimately to all humanity. Bhikkhu Bodhi wrote: "Love, it is said, can only be genuine when it is spontaneous, arisen without inner promptings or effort."[3] So this is love that is not just good will or the kind of love that is written into religious laws that is offered as a sense of duty. As Bhikkhu Bodhi said: "It must become a deep inner feeling, characterized by spontaneuous warmth rather than by a sense of obligation."[4] *Metta* incorporates all the very best kinds of selfless human friendliness, goodwill and benevolence – love that does not incorporate clinging or attachment.

While *metta* in early Buddhism and in Theravada Buddhism past and present is an important aspect of meditation, in the unprecedented times in which we live loving-kindness of the purest kind has been exemplified again and again in Covid wards in multiple hospitals around the world. Footage from hospitals in the UK has shown the remarkable level of care given by front-line staff in hospitals. For those so critically ill, and for those who succumbed to the virus and died, there could be no family support, no warmth from loved ones, but the hospital staff supplied it in abundance, compensating for the family members who could not be there. It was very moving to see hospital staff holding the hands of terrified and immensely sick patients. There was not an ounce of selfishness here only loving-kindness in abundance – and that without any thought of Buddhism or meditative practice to encourage it. Patients who began as strangers were freely offered so much boundless loving-kindness that transcended gender, race, economic status and privilege. The coronavirus levelled, and continues to level, any barriers and let us hope that the outstanding care given to its victims will never be forgotten.

For fifteen months from December 2019 to the end of February 2020, I saw first-hand the extent of loving-kindness in the care home in which my mother spent the end of her days. From the first moment we stepped into the care home we were welcomed as "family" as was my mother. The care was outstanding but it was that something extra that was remarkable and that epitomized loving-kindness. I am sure it is a facet of many nursing and care homes throughout this country and in others abroad, but we were able to see it ourselves not on the odd occasion but on every occasion. That was love given selflessly, spontaneously, generously to every resident because it came naturally from the mixed staff that were there – Romanian, Fijian, Philippine, Polish, English, Welsh. I am sure that such a level of spontaneous caring love existed in so many places but I feel fortunate to have witnessed such beauty of heart in a group of dedicated carers.

But to return to the *metta* of Buddhism, first and foremost it is important to show loving-kindness to oneself and not to be hard on oneself. We all probably have faults that we would like to get rid of but which seem to persist never mind how much we try to change. That is where Buddhist meditation can help by developing the patience to deal with faulty conditions in one's nature. Thinking more kindly of the self should aid in lessening and then ceasing the fault or faults by not reacting to them, letting them go. Much meditation is of this nature: things come into the mind both pleasant and unpleasant, but they just need observing, looking at them for what they are, and then brushing aside. Without a measure of loving-kindness for oneself there can hardly be any opportunity to extend it to others. By starting with oneself, too, it seems so obvious that the basic need of all people is to be safe, well and happy. *Metta* shares in that wish by recognizing it in the self and then projecting it outwards to understand others, wishing all to be well and happy. This in fact is a meditative process of loving-kindness directed to one-self and then radiated out first to close associates or family members, then wider to friends and acquaintances; wider still to neutral individuals; wider again to those to whom there is ordinarily hostility. Once this is mastered the radiating of loving-kindness reaches wider – perhaps north, east, south and west, or family, neighbourhood, village or town, country, nation – until one encompasses thoughts of peace for the whole world. This may seem somewhat mechanical and deliberate but practice aids the mind-shift needed to make loving-kindness a natural habit. It is a slow, gradual process of changing the way one thinks. So loving-kindness is love without the "I" of the self, that is not exclusive and selective, and that embraces all whatever their nature. This is selfless love that does not see one's own life as any more important than that of others. The

Buddhist Publication Society described it thus: "The practice of metta-bhavana is the finest expression of the fusing of self-love and love for others in Buddhism."[5]

So how does this work in practice? We probably all know an angry person, and when we take a careful look at that anger when it is being manifest it is easy to see the depth of it from the facial expressions, the ugliness of the face, and how the anger prevents discrimination between right and wrong and disables any ability to listen to reason. So if anger is directed towards an individual, it is important to remember that angry person does not own that other mind to which the anger is directed; by not reacting to the anger it is possible to stop the otherwise inevitable outcome of ending up in the same state of anger. In adapting a fellow Buddhist's text, Hammalawa Saddhatissa offers the following:

> Suppose another, to annoy,
> Provokes you with some odious act,
> Why suffer anger to spring up,
> And do as he would have you do?
>
> If you get angry, then may be
> You make *him* suffer, may be not;
> Though with the hurt that anger brings
> *You* certainly are punished now.
>
> If anger-blinded enemies
> Set out to tread the path of woe,
> Do you, by getting angry too,
> Intend to follow heel to toe?[6]

And I rather like Saddhatissa's remark "By becoming angry one is like a man throwing dust against the wind – he only soils himself."[7] Difficult as it is to be kind, pleasant and not vindictive to the angry individual with whom one is faced it is true to say that in most cases the effect of the anger is difficult to erase, and ease of mind difficult to retrace: meditation on loving-kindness is one answer. Without calming the mind in response to anger the tendency is to heap more on it to fire the furious response. I think it is "Festinger's Cognitive-Dissonance Theory" that comes into operation in the mind if we are hurt by someone, or even if we hear something bad about someone. The mind almost automatically throws up negative "others" that the hurtful individual said, or that other individuals have said against the hurtful person, so festering and supporting one's own integrity and personality against the hurtful one. It is probably not pragmatic to think that it is possible to behave calmly in the face of someone who is in an irate mode, so Ajahn Sumedho advises actually having *metta* for one's own aversion and small-mindedness – again, having loving-kindness for oneself.[8] Remembering the right speech aspect of the Eightfold Path, harsh words cannot win the kindness, trust and affection of others and only serve to sully the mind with the same poison of aversion and hatred. We are all travellers through life with its vicissitudes, its sufferings and setbacks: embracing others as fellow travellers with the same needs for happiness and well-being is what *metta* is all about.

Most if not all human beings are capable of displaying loving-kindness at some time or other, but Buddhist *metta* is a quality that becomes so ingrained in the mind that it is constant and spontaneous, which is why meditation for *metta* is so important, indeed, perhaps *the* most important meditation. And that meditation can be, as I said above, being kind to oneself by being mindful of the fears, the anger, the things not liked about one's character, observing them and letting them go. Again, loving-kindness to others cannot happen without kindness to the self. If the mind concentrates on the harmful things someone has done, one's own mind will retain harmful thoughts and will get nowhere in developing loving-kindness. But recognizing one's own harmful thoughts within meditation practice and letting them go will pave the way for a gentler, loving mind. It is worth repeating once again here the beautiful words from the *Metta Sutta*:

> Whatever living beings there be –
> Feeble or strong, tall stout or medium,
> Short, small or large, without exception –
> Seen or unseen,
> Those dwelling far or near,
> Those who are born or who are to be born,
> May all beings be happy.[9]

So *metta* is not a question of morality acquired from laws and religious or social directives, it is an *inner* state of being. The Buddha actually criticized the clinging to precepts and vows that is inimical to the kind of morality that comes from the heart. And note the word "clinging" that suggests learning loving-kindness through external pressures is the wrong means.

Aside from Buddhist meditation on *metta*, in our ordinary lives a kind word can go far in making someone else feel good, feel better, encourage a smile on someone's face. Even a passing compliment to a total stranger can achieve that. We are living in such threatening times when there is a tendency to criticize, to blame, to find some scapegoat for the ways in which the coronavirus has taken hold of our lives, preventing normal behaviour, creating stressful fears about catching it, about losing one's job, about being separated from those we love. Are we so well-informed that we know what the answers should be, what should or should not be done? Do such thoughts inculcate anger and aggression? They probably do and are better brushed to one side. So in terms of fear of the virus and *metta*, having *metta for the fear* means accepting it as there within but accepting it without reaction and then letting it go away. As Sumedho writes: "You can also minimise the fear by recognising that it is the same kind of fear that everyone has, that animals have. It's not my fear, it's not a person's, it's an impersonal fear. We begin to have compassion for other beings when we understand suffering involved in reacting to fear in our own lives," and he adds: "We can work with metta internally, with all our emotional problems."[10]

An important aspect of loving-kindness is respect for others and nowhere is this more obvious in this pandemic than respecting others sufficiently to keep them safe by wearing a mask and keeping socially distant. Those who refuse to do this are really conveying a lack of respect for the well-being of others. Then, too, another aspect of loving-kindness that is critically essential is that towards the planet. There are a few good people out there in the world who battle for change, dedicating their life works to protecting the planet. Sir David Attenborough and Bill Gates are two examples here, along with the likes of the Irish rock star, Bono, and David Beasley, Director of the United Nations World Food Programme. And there are some good companies that operate without greed, investing in programmes to supply screening, personal protective equipment for frontline workers, distributing medicines, and so on. But poverty impedes care and takes lives when viruses emerge and the whole issue of social deprivation is a serious threat to the respect due to every human being despite country or status. At the very least, the pandemic has encouraged kindness, neighbourly interaction and help where needed, but as we gain momentum into the so-called second wave now in the autumn and winter of 2020, many people have become impatient, find a second lockdown where it has occurred a real challenge, and are beginning to lose respect for others by not bothering to abide by safety regulations. The pandemic also gave nature time to breathe: and let us hope that the glimpses of a different life with birdsong in quiet cities, and creatures emboldened to enter the spaces usually taken up by the roar of normal life and traffic, will make people think about respect and kindness to nature. Nature is essential for our well-being, we just need to learn to love it in order for it to give back its many gifts to us.

Before going on to the second of the *Brahma-vihara*, I want to include two really beautiful quotations. The first is from Nyanapoika Maha Thera's words based on the *Metta Sutta* that surely resonate with the widespread suffering of those in Covid wards and the "soft firm hand" of medical staff that offered immense loving-kindness to so many:

> *Love* that lies like a soft but firm hand on the ailing beings, ever unchanged in its sympathy, without wavering, unconcerned with any response it meets. *Love* that is comforting coolness to those who burn with the fire of suffering and passion; that is life-spending warmth to those abandoned in the cold desert of loneliness; to those who are shivering in the frost of a loveless world; to those whose hearts have become as if empty and dry by the repeated calls for help, by deepest despair.[11]

And, finally, the words of Thera Piyadassi from a more Buddhist view of loving-kindness:

> If one has developed a love that is truly great, rid of the desire to hold and to possess, that strong clean love which is untarnished with lust of any kind, that love which does not expect material advantage and profit from the act of loving, that love which is firm but not grasping, unshakeable but not tied down, gentle and settled, hard and penetrating as a diamond but unhurting, helpful but not interfering, cool, invigorating, giving more than taking, not proud but dignified, not sloppy yet soft, the love that leads one to the heights of clean achievement, then, in such a one can there be no ill-will at all.[12]

Karuna: Compassion

The second of the *Brahma-vihara* is *karuna*, "compassion" and we would normally expect compassion to be evident in the face of witnessing someone or some creature that is suffering. Indeed, when suffering ourselves we look for, and need, the compassion of others to alleviate the pain, whether physical or mental. But consider these words of Nyanaponika:

> The world suffers. But most men have their eyes and ears closed. They do not see the unbroken stream of tears flowing through life, they do

not hear the cry of distress continually pervading the world. Their own little grief or joy bars their sight, deafens their ears. Bound by selfishness their hearts turn stiff and narrow. Being stiff and narrow, how should they be able to strive for any higher goal, to realize that only release from selfish craving will effect their own freedom from suffering?[13]

Buddhism has the foundational tenet that all life is suffering; and, as was seen in earlier chapters, not understanding the impermanence of all things, and the absence of any permanent self, are the contributory factors to suffering. In the normal course of life, suffering is nearly always subjective, something that happens to *me*, and for compassion to be realized, some sympathy, or even empathy, with the suffering of others has to be present. Once again as in the case of loving-kindness, we have witnessed incredible compassion so readily shown by medical staff to the sufferers of Covid-19 in hospitals around the world. But there has been compassion, too, for those isolated, those who are unable to leave their homes and who have relied on the compassion of others to supply them with the essentials they need. It is easy to see here how *metta* and *karuna* readily combine. Compassion is, to use Piyadassi's definition: "The quality which makes the heart of the good man tremble and quiver at the distress of others" and: "The quality that rouses tender feelings in the good man at the sight of others' suffering."[14] Compassion as, indeed, loving-kindness, transcends human boundaries of race, religion, nationality, gender, whenever and wherever it finds expression.

The Buddha instilled in his followers the idea of "as I am, so are others", so that compassion could be radiated out from an individual who knew others as he and she knew themselves. But remember, too, the Buddha's ideas of *volition*, the intention behind an action, which suggests that compassion that comes spontaneously and from the heart is so much better than that which is done for an ulterior motive, for praise, for promotion, or for any reason other than pure expression. Once again, I can share with the reader the incredible manifestation of selfless compassion I witnessed in the care of my mother in a truly wonderful care home. Despite my mother's deteriorating condition, dying of old age with an emaciated, corpse-like body that was immensely distressing to see, her carers had so much compassion that came from the heart – from Mariana, who never failed to put her arms around Mum and kiss her skull-like face, and she and I cried many times; Gill whose love was always evident and who tried to make Mum laugh and was so compassionate her arms were always around me, too, soothing my mental pain; Anna, who gave Mum head massages to take away her stress, and who read stories and poems to her; Bethan, who spent time bathing Mum's closed eyes so that occasionally she would open them; Maria, whose sunny smile would light up the stars; Saloti, an incredible individual who brought sunshine to my mother and to us whenever she entered the room; warm and tender-hearted Lisa, who sat quietly for a while by Mum's side after she had died; and Wendy who put beautiful designs on the wall for Mum to see when she was "turned" in her bed towards an empty wall, and who talked to Mum of the garden she had designed outside and of so many things. I saw exactly the same level of compassion, love and kindness to all the residents in that care home. I am writing of these women because they are my examples of true, honest compassion that is surely replicated by all those incredible medical staff that put their own lives on hold and at risk with compassionate care for those who are so very sick. Many of the staff who work in care homes are immigrants, and I hope that when this crisis is gone for good, everyone will remember these immigrants who showed such compassion, and who dedicated themselves to the care of others. These are men and women who work without any desire for reward or recognition but purely out of compassion and dedication to their work: I hope we are all very proud of them.

True compassion is a kind of giving; giving without thinking how good one is in doing it: true compassion is natural. Piyadassi puts this well: "Compassion is not limited merely to the giving of food and such material things to the poor and needy, or to giving a copper to a beggar. All actions done with a pure motive, free from greed, false views and pride, are reckoned as genuine acts of kindness."[15] The Sikh religion has a tradition of *langar* at its places of worship, *gurdwaras*. After worship, they share food together, a custom of giving free food to all, rich and poor and whatever class or caste. And this is not just a biscuit or two but a full cooked meal with *chapattis*, so that no one could possibly leave hungry. There are a number of *gurdwaras* that have continued *langar* during lockdown, cooking their usual meals and taking them out to the needy, to front-line workers and to non-Sikhs as an expression of true generosity and care for their local communities in lockdown. And this is just one example of the generous compassion that has been seen in communities everywhere. Piyadassi adds other examples of true compassion: "Imparting knowledge to the illiterate, guiding the muddle-headed and the uninstructed along the right path, giving strength and moral support to the weak and fearful, ministering to the sick, etc., are all humane actions."[16]

Selfless action through compassion can take many forms and has been manifest widely in communities during the pandemic. From the purely Buddhist perspective, the compassionate individual wants any suffering of another to cease, abstains from any kind of hatred, and has a gentle but profound sympathy for others that is devoid of any sense of "I". Compassion is the opposite of cruelty, aggression, and violence and is evident, as Bhikkhu Bodhi said, "by entering into the subjectivity of others, by sharing their interiority in a deep and total way". It arises he said, "by considering that all beings, like ourselves, wish to be free from suffering, yet despite their wishes continue to be harassed by pain, fear, sorrow, and other forms of dukkha".[17] For Buddhists, the means to developing compassion is meditational practice, first, as in the case of loving-kindness, for oneself, then radiating out the compassion experienced to other beings. Remembering the Four Noble Truths is helpful here by applying them to those suffering old age, sickness, death, and the general unsatisfactoriness of life.

When death occurs it is natural to grieve and that grief is almost always centred on the self. This is not compassion for the self but sorrow for the self. We generally do not extend the same kind of feeling of grief for the death of those we did not know well. These more distant individuals do not belong to *us*, so *we* have not really lost anyone and our lives can proceed without too much upset, if any. Given the nature of the coronavirus that defies full scientific understanding as yet, and no cure other than one's own immune system – some stronger than others – I have some sympathy here with the sombre words of Piyadassi: "Our life is so dark with ageing, so smothered with death, so bound with change, and these qualities are so inherent in it – even as greenness in grass, and bitterness to quinine – that not all the magic and witchery of science can ever transform it. The immortal splendour of an eternal sunlight awaits only those who can use the light of understanding and the culture of conduct to illuminate and guard their path through life's tunnel of darkness and dismay."[18] Piyadassi's words offer light at the end of the tunnel of life but are relevant in our difficult contemporary lives where the aged are particularly vulnerable to Covid, and death from it so rife around the world. Compassion has become rather localized in nations and we seem to have long forgotten any compassion for war-torn countries, the plight and suffering of refugees and the massive displacements of peoples. It seems we can only parcel out tiny amounts of compassion unless we have a direct hit with illness and death of those close to us. Even with global infection and death rates, there is little evidence of the kind of internationalism that would encompass collective understanding and change to work for the greater good of all humanity and, crucially, for the planet. But nationalism is a greedy mind-set and already the race for a vaccine for Covid is mainly a selfish and greedy one. The USA, Russia, and possibly China here are certainly portraying what we can only term vaccine nationalism. The USA has tried to buy *all* of the pending German vaccine. But regardless of such a statement, it has been a great joy to witness the many, many, truly compassionate acts of generosity and kindness that we have seen in communities around the world in the face of the pandemic.

Metta, loving-kindness, and *karuna*, compassion, are the qualities of the very best of individuals for they get rid of selfishness and disharmony and promote peace and well-being. As all the *Brahma-vihara* they are boundless, meaning they are not limited to particular groups of people, not bound by nationality, race, gender and the like. The aspects of life that normally divide and differentiate people disappear here and even the lives of the creatures and animals that inhabit our planet are encompassed by the boundless nature of these first two of the *Brahma-vihara*.

Mudita: Sympathetic joy

The third of the *Brahma-vihara* is *mudita*, which is "sympathetic joy" in a really empathetic way. It is sheer delight and joy in the happiness of others. We have seen much footage of such moments of utter joy as the result of so many kindnesses at this difficult time especially when there are tears of profound joy by a recipient of kindness. Perhaps the most profound of times when this is evident is when a life is saved in a hospital and one individual has returned from the brink of death on a ventilator to survive and emerge free of the virus to a watching world. Scenes of medical staff lining the corridors and applauding the survivor epitomize the complete sympathetic joy they have that a life has been saved. And for the waiting relatives whose lives have been changed from fear and immense dread their joy is overwhelming. Not so many make it back into life after being placed on ventilators, their lives suspended in temporary comas until they finally pass away. Nyanaponika's words here are so apt for the current climate and the hidden virus lingering among us: "Small, indeed, is the share of happiness and joy allotted to beings! Whenever that little of happiness comes to beings, then you may rejoice with them that, at least, one ray of joy has pierced through the darkness of their life, and dispelled the gray and gloomy mist that enwraps their heart."[19]

Sympathetic joy is also sympathetic *understanding*. The adage that one should "walk a mile in a person's shoes before you judge him or her" is an appropriate one for getting rid of the prejudices and criticisms we may have of others. Understanding others without discrimination can open the heart to their sorrows, but also to their joys. Those who see Buddhism as pessimistic and joyless should gaze on the Buddha's face in the abundant iconographic portrayals of him. There is no fierce look, but gentleness, peacefulness, tranquillity, and a faint smile. He may have taught that all life is suffering but his image is suffused with the joy of an answer to it. In words again from Nyanaponika:

> Your life will gain in joy by sharing the happiness of others as if it were yours. Did you never observe how in moments of happiness men's features change and become bright with joy? Did you never notice how joy rouses men to noble aspirations and deeds, exceeding their normal capacity? Did not such experience fill your own heart with bliss? It is in your power to increase such experience of *Sympathetic Joy*, by producing happiness in others, by bringing them joy and solace.[20]

I am sure the many lives saved by medical staff in intensive care wards have encouraged them even more in their "noble aspirations and deeds".

Upekkha: Equanimity

The fourth of the *Brahma-vihara* is *upekkha*, "equanimity", which is the epitome of the true Buddhist mind in perfect balance. Here, there is a full understanding of the wisdom of Buddhism, with a foundation of insight into the heart of the Buddha's *Dhamma*. Our lives are full of dualities, not just because we understand light in contrast to darkness, heat in contrast to cold and so on, but also because we have so many dualities of emotions, of success and failure, happiness and sadness, satisfaction and disappointment, hope and despondency. Nyanaponika wrote on such dualities: "These waves of emotion carry us up, and fling us down; and no sooner do we find some rest, than we are in the power of a new wave again. How can we expect to get a footing on the crest of the waves? How shall we erect the building of our life in the midst of this ever restless ocean of existence, if not on the Island of Equanimity."[21] For Buddhism, that which is inimical to equanimity is the self. All those dualities of which Nyanaponika wrote belong to the many arenas of life experiences, and we react to every one of them that comes our way. So many times in earlier chapters we have met the dangers of reactions in the mind to the stimuli that enter it, and so many times we have been given the answer that *not* to react will stem the tide of suffering. Even in times of joy the reaction should not be there, otherwise it is self-enjoyment and not sympathetic, selfless joy. We take ownership of failure or success, happiness or sorrow but equanimity brings the half-way balance of neither this nor that. This is not indifference but just a change in mind to bring it to a state of balance, a *mindful* equanimity. Consider the three evils, greed/desire, hatred/aversion and delusion/stupidity; most of what comes into the mind elicits a response that is positive, negative or neutral to some stimulus from these categories. We can be carried away by them or ignore them. But Buddhism advises bare attention to such stimuli, objectifying them not reacting to them, not pushing them down into the subconscious and repressing them but examining them for what they are and brushing them gently aside. And that obtains as much with positive stimuli as negative ones. To do this puts one's mind in equanimity.

In a state of equanimity the mind does not have to fear dualities since it is realized that all that happens in the mind is an outcome of our own thoughts and actions. Staring into the mind we can only be faced with what we have made ourselves into: there is nothing permanent there and what is there is capable of being changed since everything, including the mind, is impermanent. And suffering is no different here: to treat it with equanimity and calm is to lessen it: difficult as that may be with raging toothache, the more mental states of suffering are far better dealt with through equanimity rather than reaction. Even the toothache will seem less when the body is calmed and not tensed and fearful.

We are such creatures of habit, reacting habitually to stimuli and habitually building up our personalities. Put a thought in the mind and an action will so often follow; the action if repeated will result in a habit; deepen the habit and the result is a personality. The Buddha did not have a successor, but he had his teaching, his *Dhamma*, for eternity. Piyadassa wrote here: "The *Dhamma* is not an invention, but a discovery. It is an eternal law; it is everywhere with each man and woman, Buddhist or not Buddhist, Eastern or Western. The *Dhamma* has no labels, it knows no limit of time, space or race. It is for all time."[22] The Buddha's *Dhamma* is not just teaching but also a journey with levels of truth to be plummeted on the way. Nothing here is left behind but, just like pieces of a jigsaw, everything ultimately fits together to make a perfect whole, an ultimate Truth. Those who fully embody the Path and the *Dhamma* become enlightened beings in full perfection and are fully delivered from suffering. This will probably never be the case for so many of us but to try, to practise, to absorb the goodness of the *Dhamma* as much as possible is to take a step in the right direction and to move towards happiness. Equanimity means that there is no worrying or repenting about the past and no fearfulness and brooding over the future. The message is to let go of desires, aversions, let go of fears and root out habits and conditioned behaviour through mindfulness. We may never be able to let go of the idea of self even if we recognize its impermanence, and we may have to remain in part the conditioned beings that we have made for ourselves: we would probably need many lifetimes – if such there be – to reach the ultimate goal of *nibbana*. But that there is an "unconditioned" the Buddha was certain:

> For the conditioned, motion exists; but for the unconditioned there is no motion. Where no motion is, there is stillness. Where stillness is, there is no craving. Where no craving is, there is neither coming nor going. Where no coming or going is, there is neither arising nor passing away. Where neither arising not passing away is, there is neither this world nor a world beyond, nor a state between. This, verily, is the End of Suffering.[23]

Human folly

It may well seem that humanity has evolved such a long way in so many directions, not least in our incredible technical abilities. However, let us think back to the ancient hunter-gatherers living thousands of years ago: their move to a more settled existence and their domestication of animals was what opened the door to infections from viruses. They can be excused in that they knew no better. But here we are in the so-called civilized world opening the doors to lethal viruses again and again by stupidity and ignorance on the one hand, and the total lack of any respect for animal life and for the ecosystems of the planet on the other. What do we expect with such irrational behaviour? Viruses preceded us on the planet and will be here when we are all gone unless we change and have some sympathy for our home on Earth. Human folly seems to know no bounds and the Buddha is right; we create our own suffering. And while viruses are essential to our survival through the DNA blending that takes place, for the most part they should be kept where they belong in the creatures they symbiotically inhabit without harm, not passed to humans because of the negligent treatment of those creatures. If we invade the territories of animals to build our cities, to use the animals for food, and destroy the rainforests in which they live, we are inviting lethal viruses to take up home within us. We do not seem to have progressed much from the hunter-gatherers in this respect. Dorothy Crawford makes the important point that: "Animal viruses also thrive on overpopulation. For them, intensively farmed animals equate to crowded cities and present the opportunity to spread easily among their hosts."[24] And elsewhere, she echoes the comparison with early hunter-gatherers with the frequency of new infections and lethal microbes emerging, "they have hit us at the rate of around one a year, and now the frequency is increasing, a scenario that seems to mirror events of 10,000 years ago when animal domestication prompted a spate of new infections. And the reasons today are broadly the same as they were then – environmental changes that bring us into contact with 'new' microbes which are then spread by travellers."[25]

The balance between nature and humanity is a delicate one and humanity has always got the balance wrong, assuming that it has the right to invade and harm nature without consequence. Christopher Wills, in fact, says: "It is after all a truism that the plagues that afflict us do so because we have upset the balance of nature."[26] Wherever humanity treads it causes extinctions of species, devastation of lands, and decimation of peoples. We have become the virus of the planet. Consider, too, Wills' words here for he writes that,

> we have also surrounded ourselves with less obvious creatures, like the teeming micro-organisms that have invaded the estuaries we have polluted, and the new mix of soil bacteria that is now found in the fields we have cultivated and altered with the addition of pesticides and fertilizers. These new combinations of micro-organisms provide new evolutionary opportunities. Pathogens with which we have previously been coexisting can be catapulted into new, short-term but terrible modes of existence. In short, they can become plagues.[27]

Sadly, in the ecological changes we have forced on the planet, new viruses have invaded creature species, too, endangering their existence. Wherever humanity ventures it disturbs the natural ecosystems. Thus, Crawford advises: "At the moment we are severely out of balance with the natural environment and this is directly responsible for the recent rise in 'new' virus infections. The situation will only change for the better if we redress the balance and restore harmony with our surroundings."[28]

Humanity's invasion of the rainforests has continued unabated for decades. The diverse trees in these forests have enabled equally diverse species to survive and evolve in appropriate niches. We all know of the elastic-like material of latex that comes from rubber trees that is mixed with sulphur to harden it. But wherever latex was harvested plantations took over from the natural ecosystems and entirely ruined natural forests. We have all heard of global warming and the subsequent climate change it is bringing and will continue to bring. And we know, too, that deforestation is one radical cause of climate change apart from our own very poor carbon footprints. The problem partially lies in the fact that so many do so little about it, and do not concern themselves with what happens on the other side of the world. At least a small percentage of the youth of today seems to be focusing on the issue with inspiration from activists such as Greta Thunberg. Perhaps when we are invaded by disease-bearing mosquitoes because of the tropical and subtropical climes moving further north and south, we will take more notice. At one time, the *Aedes* mosquito of the disease-bearing and biting variety that causes Zika virus was fairly confined to Africa, but it reached over thirty states in the USA and even Europe through a warming climate.

In news coverage of the virus, there is never any mention of the fundamental problem of humanity itself being so responsible for infectious diseases, epidemics and pandemics. If I mention such a thing to family and friends, they stare at me oddly. How can they as individuals have any effect on something that is happening on the other side of the world, apart from offering a little sympathy? Individuals in the West generally fail to see any connection between the ways in which they live and the virus that is now infecting and killing so many people. They fail, too, to take seriously any responsibility in effecting changes in thought and lifestyle in order to prevent the suffering of the planet. But the message of the Buddha here is so relevant. It is a message to each *individual*, advising and guiding each man and woman to bring about changes in attitudes to understand who we are and how our individual greed and desires affect the wider world. It is critical that we overcome the delusion that what each of us does will have minimal effect on the global scale and will fail to influence governments and corporate industries that are killing our planet. Change begins with individuals, with you and me: we have to try.

The socio-economic factors affecting societies because of the pandemic need urgent attention. The sad fact about viruses and their spread is that they favour dense populations – again, not so different from the hunter-gatherers who moved to denser living. And dense populations are so often concomitant with social disparities. If Covid has done nothing else, it should make us focus on the social conditions and poverty that provide breeding grounds for any virus. In Wales in the UK where I live, and in many other areas around the world, black, Asian and minority ethnic, BAME, groups have been disproportionately affected by Covid. While that is a fact *irrespective* of social disadvantages, many of these individuals *had* to work during lockdown and, in the early days of the pandemic with little other protection than a mask. And it also has to be said that BAME individuals have greater health problems than their white counterparts, and they also provide more care than white care workers. Grangetown, in an area of the capital city of Wales, Cardiff, is a very deprived area that had a disproportionate number of Covid cases at the beginning of the pandemic. In Grangetown, ethnic minority workers are twice as likely to be on agency contracts and in low-paid jobs, and Bangladeshi men are four times as likely to be working in industries that close down during lockdown. The impact of such facts is suggestive of far more detrimental economic consequences for BAME than for white individuals: there is certainly structural inequality here. And in Africa, where viruses are rife, areas where there is poverty, crowded living conditions and instability are favoured places for viruses to thrive. Christian McMillen has an interesting comment here. "The very simple point is that there is a relationship between disease and social conditions, conditions that do not exist everywhere and that will not be alleviated with biomedicine."[29] Viruses will invade the poor first and affect them more severely, as demonstrated in the case of Brazil,[30] and Africa.[31] Crawford comments on this:

> It is glaringly obvious from a glance at the figures that poverty is *the* major cause of microbe-related deaths. On a worldwide scale microbes are still major killers, accounting for one in three of all deaths. But the huge discrepancy in the death rates between rich and poor nations reveals the stark reality. Whereas only 1–2 per cent of all deaths in the West are caused by microbes, this figure rises to over 50 per cent in the poorest nations of the world, and it is in these highly microbe-infected areas where over 95 per cent of the global deaths from infections occur.[32]

Filthy slums are breeding grounds of virus disease. Then, too, where natural forest jungles are replaced by concrete ones, viruses have plenty of scope for massive infection.

We now have a moral obligation to change the world for the better, and with a present population of more than 1.5 billion expected to increase exponentially in the decades to come the solution to dense populations is exigent. That reminds me of something I said in Chapter 2 that is worth repeating here: viruses depend on two facts (1) how dense the population is, and (2) how dense the population is! The stark reality is the greater the population the greater the number of viruses. If humanity is to survive it has to change. Michael Oldstone has these wise words: "In the end, the splendour of human history is not in wars won, dynasties formed, or financial empires built, but in improvement of the human condition. The obliteration of diseases that impinge on our health is a regal yardstick of civilization's success, and those who accomplish that task will be among the true navigators of a brave new world."[33] Viruses have no brains but it is a no-brainer to say that we will never totally outwit them: they are here to stay, to evolve in new ways and to be opportunist in mutating to survive. At present, the tables are turned: humanity is the virus of the planet, slowly killing it for all humanity's ability to think.

As we approach winter in the northern hemisphere, Covid is on the rise once again but with people less willing to have restrictions placed on their lives this time. Even if we get through this pandemic, massive social change is inevitable, along with equally massive economic hardship. Will people have the will to reflect on wider issues of the harm they do to the planet by humanity's ignorance and greed, or will they be carried along in waves of blame and social unrest? The huge animal farms with creatures squashed together would have to close if people no longer ate so much meat. Deforestation to produce soy for animal feed and grazing for cattle production for the table would be so much lessened if people could agree to give up eating meat. That would be something *every* individual could do for the planet. But most individuals seem to have missed the connection between what they eat and the causes of the virus out there affecting so many peoples globally. More virus pandemics will come our way unless there is reflective understanding of how and why viruses emerge. If Covid is believed to be a dangerous enemy and a destructive force, then humanity is equally so – again, humanity itself is the dangerous and destructive virus of the planet.

Epilogue

I began writing this book early in the spring of 2020 when the trees were still leafless after winter, though the promise of summer was evident in nature. When the spring ripened, the summer came, and then the autumn, much of that long spell was spent in lockdown and now, as we are passing into winter, the leafless trees are there again and many of us are, once again, in another phase of Covid and another lockdown. Wales, where I live in the UK, has just emerged from a "fire breaker" lockdown, and England has recently gone back into one, as have many countries around the world. There are success stories such as from Victoria in Australia, which has not had a single Covid infection for three weeks, but there are other countries, such as France, where cases have surpassed two million. In the US, there have been 250,000 deaths and 10 million have been infected. In Europe, 29,000 people have lost their lives. Professor Neil Ferguson of Imperial College London has projected that there could be 1,000 deaths a day by the end of December in the UK: currently, there are around 600, but with the UK having the highest number of deaths in Europe – over 60,000 – Ferguson's prediction may well be right. According to the WHO, the World Health Organization, someone dies from Covid every 17 seconds in Europe. Globally, there have been 58,081,322 infections as of the third week of November 2020, and 1,380,643 deaths.

There are some individuals who argue that death rates are no higher than average for each month of the year. That is misinformation that would do justice to the Buddha's tenet concerning false speech. In the UK, for example, the average number of deaths from all causes per month is around 14,000–15,000. In April because of the pandemic, that figure rose to 24,000, of which 20,000 were Covid deaths. Some of the remaining 4,000 may also have been Covid related. Now, in the second phase, deaths are up beyond the average again but not, as yet, as numerous as in April 2020. In the first phase of the pandemic here in Wales, deaths were a third higher than the number of deaths for the same period in the previous year. One statistic that is now different is that in the first phase, 40 percent of the deaths in the UK were of individuals in care homes. Since then, the second phase is proving to stimulate proper procedures to protect residents and staff in care homes. The sad fact for those non-Covid patients who urgently need operations is that, as hospitals are filling up with Covid cases, those in need of such care are put to one side. In Wales, 54 percent fewer operations took place in the first phase of the pandemic. Deaths are raised between 16–30 percent for every month's delay for a cancer patient.

While we do not know everything this SARS–CoV-2 virus has yet to reveal, some facts are now clearer. In terms of its infection, transmission and spread, according to Muge Cevik *et al.* the virus is at its highest potential for infection "just before or within the first five days of symptom onset".[1] Tests have shown that infection seems to die away after the first week of symptomatic illness, even though the virus stays in the upper respiratory tract for an average of 17 days. Samples, say the researchers "have rarely been positive beyond nine days of illness", and: "Symptomatic and pre-symptomatic transmission (1–2 days before symptom onset), is likely to play a greater role in the spread of SARS–CoV-2 than asymptomatic transmission."[2] These facts have considerable consequence for the spread of the virus, suggesting that those who have contracted the virus but do not have symptoms for a few days are the ones who are really spreading the virus. Those who do have the virus symptoms will isolate but those who have no idea as yet that they are infected are considerably endangering others. That is why we *all* need to protect each other by social distancing, by wearing masks, and by limiting contact with people indoors because that is where superspreading of the virus takes place. That does not augur well for those who are wishing to have large family gatherings for the celebration of Christmas this 2020. Contact tracing has also proved that transmission is likely to be during the first week of illness but is not well-documented after that time.[3] However, the greater the virus affects an individual, the more it is able to shed, so it is in the interests of the virus to make us more seriously ill.

Covid reproduces faster than SARS and so its spread is more virulent. It is also more efficient in getting into the host cells than was the case with SARS, particularly with its efficient spike glycoprotein. Coronaviruses are RNA (ribonucleic acid) viruses that are known for their rapid replication and, alongside that replication, rather a lot of mutations. Now, coronaviruses are a bit different, even though they are RNA viruses. Our own DNA cells reproduce at a far slower rate but are "checked" to ensure they are copied exactly. While most RNA viruses have no such checking ability, coronaviruses do: they proofread their replication and that, thankfully, as we shall see below, means that they do not mutate as much as other RNA viruses. We know that there are some mutations – the human > mink > human one in Denmark and the Netherlands, as well as the mutated strand of the Spanish Covid – but these mutations do little to affect the major power of the virus with its glycoprotein spikes that so easily invade cells.

Vaccines

As we approach the winter of 2020, the world has woken up to the possibility of the end of the virus through a number of vaccines that look to be available relatively shortly. I say relatively shortly because they will be with us perhaps in the next few weeks, rolling out until next spring or summer, but also relatively shortly in that it usually takes years – five or ten – to produce a vaccine that has gone through the various phases and safety checks to make it viable for use. The vaccines that will shortly be available, however, have been developed using new techniques that reduce the time needed for testing and production. Two are similar in the processes that have been used – Pfizer/BioNTech and Moderna.

Pfizer BioNTech

The Pfizer BioNTech vaccine is the result of the work of German husband and wife scientists, Ugur Sahin, Chief Executive of BioNTech, and his wife Ozlem Tureci. BioNTech is an independent company that has remained politically neutral throughout its research on the vaccine and certainly had no funding from the Trump administration, even though the pharmaceutical company that will manufacture the vaccine is the US Company Pfizer. Pfizer used 2 billion dollars of its own finances to produce the vaccine. So how will the Pfizer BioNTech vaccine work? It focuses on the RNA protein of the virus, specifically, its spike protein. The researchers took the virus blueprint for the protein, the genetic code that makes the spike protein, and wrapped the fragments in a lipid, oily wrapper. The resulting vaccine does not contain any part of the virus and is completely synthetic. When injected into the body, the fragment particles will invade the cells and replicate the spike proteins, then die away, but not before they have stimulated the immune system to engage with the virus and overcome it. This remarkable vaccine has come through phase 3 trials and has been shown to have over 90 percent efficacy 7 days after the second dose. Some things are, however, unknown. In the 10 percent of cases of individuals who developed symptoms of the virus it is unknown whether their infection was lessened as a result of the vaccine. Then, too, it is unknown whether those vaccinated can still transmit the virus as asymptomatic cases, though Sahin thinks that transmission could, at the very least, be reduced by 50 percent. It is also unknown how much immunity is retained over time. Will it be as the cold coronaviruses and not last long? As yet, we do not know. The main problem with the Pfizer BioNTech vaccine is that it has to be stored at −70 C, though ongoing research is concentrating on this problem. It is also an expensive vaccine – $39 for a two-shot course per person – the vaccine being given in two doses, three weeks apart. The vaccine has been tested on 43,538 volunteers and there seem to be no adverse effects other than a sore arm at the injection site and a possible fever for two or three days. Other advantages of this vaccine are that it should prevent cases of long-Covid, and it is apparently effective across age, ethnicity and race by as high as 95 percent. As far as immunity is concerned, that should be possible for one year: T-cell response is good, but it is thought antibody response may decline over time. The UK has bought 40 million of the vaccine, sufficient for the two doses of 20 million individuals. It is not known, however, whether the vaccine can stop asymptomatic infections and, therefore, the shedding of the virus in such cases. Pfizer is hoping to produce up to 50 million vaccine doses in 2020 and up to 1.3 billion in 2021; the vaccine has now passed regulatory procedures for immediate use in the UK.

Moderna

The Moderna and the National Institutes of Health vaccine works on the same principles as the BioNTech research, targeting the virus spikes – a new technique for both research companies. In our human biochemistry, we have an RNA messenger, mRNA, which carries the DNA genetic code in the nucleus of a cell to ribosomes that make protein. That messenger gene complements one of the virus genes. Using mRNA is not new, and vaccines have been developed along these lines since the 1990s. Both Moderna and BioNTech have constructed synthetic mRNA that contains the genetic information of the virus spikes. Injected into the body, the synthetic virus particles invade the cells, which read the genetic code of the spikes and relay that code to the body. That stimulates the body to produce antibodies and T-cells against it, to destroy the protein, and to set up the immune system to recognize the virus in the future. Importantly, the vaccine does not contain any part of the virus; it is synthetically manufactured mRNA that, as most vaccines, would be eliminated from the body in about three days. Side effects of the Moderna vaccine are rare – just 1 in 10,000 people recorded some adverse effect, though mild pain at the site of the injection, chills, myalgia, and fever have been noted. It is 90 percent effective and in the remaining 10 percent who were positive for the virus, it is as yet unknown whether the vaccine lessened the infection for them. The UK has orders for 5 million doses of this vaccine, sufficient for 2.5 million people since it, too, is a double-dose vaccine, but it has yet to undergo safety checks and, if positively regulated, production and arrangements for distribution will not be in process until the spring 2021.

The Oxford vaccine

In the last few days, in the third week of November, 2020, UK researchers at Oxford University led by Chief Investigator Professor Andrew Pollard collaborating with colleagues in South Africa and Brazil have revealed the results of their phase 3 vaccine involving 30,000 volunteers. At first, it seemed less effective than the Pfizer BioNTech and Moderna vaccines, with just 70 percent efficacy after two equal doses. With a trialled, novel approach, however, where volunteers were given half a dose of the vaccine and then weeks later, a full dose, that turned out to be 90 percent effective. It looks as if immune response starts well with the half dose with a fuller response at the second dose. Data is now being put together by the partner pharmaceutical company, AstraZeneca, to present to the regulators with the possibility of production and distribution fairly soon. This vaccine has the advantage over Pfizer BioNTech and Moderna in that it can be stored in normal refrigerator temperature. Oxford's contract with AstraZeneca is a not-for-profit-one that will hopefully eventually reach more underprivileged countries, and it is much, much cheaper than the others. The vaccine had a robust response across all age groups and is viable for the elderly for whom immune response weakens with increasing age. The UK has ordered 100 million of this vaccine, its two doses catering for 50 million, and it could be approved for use sometime in December. This is not an expensive vaccine – $3 to $5 per dose.

Similar to the Pfizer-BioNTech and Moderna vaccinations, the Oxford team has targeted the spike protein of the virus, but not in the same way. The team at Oxford's Jenner Institute, more specifically with its associated team of Vaccitech, has been working on a possible vaccine for a hypothetical pandemic for many years, so the research for their present vaccine did not just begin at the start of the pandemic. The approach here was to work with an adenovirus, a cold, isolated from chimpanzees (to be precise, the stools of the chimpanzees – *quelle merde*!), and modified so that the virus itself does not replicate in cells.

So the chimp virus, ChAdOx1, Chimpanzee Adenovirus Oxford One, is a genetically modified base from which further modifications can be made to target specific viruses.[4] Just as with Pfizer-BioNTech and Moderna vaccinations, the spike proteins of the virus are the key to its defeat. After vaccination, the cells of the body will begin to manufacture the spike protein but Y-shaped antibodies and T-cells will attack effectively and, crucially, remember the virus for any future infection in order to destroy it.[5] Side effects seem to be very mild from the vaccination and include soreness and pain at injection site, fatigue, chill and fever, headache, myalgia, nausea and malaise for up to five days after vaccination.

There are a number of other research efforts that are also close to vaccine production, a few in phase 3 trials so there may well be other vaccines available for regulation in the near future. Certainly, a high vaccination rate is exigent before next autumn. The virus will probably still exist out there and could do for a further five to ten years. Herd immunity would at least be viable with prolific vaccination, and may halt the rate of spread of the virus. And perhaps a variety of vaccines would be needed because they work differently on different people. So will people take up the offer of vaccination? There is a good deal of misinformation out there on social media: two of the most prolific anti-vaccination movements are World Mercury Project and Stop Mandatory Vaccinations (though mandatory vaccines are minimal if any). The speed at which the vaccines are being developed fuels their cause.[6] In 2019, the WHO claimed that vaccine hesitancy was one of the top ten threats to world health.

Immunity

One of the important issues in the use of any vaccine is how long immunity would last: as I said above, it does not last long in cold coronaviruses. One of the problems with Covid is that the immune system controls mild infection extremely well, but in hosts where the infection is severe the immune response can become excessive and cause organ damage, necessitating intensive care and even lead to death. The first response of the immune system to Covid is the targeting of the virus by antibodies – mostly in the respiratory tract, causing inflammation, but slowly in the first four days of the disease.[7] Then important T-cells are attracted to the inflammatory areas and if any cells are infected, they are destroyed by them. But it is the over-response of the antibodies causing excessive inflammation in the lungs that makes the disease severe. It is now known that women have more robust T-cell activity than men, and that is maintained as they age.

With men, however, T-cell activity declines as they get older. That is partly why men are at a greater risk with the virus. The whole question of immunity after contracting Covid or, post-vaccination, is a hidden area. Immunity to other coronaviruses is short in duration.[8] Immunity with both SARS and MERS lasted for 2–3 years only. None of the impending vaccines can guarantee immunity in any clear way. Further, it seems immunity might not be very long lasting for individuals who have had only a mild disease.[9] Gregory Poland *et al.* point out that vaccine manufacture has an Achilles heel, which is the possibility that the virus could mutate in a way that evades immunity to the spike protein.[10] The many mutations of SARS–CoV-2 have, thus far, not shown changes to the protein spikes so vaccines remain viable for the present.

More human folly

While it may seem that I have left Buddhism aside for too long in this Epilogue, the tenets of early Buddhism should never be far from mind and, at the very least, should always engender as much right thought and right attitude as possible. Human beings have the ability to reflect, consider options, think about choices they make and the actions they undertake. I was alarmed recently to hear that famous brands are still guilty of acquiring products through slave labour. Ralph Lauren Fashion, Marks and Spencer, Tesco and Sainsbury's have their clothing products made by people in South India, who are working under terrible constraints – long, long hours, no time to eat, pee, or get home – for a pittance of money and for taskmasters who terrify them. This is sheer greed on the part of the companies who turn a blind eye to the ways in which they can procure their products cheaply and sell them at comparatively exorbitant prices. Those three evils of early Buddhism – greed, hatred/aversion, and delusion/stupidity – are still evident at a time when a pandemic should be fostering empathy and compassion for humanity.

I confess to having no idea about technical greed and was shocked to see footage of how greedy we are in using our technical aids – the smartphones, iPads, tablets, social media and Zoom. It is something that has acquired attention in a number of newspapers and television and radio broadcasts. Throughout the lockdown of the past and now of the present, our devices were and are our door to the outside world. I have asked a number of people what "the cloud" is and, without exception, they all gazed up into the sky! No, the cloud is not up there but absolutely on *terra firma*. And there are about 8 million so-called "clouds", data centres that store all the information we send out, send on, source and store. Such data centres are massive, massive computers that gobble up energy. And while these data centres like us to believe they are sourcing the incredible energy they need in responsible ways, it is always something they project for the future, not the here and now. Like so many of these companies, their energy sourcing is deliberately nebulous with fudged statements. In fact, Dr Rabih Bashroush of Uptime Institute and University of East London says that: "Staying on line could cost us the Earth." The energy usage of Zoom, for example, is colossal. Have we ever thought of such greed? Probably not, and we probably will not lessen our time on such appliances in the future even if we correct our ignorance with the knowledge of the position of "the cloud" and of our hefty carbon footprints here.

And when it comes to ignorance, delusion, stupidity, China is now claiming that the virus was imported from outside China in seafood! If China does not change its tactics concerning animal markets we are highly likely to be at the receiving end of other lethal viruses spawned there. Then, too, after a three-week delay, Donald Trump is finally allowing the President Elect to take over important administration. His delay in doing this has been disastrous for the pandemic, preventing any clear forward policy to control it. Joe Biden is keen to begin getting Covid under control in the US, and from a global perspective he seems keen to build bridges with those nations engaged in reducing global warming and pollution through fossil fuels: it is hoped he will think about the ways in which animal farming is creating the milieu for global pandemics. Donald Trump has been disastrous for conservation, disastrous for stemming Covid, and disastrous for truth. Indeed, the former president Barack Obama has spoken of "truth decay" in relation to the outgoing President.

We are not getting to grips with the pandemic in the UK either. The lockdown in the first phase was too late and exactly the same happened with the present lockdown. Prime Minister Johnson was advised by SAGE, Scientific Advisory Group for Emergencies, on 21 September to impose a lockdown for England, but that advice was ignored and the virus spread. It was not until 5 November 2020 that a second lockdown for England began: that was not "following the science" as the government so often says it does. Then, too, the system of test, track and trace in the UK has been appallingly badly handled. To date it has failed to trace more than half of contacts and so has failed to stop the virus: and there is no abstention from false speech here for the UK boasted a world-beating system! The consultant anaesthetist I wrote of in Chapter 4 has still failed to be tested for Covid even though a few days ago she was in theatre with a Covid patient. The government outsourced testing but that did not work. For example, Randox Science Park is one centre that receives tests but is poorly managed with leakages in test-kit samples. The inefficiency there and a cavalier attitude result in possibilities of cross-contamination of tests. The company Serco was given a contract for testing and sub-contracted the work to twenty other companies, some of whom had no prior experience with testing and public health. Neither the government nor Serco seem happy to reveal who these sub-contracted companies are. And Serco was paid £410 million to do the job. Delusional behaviour might also be laid at the feet of government minister Baroness Dido Harding who really has failed to live up to her position as the person responsible for testing and tracing. It would have been sensible to have made it available in September 2020 when schools and universities restarted, but she waited until October. Thinking back to the Cheltenham Festival for horse racing that took place at a critical time for Covid infections in mid-March 2020, it took place just *before* lockdown and was a huge contributory factor to the spread of Covid. And who is a racecourse committee director at Cheltenham Racecourse and a director of Jockey Club Racecourses? Dido Harding fills both those posts. Many lives could have been saved and the virus spread with less virulence had that race meeting been cancelled.

In terms of *right speech*, it seems much of what is right for scientists is suppressed, according to Kamran Abbasi, who claims that science concerning Covid is being suppressed for political and financial gain. The identity of members of SAGE, he said, was kept a secret until a press leak forced transparency. Further, members and authors of research papers in Public Health England were prevented from talking to the media. And Abbasi writes: "The UK's pandemic response relies too heavily on scientists and other government appointees with worrying competing interests, including shareholdings in companies that manufacture Covid-19 diagnostic tests, treatments, and vaccines. Government appointees are able to ignore or cherry pick science – another form of misuse – and indulge in anti-competitive practices that favour their own products and those of friends and associates."[11] Without fairness for valid scientific outlets, the public may well be drawn to misinformation.

At the close of Chapter 8, I dealt with what I consider to be human folly, and the gist of that section and closing of this book was the repetition of the main thesis that runs throughout it, that human behaviour is harmful to the planet and to itself and, very specifically, because of the way in which we herd animals into factories for our meat consumption. We may want to think that this kind of stupidity takes place in horrendous animal markets in China but I was surprised and shocked to find that Denmark, the Netherlands and Ireland profit from the sale of mink. Leaving aside for the moment the staggering number of mink bred just to provide the furs of the clothing industry – of the very rich, I presume – the mink in Denmark and the Netherlands were found to be infected with Covid early in November 2020. And they had got Covid from humans who were breeding them. But the cross-infection does not end there because the virus mutated in the mink and then crossed back into humans, a few hundred of them. In the Netherlands there were fewer human infections since those who worked on the mink farms were given personal protective equipment to prevent infection! 17 million mink were culled in Denmark alone, a figure that is indicative of the prolific nature of mink farming. Mink are bred in large numbers and in close living conditions. Are they treated well? No, the UK *Independent* has a video of mink being pulled from their cages "like rubbish" and thrown into gas chambers on Dutch farms: I could not watch it.[12] Three mink farms in Ireland have been told by the Department of Agriculture that the mink on their farms will have to be culled to prevent the potential of a mutated version of the coronavirus spreading. Mink farms in Spain and Greece have also been advised to conduct a cull. Other animals are also possible transmitters of coronaviruses, including Covid. There are farms of foxes and raccoon dogs kept for their fur, raccoon dogs especially being possible transmitters of Covid.[13] And China is the biggest fur-producing country. The Buddha would have been saddened to know that abstention from taking life is so readily ignored by those engaged in this kind of work and it brings the issue of *right livelihood* very much into the present.

The Buddha said that no creature, human or animal, wants to suffer, but humanity causes so much suffering, so widely and so carelessly. The words of Nyanaponika Thera that I cited in Chapter 8 are so worth iterating here: "The world suffers. But most men have their eyes and ears closed. They do not see the unbroken stream of tears flowing through life, they do not hear the cry of distress continually pervading the world."[14] In an interview on BBC television, David Attenborough said: "Human beings have overrun the world" and "humanity is capable of exterminating whole communities, enormous communities of living creatures". We seem to be killing off so many creatures yet breeding millions of those that can supply profitable gain. What sort of people are we? Attenborough says that if we damage the planet, we really damage ourselves, and that the natural world should be treated as if it is precious.[15]

I would have so wished to end the Epilogue of this book on a cheerful and optimistic note, but I have to fail in that wish. I have said that Buddhism is optimistic despite the Buddha's tenet that all life is suffering. The cure and the experience of happiness instead of suffering lie firmly *with each individual* and until individuals change the way they think, change their desires, their intentions, and temper unkindness to humankind and creatures, I hold out no hope for the future of humanity. We will kill ourselves by our own stupidity, by the delusion that we are the pinnacles of evolution through our technological advances. But we will never win against viruses and if we do not want another pandemic then we will *have* to change our attitudes or pay a very hard price for our stupidity. Again, humanity is the virus of the planet.

As I close this Epilogue on 3 December 2020, the UK has just recorded over 60,000 Covid deaths, the fifth highest in the world. And in the United States, if deaths from Covid continue at the present rate, by mid-December they will be almost, or more than, 300,000.

Notes

1 The Buddha

1. Rupert Gethin, *The Foundations of Buddhism* (Oxford and New York: Oxford University Press, 1998, p. 16.
2. See Edward Conze, translator, *Buddhist Scriptures* (London and New York: Penguin Classics, 1959).
3. *Ibid.*, p. 39.
4. *Ibid.*
5. *Ibid.*, p. 40.
6. *Ibid.*
7. *Ibid.*, p. 41.
8. *Ibid.*, p. 42.
9. *Dharma* is the Sanskrit form of Pali *Dhamma*. Since I am dealing solely with early Buddhism, I am retaining the more accurate Pali throughout this book.
10. Conze, *Buddhist Scriptures*, pp. 42–3.
11. Valerie J. Roebuck, translator, *The Dhammapada* (London and New York: Penguin Books, 2010), p. 32.
12. Such communities were probably located in woods, forests or caves in the early stages rather than the later monasteries: see Hajime Nakamura, *Indian Buddhism: A survey with biographical notes* (Delhi: Motilal Banarsidass Publishers Private Limited, 1996 reprint of 1987 edn, first published 1980), p. 58.
13. *Potthapada Sutta* 9:27:188, translator Maurice Walshe, *Thus Have I Heard: The Long Discourses of the Buddha Digha Nikaya* (London: Wisdom Publications, 1987), p. 164.
14. Richard F. Gombrich's words are noteworthy here: "The *suttas* are artefacts, not perfect records of actual conversations": see *How Buddhism Began: The conditioned genesis of the early teachings* (London & Atlantic Highlands, New Jersey: Athlone, 1996), p. 29. Not all the words we find in the *Suttas* came from the Buddha or his disciple Ananda, though the latter is reputed to be the main source of the oral recitations of the Buddha's teachings.
15. Traditionally, it was at a Council held by monks shortly after the Buddha died that the Pali canon was finalized, though orally at first. However, the canon as we have it today probably evolved over a much longer period: see Walshe, translator, *Thus Have I Heard*, p. 46, and Gombrich, *How Buddhism Began*, p. 9. There are, however, problems with such

systematizing of what was thought to be the Buddha's words. As Gombrich notes, the Buddha adapted his teaching to his audience, the "skill in means" of later Mahayana Buddhism (p. 17), and attempts to systematize such varied, contradictory teachings give false impressions of early Buddhism. As Gombrich says of the Buddha: "He had had a clear and compelling vision of the truth and was trying to convey it to a wide range of people with different inclinations and varying presuppositions, so he had to express this message in many different ways" (p. 18). And then: "I think we would find that during this preaching career of forty-five years he had expressed himself in an enormous number of different ways" (p. 19).

16 *Dhammapada* 6:79, translator Roebuck, *The Dhammapada*, p. 17.
17 *Majjhima Nikaya* 1:167:31: see Henry Clarke Warren, ed., *Buddhism in Translations*, from 1888 edited work of V. Trenckner (Delhi: Motilal Banarsidass, 1987 reprint of 1896 edn), p. 339.
18 Conze, translator, *Buddhist Scriptures*, p. 145.
19 Peter Harvey, *An Introduction to Buddhism: Teachings, history and practices* (Cambridge: Cambridge University Press, 1992 reprint of 1990 edn), p. 37.

2 Viruses: Friends and Enemies

1 See Edward C. Holmes, "What Does Virus Evolution Tell Us about Virus Origins?" In *Journal of Virology* 85(2011), p. 5251.
2 Juris A. Grasis, "The Intra-Dependence of Viruses and the Holiobont." In *Immunology* Nov (2017), p. 1. https://www.frontierin.org/ people/ u/118353
3 Richard Horton, *The COVID-19 Catastrophe: What's gone wrong and how to stop it happening again* (Cambridge and Medford MA: Polity Press, 2020), p. 96.
4 Cited by Dorothy Crawford, *Viruses: A very short introduction* (Oxford: Oxford University Press, 2018 reprint of 2011 edn), p. 132.
5 Cited by Michael B. A. Oldstone, *Viruses, Plagues, & History: Past, present and future* (Oxford and New York: Oxford University Press, revised and updated edn 2010), p. 10.
6 Judy Diamond and Charles Wood in the *Foreword* to Carl Zimmer, *A Planet of Viruses* (Chicago and London: Chicago University Press, second edn 2015, first published 2011), p. ix.
7 Dorothy H. Crawford, *The Invisible Enemy: A natural history of viruses* (Oxford and New York: Oxford University Press, 2009 reprint of 2000 edn), p. 31.
8 See Christian W. McMillen, *Pandemics: A very short introduction* (Oxford and New York: Oxford University Press, 2016), p. 2.
9 See Dorothy H. Crawford, *Deadly Companions: How microbes shaped our history* (Oxford and New York: Oxford University Press, 2018 second edn, first published 2007), pp. 10–11.
10 Arinjay Banerjee, Karen Mossman, Vikram Misra, "Viruses Can Cause

Notes 223

   Global Pandemics, But Where Did The First Virus Come From?" In *The Conversation* May (2018), p. 5.
11 Holmes, "What Does Virus Evolution Tell Us about Virus Origins?", p. 5247.
12 *Ibid.*, p. 5248.
13 Discovered in the Pilbara area of Western Australia.
14 Paul Davies, *The Origin of Life* (London and New York: Penguin Books, 2000, first published 1999), p. 2.
15 Jim Al-Khalili and Johnjoe McFadden, *Life on the Edge* (London: Penguin Random House, 2015), p. 269. Mars is beginning to show evidence of such subterranean water, perhaps with its own microbes.
16 For further information on what Davies calls "Superbugs", see *The Origins of Life*, chapter 7, pp. 144–68.
17 Davies, *The Origin of Life*, p. 211.
18 Zimmer, *A Planet of Viruses*, p. 4.
19 *Ibid.*
20 See Crawford, *Deadly Companions*, p. 29.
21 Julia Durzyńska and Anna Goździcka-Józefiat, "Viruses and Cells Intertwined Since the Dawn of Evolution". In *Virology Journal* 12 169(2015), p. 1.
22 Crawford, *Deadly Companions*, pp. 54–5.
23 *Ibid.*, p. 67.
24 See Zimmer, *A Planet of Viruses*, p. 53.
25 Crawford, *The Invisible Enemy*, pp. 7–8.
26 Durzyńska and Goździcka-Józefiat, "Viruses and Cells Intertwined Since the Dawn of Evolution", p. 6.
27 Oldstone, *Viruses, Plagues, & History*, p. 10.
28 Crawford, *Viruses*, pp. 11–12.
29 See Christopher Wills, *Plagues: Their origin, history and future* (London: HarperCollins, 1996), p. 224.
30 *Ibid.*, pp. 151–2.
31 Crawford, *The Invisible Enemy*, p. 6.
32 *Ibid.*, p. 7.
33 Michael Mosley, *COVID-19: What you need to know about the coronavirus and the race for the vaccine* (London: Short Books, 2020), p. 10.
34 *Ibid.*, pp. 62–3.
35 Wills, *Plagues*, p. 223.
36 Matti Jalasvuori, "Revolutionary Struggle for Existence: Introduction to Four Intriguing Puzzles in Virus Research", in Günther Witzany, ed., *Viruses: Essential Agents of Life* (Berlin: Springer, 2012), p. 3.
37 Crawford, *The Invisible Enemy*, p. 15.
38 Mosley, *COVID-19*, p. 11.
39 See Oldstone, *Viruses, Plagues, & History*, for a detailed account of virus access to cells, pp. 12–14.
40 Zimmer, *A Planet of Viruses*, p. 22.
41 *Ibid.*, p. 22.

42 Crawford, *Viruses*, p. 24.
43 Crawford, *Deadly Companions*, p. 19.
44 Jonathan Quick, *The End of Epidemics: The looming threat to humanity and how to stop it* (Victoria, Australia: Scribe, 2018), p. 26.
45 *Ibid.*
46 *Ibid.*
47 Crawford, *The Invisible Enemy*, p. 95.
48 *Ibid.* p. 26.
49 *Ibid.*, p. 98.
50 *Ibid.*, p. 102.
51 Crawford, *Deadly Enemies*, p. 15.
52 Durzyńska and Goździcka-Józefiat, "Viruses and Cells Intertwined Since the Dawn of Evolution", p. 7.
53 *Ibid.*, p. 9.
54 See Zimmer, *A Planet of Viruses*, pp. 4–5.
55 Crawford, *The Invisible Enemy*, p. 35.
56 Wills, *Plagues*, p. 46.
57 Zimmer, citing the work of Thierry Heidmann in *A Planet of Viruses*, p. 58.
58 *Ibid.*, p. 17.
59 Crawford, *Viruses*, p. 51.
60 Zimmer, *A Planet of Viruses*, p. 58.
61 Oldstone, *Viruses, Plagues, & History*, p. 56.
62 *Ibid.*
63 Quick, *The End of Epidemics*, p. 99.
64 See Crawford, *Viruses*, p. 64.
65 See Mosley, COVID-19, p. 107.
66 Crawford, *Viruses*, pp. 64–5.
67 See Crawford, *The Invisible Enemy*, p. 112.
68 See Oldstone, *Viruses, Plagues, & History*, pp. 318–19.
69 Quick, *The End of Epidemics*, p. 43.
70 Crawford, *Viruses*, p. 45.
71 Quick, *The End of Epidemics*, p. 49.
72 Crawford, *Viruses*, p. 46.
73 See Crawford, *ibid.*, p. 76.
74 See Zimmer, *A Planet of Viruses*, p. 31.
75 Crawford, *Viruses*, p. 51.
76 Crawford, *Deadly Companions*, p. 190.
77 Oldstone, *Viruses, Plagues, & History*, p. 240.
78 Wills, *Plagues*, p. 217.
79 See Paul Klenerman, *The Immune System: A very short introduction* (Oxford: Oxford University Press, 2017), pp. 65–6.
80 Crawford, *Deadly Companions*, p. 188.
81 Oldstone, *Viruses, Plagues, & History*, p. 269.
82 *Ibid.*, p. 253.
83 Crawford, *The Invisible Enemy*, pp. 68–9.

84 Quick, *The End of Pandemics*, p. 52.
85 Ibid., p. 52.
86 See Oldstone, *Viruses, Plagues, & History*, p. 231.
87 Horton, *The COVID-19 Catastrophe*, p. 30.
88 Oldstone, *Viruses, Plagues, & History*, p. 230.
89 Quick, *The End of Pandemics*, p. 16.
90 BMJ Best Practice, "Coronavirus Disease 2019 (COVID-19)" (British Medical Journal: BMJ Publishing Group, 2020), p. 5.
91 Mosley, *COVID-19*, p. 8.
92 For the current Covid-19 situation update worldwide country by country, see ecdc.eu/en/geographical-distribution-2019-ncov-cases
93 Alexandre Hassanin, "Coronavirus Origins: Genome Analysis Suggests Two Viruses May Have Combined". In *The Conversation*, March 18, 2020.
94 Mosley, *COVID-19*, pp. 26–7.
95 BMJ Best Practice, "Coronavirus Disease 2019 (COVID-19)", p. 8.
96 "Scientists warn of new coronavirus variant spreading across Europe", ft.com/content/2782655a-438-6603-5c4e67ead110
97 Richard L. Tillett, Joel R. Sevinsky, Paul D. Hartley, Heather Kerwin, Natalie Crawford, Andrew Gorzalski *et al*.https://doi.org/10.1016/S1473–3099(20)30764–7, published 12 October 2020. See also thelancet.com/journals/lanif/article/PIIS1473–3099(20)30764–7fulltext
98 Interviewed on British Broadcasting Corporation television, 27 October 2020.
99 Nevertheless, it has to be said that there is some evidence that early cases of Covid had no connection with the animal market. China is very sensitive about the origins of Covid being there, so perhaps evidence is uncertain.
100 See Horton, *The COVID-19 Catastrophe*, pp. 19–20.
101 *The Epoch Times*, May, 2020.
102 Hassanin, "Coronavirus Origins: Genome Analysis Suggests Two Viruses May Have Combined", p. 4.
103 Klenerman, *The Immune System*, p. 1.
104 See Mosley, *COVID-19*, pp. 30–4.
105 Wills, *Plagues*, p. 255.
106 Crawford, *The Invisible Enemy*, p. 39.
107 Horton, *The COVID-19 Catastrophe*, p. 64.
108 Ibid., p. 16.

3 The Noble Truth of Suffering

1 Walpola Rahula, *What the Buddha Taught* (Oxford: Oneworld, 1997, first published 1959), p. 17.
2 *Dhammapada* 25:372, translator Valerie J. Roebuck, *The Dhammapada* (London and New York: Penguin Books, 2010), p. 73.
3 Steven Collins, *Selfless Persons: Imagery and thought in Theravada*

Buddhism (Cambridge, London, New York, New Rochelle, Melbourne, Sydney: Cambridge University Press, 1982), p. 83.
4   Rahula, *What the Buddha Taught*, p. 40.
5   *Udana* 80, translator Rupert Gethin, *The Foundations of Buddhism* (Oxford and New York: Oxford University Press, 1998), pp. 76–7.
6   Cited here by Francis Story, *The Four Noble Truths* (Kandy, Sri Lanka: Buddhist Publication Society, 1983 reprint of 1961 edn), p. 16.
7   From the *Visuddhimagga*, cited in Bhikku Khantipālo, "A Description of Dukkha" in *The Three Basic Facts of Existence II Suffering (Dukkha) Collected Essays* (Kandy, Sri Lanka: Buddhist Publiation Society, 1983 reprint of 1973 edn), p. 19.
8   See Richard Horton, *The COVID-19 Catastrophe: What's gone wrong and how to stop it happening again* (Cambridge: Polity Press, 2020), p. 112.
9   Jonathan Quick with Bronwyn Fryer, *The End of Pandemics: The looming threat to humanity and how to stop it* (Victoria: Scribe, 2018), p. 45.
10 Michael Mosley, *COVID-19: What you need to know about the Coronavirus and the race for a vaccine* (London: Short Books, 2020), p. 40.
11 Horton, *The COVID-19 Catastrophe*, p. viii.
12 Quick, *The End of Pandemics*, p. 46.
13 Horton, *The COVID-19 Catastrophe*, p. 21.
14 *Ibid.*, p. 23.
15 Natasha Jackson, "The Pursuit of Happiness and the Fact of Suffering" in *The Three Basic Facts of Existence II Suffering (Dukkha) Collected Essays*, p. 55.
16 *Ibid.*
17 Rahula, *What the Buddha Taught*, p. 28.
18 Quick, *The End of Pandemics*, pp. 18–19.
19 Mark Csikszentmihalyi, *Flow: The psychology of optimal experience* (New York, London, Toronto, Sydney, New Delhi, Auckland: Harperperennial, 2008, first published 1990), p. 24.
20 Susan Greenfield, *Brain Story: Unlocking our inner world of emotions, memories, ideas and desires* (London: BBC Worldwide Limited, 2000), p. 171.
21 Susan Blackmore, *Consciousness: A very short introduction* (Oxford and New York: Oxford University Press, 2005), p. 15.
22 Anmar Al-Chalabi, Martin R. Turner and R. Shane Delamot, *The Brain* (London: Oneworld, 2015 reprint of 2008 edn), p. 112.
23 Simon Blackburn, *What Do We Really Know: The big questions of philosophy* (London: Quercus, 2012, first published 2009), p. 16.
24 I am retaining the Pali form throughout, though the word is popularly known in its Sanskrit form, *karma*.
25 *Dhammapada* 1:1–2. The translation here that I particularly like is that of Max Müller recorded in Edward Arthur Burtt ed., *The Teachings of*

Notes 227

the Compassionate Buddha: Early discourses, the Dhammapada and later basic writings (New York, London, Ontario, Victoria, Auckland: New American Library, 2000, first published 1955), p. 28.
26 V. F. Gunaratne, The Significance of the Four Noble Truths (Kandy, Sri Lanka: Buddhist Publication Society, 1973 reprint of 1968 edn), p. 15.
27 Dhammapada 25:370 and 373, translator Roebuck, The Dhammapada, pp. 72–3.
28 Story, The Four Noble Truths, p. 24.

4 The Second Noble Truth of the Cause of Suffering

1 Dhammacakkappavattana Sutta translated here by Francis Story, The Four Noble Truths (Kandy, Sri Lanka: Buddhist Publication Society, 1983 reprint of 1961 edn), p. 34.
2 Walpola Rahula, What the Buddha Taught (London and Bedford: Gordon Fraser, 1982 reprint of second enlarged edn 1967, first published 1959), p. 30.
3 Ibid., pp. 31–2.
4 Rupert Gethin, The Foundations of Buddhism (Oxford and New York: Oxford University Press, 1998), p. 73.
5 Ibid., p. 70.
6 Story, The Four Noble Truths, p. 25.
7 Digha Nikaya 16 translator O. H. de A. Wijesekera, The Three Signata: Anicca, Dukkha, Anatta (Kandy, Sri Lanka: Buddhist Publication Society, 1982), p. 25.
8 Samyutta Nikaya XII, 15 translator Wijesekera, ibid., p. 26.
9 Damien Keown, Buddhism: A very short introduction (Oxford and New York: Oxford University Press, 1996), p. 53.
10 Phra Khantipalo, "A Walk in the Woods" in The Three Basic Facts of Existence I Impermanence, Collected Essays (Kandy, Sri Lanka: Buddhist Publication Society, 1981 reprint of 1973 edn), p. 43.
11 Ibid.
12 Samyutta Nikaya III, 44 translator Piyadassi Thera, "The Fact of Impermanence" in The Three Basic Facts of Existence I Impermanence, Collected Essays, p. 4.
13 Ibid., XXII, 102.
14 See Jeaneane Fowler, Causality: Macrocosmic and microcosmic theories of cause and effect in belief systems (Brighton, Chicago, Toronto: Sussex Academic Press, 2020), pp. 298–301.
15 Paul Williams with Anthony Tribe, Buddhist Thought: A complete introduction to the Indian tradition (London and New York: Routledge, 2000), p. 63.
16 G. P. Malalasekera, The Truth of Anatta (Kandy, Sri Lanka: Buddhist Publication Society, 1966), p. 15.
17 David Kalupahana, A History of Buddhist Philosophy: Continuities and discontinuities (Honolulu: University of Hawaii Press, 1992), p. 89.
18 See Jonathan Quick with Bronwyn Fryer, The End of Pandemics: The

looming threat to humanity and how to stop it (Victoria and London: Scribe Publications, 2018), pp. 167–8.
19 *Ibid.*, p. 19.
20 *Ibid.*, p. 54.
21 *Ibid.*, p. 50.
22 Cited by Quick, *ibid.*, p. 55.
23 Richard Horton, *The COVID-19 Catastrophe: What's gone wrong and how to stop it happening again* (Cambridge: Polity Press, 2020), p. 99.
24 *Ibid.*, p. 27.
25 *Ibid.*, p. 97.
26 Christopher Wills: *Plagues: Their origin, history and future* (London: HarperCollins, 1996), p. 245.
27 Horton, *The COVID-19 Catastrophe*, p. 35.
28 *Ibid.*, pp. 46–7.
29 *Ibid.*, p. 12.
30 Quick, *The End of Pandemics*, p. 19.
31 David Attenborough, "Meat is Murder", *Radio Times*, 3–9 October 2020, p. 132.
32 See Williams with Tribe, *Buddhist Thought*, p. 57.
33 Gethin, *The Foundations of Buddhism*, p. 139.
34 Malalasekera, *The Truth of Anatta*, p. 13.
35 *Samyutta Nikaya* XXII, 33.
36 David Eagleman, *The Brain: The story of you* (Edinburgh and London: Canongate, 2016, first published 2015), p. 23.
37 Julian Jaynes, *The Origins of Consciousness in the Breakdown of the Bicameral Mind* (Boston: Houghton Mifflin Company, 1990 reprint of 1976 edn), p. 30.
38 *Ibid.*, p. 28.
39 Gethin, *The Foundations of Buddhism*, p. 142.
40 *Ibid.*, p. 144.
41 G. P. Malalasekera, *Aspects of Reality as Taught by Theravada Buddhism* (Kandy, Sri Lanka: Buddhist Publication Society, 1982 reprint of 1968 edn, taken from *Essays in East and West Philosophy*, Honolulu: University of Hawaii Press, 1951), p. 10.
42 Nyanatiloka Mahathera, "Egolessness" in *The Three Basic Facts of Existence III Egolessness* (Kandy, Sri Lanka: Buddhist Publication Society, 1984, first published 1974), p. 4.
43 *Samyutta Nikaya* 163, translator Mahathera, "Extracts from the *Samyutta-Nikaya* Dealing with Egolessness" in *The Three Basic Facts of Existence III Egolessness* p. 47.
44 Malalasekera, *Aspects of Reality as Taught by Theravada Buddhism*, pp. 26–7.
45 Williams with Tribe, *Buddhist Thought*, p. 60.

5 The Third Noble Truth of the Cessation of Suffering

1. Paul Williams with Anthony Tribe, *Buddhist Thought: A complete introduction to the Indian tradition* (London and New York: Routledge, 2000), p. 68.
2. *Udana* VIII, 3.
3. Joanna Macy, *Mutual Causality in Buddhism and General Systems Theory: The dharma of natural systems* (Albany, New York: State University of New York Press, 1991), p. 19.
4. Alfonso Verdu, *Early Buddhist Philosophy in the Light of the Four Noble Truths* (Delhi, Varanasi, Patna, Madras: Motilal Banarsidass, 1985), p. 97.
5. Peter Harvey, *An Introduction to Buddhism: Teachings, history and practices* (Cambridge: Cambridge University Press, 1992 reprint of 1990 edn), p. 57.
6. Sue Hamilton, *Identity and Experience: The constitution of the human being according to early Buddhism* (London: Luzac Oriental, 1996), p. 70.
7. Bhikkhu Bodhi translator, *The Great Discourse on Causation: The Mahanidana Sutta and its commentaries* (Kandy, Sri Lanka: Buddhist Publication Society, 2000 reprint of 1984 edn), p. 18.
8. *Questions of Milinda* 40:17, translator Henry Clarke Warren, *Buddhism in Translations*, from 1888 edited work of V. Trenckner (Delhi: Motilal Banarsidass, 1987 reprint of 1896 edn), pp. 149–50.
9. *Dhammapada* 17:221, translator Valerie Roebuck, *The Dhammapada* (London and New York: Penguin Books, 2010), p. 44.
10. Hamilton, *Identity and Experience*, p. 22.
11. Macy, *Mutual Causality in Buddhism and General Systems Theory*, p. 122.
12. Hamilton, *Identity and Experience*, p. 43.
13. Bhikkhu Bodhi, *The Great Discourse on Causation*, p. 10.
14. Francis Story, *The Case for Rebirth* (Kandy, Sri Lanka: Buddhist Publication Society, 1973), p. 10.
15. Thera Piyadassi, *Dependent Origination* (Kandy, Sri Lanka: Buddhist Publication Society, 1981), p. 4.
16. *Ibid.*, p. 31.
17. *Ibid.*, p. 32.
18. Verdu, *Early Buddhist Philosophy in the Light of the Four Noble Truths*, p. 101.
19. *Ibid.*, p. 96.
20. *Ibid.*
21. Theodore Stcherbatsky, *Buddhist Logic Volume I* (Delhi: Motilal Banarsidass Publishers Private Limited, 1994 reprint of 1993 edn), p. 119.
22. Bhikkhu Bodhi, *The Great Discourse on Causation*, p. 2.
23. Macy, *Mutual Causality in Buddhism and General Systems Theory*, p. 55.

24 Prayadh A. Payutto, *Dependent Origination: The Buddhist Law of Conditionality* (Bangkok, Thailand: Buddhadhamma Foundation, 1944), p. 15.
25 David J. Kalupahana, *Causality: The central philosophy of Buddhism* (Honolulu: The University Press of Hawaii, 1975), p. 56.
26 Williams with Tribe, *Buddhist Thought*, p. 63.
27 See A. K. Warder, *Indian Buddhism* (Delhi: Motilal Banarsidass Publishers Private Limited, 1997 reprint of second revised edn, first published 1970), p. 143.
28 Bhikkhu Bodhi, *The Great Discourse on Causation*, p. 25.
29 From the Sanskrit *Dharmapada* 4a, the chapter on *Karma*, translator Edward Conze, *Buddhist Scriptures* (London and New York: Penguin Books, 1959), p. 83. See also the Pali *Dhammapada* 9:127–8.
30 Francis Story, "Action" (Kandy, Sri Lanka: Buddhist Publication Society, 1975), p. 7.
31 Nyanatiloka Mahathera, *Karma and Rebirth* (Kandy, Sri Lanka: Buddhist Publication Society, 1982), p. 18.
32 See Verdu, *Early Buddhist Philosophy in the Light of the Four Noble Truths*, p. 79.
33 K. N. Jayatilleke, *Survival and Karma in Buddhist Perspective* (Kandy, Sri Lanka: Buddhist Publication Society, 1980), p. 27.
34 Leonard A. Bullen, "Action and Reaction in Buddhist Teachings" (Kandy, Sri Lanka: Buddhist Publication Society, 1975), p. 66.
35 *Ibid.*
36 *Ibid.*, p. 59.
37 Francis Story, *Kamma and its Fruit* (Kandy, Sri Lanka: Buddhist Publication Society, 1975), p. 106.
38 Reverend Richard Coles, *Radio Times*, 11–17 April, 2020, p. 23.
39 *Ibid.*
40 See Bhikkhu Khantipalo, "A Description of Dukkha" in *The Three Basic Facts of Existence II Suffering Collected Essays* (Kandy, Sri Lanka: Buddhist Publication Society, 1983 reprint of 1973 edn), p. 16.
41 *Ibid.*, p. 14.
42 Walpola Rahula, *What the Buddha Taught* (London and Bedford: Gordon Frazer, 1982 reprint of second, enlarged edn 1967), p. 33.
43 *Visuddhi-Magga* XVII.
44 William Gilbert, "Soul and Substance" in *The Three Basic Facts of Existence III Egolessness Collected Essays* (Kandy, Sri Lanka: Buddhist Publication Society, 1984 reprint of 1974 edn), p. 69.
45 *Visuddhi-Magga* chapter XVII, translator Warren, *Buddhism in Translations*, p. 238.
46 Verdu, *Early Buddhist Philosophy in the Light of the Four Noble Truths*, p. 70.
47 Richard Gombrich, *How Buddhism Began: The conditioned genesis of the early teachings* (London and Atlantic Highlands, New Jersey: Athlone, 1996), p. 51.

48 Maria Heim, *The Forerunner of All Things: Buddhaghosa on mind, intention, and agency* (Oxford and New York: Oxford University Press, 2014), p. 221.
49 *Ibid.*, p. 105.
50 Peter Harvey, *The Selfless Mind: Personality, consciousness and nirvana in early Buddhism* (Richmond, Surrey: Curzon Press, 1995), p. 115.
51 Rupert Gethin, *The Foundations of Buddhism* (Oxford and New York: Oxford University Press, 1998), p. 144.
52 Macy, *Mutual Causality in Buddhism and General Systems Theory*, p. 48.
53 Payutto, *Dependent Origination*, p. 62.
54 Bhikkhu Bodhi, *The Great Discourse on Causation*, pp. 18–19.
55 Harvey, *The Selfless Mind*, p. 76.
56 Gethin, *The Foundations of Buddhism*, p. 126.
57 *Ibid.*, p. 132.
58 Gethin, *The Foundations of Buddhism*, p. 142.
59 *Ibid.*, p. 143.
60 *Ibid.*, pp. 143–4.
61 M O' C. Walshe, *Buddhism and Death* (Kandy, Sri Lanka: Buddhist Publication Society, 1978), p. 23.
62 Nyanaponika Thera, "Reflections on Kamma and its Fruit", in *Kamma and its Fruit*, p. 119.

6 The Fourth Noble Truth: The Noble Eightfold Path

1 See Jeaneane Fowler, "Spirituality" in Andrew Copson and A. C. Grayling, eds., *The Wiley Blackwell Handbook of Humanism* (Chichester, West Sussex: Wiley Blackwell, 2015), p. 348.
2 *Ibid.*, p. 356.
3 Rupert Gethin, *The Foundations of Buddhism* (Oxford and New York: Oxford University Press, 1998), p. 166.
4 Bhikkhu Bodhi, *The Noble Eightfold Path* (Kandy, Sri Lanka: Buddhist Publication Society, 1984), p. 1.
5 Thera Piyadassi, *The Buddha's Ancient Path* (Sri Lanka, 1987 edn of original UK: Rider and Company edn, 1964), p. 79.
6 *Ibid.*, p. 143.
7 Gethin, *The Foundations of Buddhism*, p. 164.
8 Bhikkhu Bodhi, *The Noble Eightfold Path*, p. 14.
9 *Anguttara Nikaya* III, 33, cited in Ledi Sayadaw, *The Noble Eightfold Path and its Factors Explained* (Kandy, Sri Lanka: Buddhist Publication Society, 1985 reprint of 1977 edn), p. 6.
10 Nyanaponika Thera, "Reflections on Kamma and its Fruit" in *Kamma and its Fruit*, collected essays (Kandy, Sri Lanka: Buddhist Publication Society, 1975), p. 120.
11 See Jeaneane Fowler, *Causality: Macrocosmic and microcosmic theories of cause and effect in belief systems* (Eastbourne and Chicago: Sussex Academic Press, 2020), pp. 327–8.

12. Bhikkhu Bodhi, *The Noble Eightfold Path*, p. 30.
13. Gianluca Vialli, *Goals: Inspirational stories to help tackle life's challenges*, translated by Gabriele Marcotti (London: Headline, 2020), p. 132.
14. *Ibid.* p. 225.
15. Bhikkhu Bodhi, *The Noble Eightfold Path*, p. 44.
16. See *ibid.*, p. 47.
17. Vialli, *Goals*, p. 118.
18. Richard Horton, *The COVID-19 Catastrophe: What's gone wrong and how to stop it happening again* (Cambridge: Polity Press, 2020), pp. 38–9.
19. See Michael B. A. Oldstone, *Viruses, Plagues, & History: Past, Present, and Future* (Oxford: Oxford University Press, revised and updated edn 2010), pp. 276–8.
20. Horton, *The COVID-19 Catastrophe*, pp. 78–81.
21. *Ibid.*, p. 50.
22. Piyadassi, *The Buddha's Ancient Path*, p. 143.
23. *Suttanipata* 705.
24. Piyadassi, *The Buddha's Ancient Path*, p. 147.
25. Dorothy H. Crawford, *Deadly Companions: How microbes shaped our history* (Oxford: Oxford University Press, 2018 second edn, first published 2007), p. 189.
26. Jane Goodall and Marc Bekoff, *The Ten Trusts: What we must do to care for the animals we love* (New York: HarperOne, 2003), p. 97.
27. *Ibid.*, Contents page.
28. *Ibid.*, p. 182.
29. See Damien Keown, *Buddhism: A very short introduction* (Oxford and New York: Oxford University Press, 1996), pp. 108–9.
30. Sangharakshita, *The Ten Pillars of Buddhism* (Glasgow: Windhorse Publications, 1989 reprint of 1984 edn), p. 67.
31. Sayadaw, *The Noble Eightfold Path and its Factors Explained*, p. 50.
32. Vialli, *Goals*, p. xiii.
33. *Ibid.*, p. 14.
34. Cited in Piyadassi, *The Buddha's Ancient Path*, pp. 174–5.

7 The Noble Eightfold Path: Mindfulness and Concentration

1. Ajahn Sumedho, *Mindfulness: The path to the deathless* (Hemel Hempstead: Amaravati Publications, 1985), p. 19.
2. *Anguttara-nikaya* II, 177 translated here by Thera Piyadassi, *The Buddha's Ancient Path* (1987 reprint of 1974 Sri Lankan edn, first published by Rider & Company, 1964), p. 198.
3. Sumedho, *Mindfulness*, p. 19.
4. Jeremy Paxman, *Saga*, June 2020, p. 11.
5. Piyadassi, *The Buddha's Ancient Path*, pp. 200–1.
6. Rupert Gethin, *The Foundations of Buddhism* (Oxford and New York: Oxford University Press, 1998), p. 174.

7   Damien Keown, *Buddhism: A very short introduction* (Oxford and New York: Oxford University Press, 1996), p. 88.
8   Edward Conze, *The Way of Wisdom: The five faculties* (Kandy, Sri Lanka: Buddhist Publication Society, 1980), p. 14.
9   *Samyutta-nikaya* V, 115 translator Piyadassi, *The Buddha's Ancient Path*, p. 183.
10 Bhikkhu Bodhi, *The Noble Eightfold Path* (Kandy, Sri Lanka: Buddhist Publication Society, 1984), p. 84.
11 *Ibid.*, p. 86.
12 Mihalyi Csikszentmihalyi, *Flow: The psychology of optimal experience* (New York: HarperPerennial, 1990), p. 64.
13 *Satipatthana-sutta* I, 8 translated here by Walpola Rahula, *What the Buddha Taught* (London and Bedford: Gordon Frazer, 1982 reprint of second enlarged edn 1967, first published 1959), p. 97.
14 Conze, *The Way of Wisdom*, p. 13.
15 See Jeaneane Fowler, "Spirituality" in Andrew Copson and A. C. Grayling eds., *The Wiley Blackwell Handbook of Humanism* (Chichester, West Sussex: Wiley Blackwell, 2015), p. 356.
16 Bhikkhu Bodhi, *The Noble Eightfold Path*, p. 90.
17 Rahula, *What the Buddha Taught*, p. 70.
18 *Ibid.*, p. 71.
19 *Ibid.*, p. 72.
20 Bhikkhu Bodhi, *The Noble Eightfold Path*, p. 97.
21 Rahula, *What the Buddha Taught*, p. 73.
22 Keown, *Buddhism*, p. 100.
23 Rahula, *What the Buddha Taught*, p. 73.
24 *Dhammapada* 35 translator Valerie J. Roebuck, *The Dhammapada* (London and New York: Penguin Books, 2010), p. 9.
25 Sumedho, *Mindfulness*, p. 49.
26 Damien Keown, *The Nature of Buddhist Ethics* (Basingstoke, Hampshire: Macmillan, 1992), p. 76.
27 Piyadassi, *The Buddha's Ancient Path*, p. 197.
28 *Ibid.*, p. 84.
29 Conze, *The Way of Wisdom*, p. 104.
30 Bhikkhu Bodhi, *The Noble Eightfold Path*, p. 21.
31 Csikszentmihalyi, *Flow*, p. 64.
32 Ursula King, "Women's Contribution to Contemporary Spirituality". In *Teaching Spirituality*, The Way Supplement 84(1995), p. 30.
33 Csikszentmihalyi, *Flow*, p. 3.
34 *Ibid.*, p. 4.
35 *Ibid.*, pp. 88 and 106.
36 Daniel Goleman, *Emotional Intelligence* (London: Bloomsbury, 1996), p. 92.
37 See Jeaneane Fowler, *Pathways to Immortality: An introduction to the philosophy and religion of Taoism* (Brighton, Sussex and Portland, Oregon: Sussex Academic Press, 2005), pp. 119–124.

38 I am immensely grateful to Dr Meirion B. Llewelyn, Consultant Physician General Medicine/Infectious Diseases in the Aneurin Bevan Health Board for providing me with the relevant data on neuroscience that informs this section of the chapter.
39 Britta K. Hölzel, James Carmody *et al.* "Stress Reduction Correlates with Structural Changes in the Amygdala", SCAN 5(2010), pp. 11–17.
40 *Ibid.*, p. 15.
41 Sara W. Lazar, Catherine E. Kerr *et al.*, "Meditation Experience is Associated with Increased Cortical Thickness", NIH Public Access Author Manuscript, February 6, 2006.
42 *Ibid.*, p. 1.
43 F. Zeidan, K. T. Martucci, R. A. Kraft, N. S. Gordon, J. G. McHaffie and R. C. Coghill, "Brain Mechanisms Supporting Modulation of Pain by Mindfulness Meditation", NIH Public Access Author Manuscript, October 6, 2011.
44 *Ibid.*, pp. 1–2.
45 In medical terms, the authors put it this way: "Because meditation likely alters pain by enhancing cognitive control and reframing the contextual evaluation of nociceptive [sensations of noxious stimuli associated with injury or threatened injury such as heat, pain or cold] information, the constellation of interactions between expectations, emotions, and cognitive appraisals intrinsic to the construction of the sensory experience can be regulated by the meta-cognitive ability to non-judgmentally sustain focus on the present moment." *Ibid.*, p. 11.
46 "Integrative Body–Mind Training (IBMT) Meditation Found to Boost Brain Connectivity", *Science Daily*, August 18, 2010.
47 "The technique also reduces activity in the thalamus and the medial occipital lobe, apparently related to withdrawal of the mind from sensory processing, and it reduces hippocampal activity, related to reduced mental processing of short-term into long-term memory. Respiratory rate and plasma lactate decrease and basal skin resistance increases, indicating a state of psychophysiological quiescence during which the endogenous sources of pain could resolve via the action of homeostatic mechanisms." David W. Orme Johnson *et al.*, "Neuroimaging of Meditation's Effect on Brain Reactivity to Pain", NIH Public Access Author Manuscript, January 2, 2008, p. 2.
48 Piyadassi, *The Buddha's Ancient Path*, pp. 199–200.
49 Sumedho, *Mindfulness*, p. 55.
50 *Ibid.*, p. 32.
51 Gethin, *The Foundations of Buddhism*, p. 189.
52 *Ibid.*
53 *Ibid.*, p. 190.
54 Sumedho, *Mindfulness*, p. 52.
55 Bhikkhu Bodhi, *The Noble Eightfold Path*, p. 27.
56 Piyadassi, *The Buddha's Ancient Path*, p. 202.

57 Sumedho, *Mindfulness*, p. 49.
58 *Dhammapada* 275.

8 The *Brahma-vihara*: Love, Compassion, Sympathetic Joy, Equanimity

1   Francis Story, "Karma and Freedom" in *Kamma and its Fruit* (Kandy, Sri Lanka: Buddhist Publication Society, 1975), p. 105.
2   *Ibid.*
3   Bhikkhu Bodhi, *The Noble Eightfold Path* (Kandy, Sri Lanka: Buddhist Publication Society, 1984), pp. 38–9.
4   *Ibid.*, p. 38.
5   Buddhist Publication Society, *The Three Basic Facts of Existence III Egolessness* (Kandy, Sri Lanka: Buddhist Publication Society, 1984 reprint of 1974 edn), p. 35.
6   Hammalawa Saddhatissa, *Buddhist Ethics* (London: Wisdom Publications, 1987, first published by George Allen & Unwin in 1970), p. 81 adapted from Bhikkhu Nanamoli's *The Path of Purification*.
7   *Ibid.*, p. 82.
8   Ajahn Sumedho, *Mindfulness, The path to the deathless* (Hemel Hempstead: Amaravati Publications, 1987, first published 1985), p. 57.
9   *Suttanipata*, here translated by Saddhatissa, *Buddhist Ethics*, p. 78.
10 Sumedho, *Mindfulness*, p. 38.
11 Nyanaponika Maha Thera, *The Four Sublime States* (Kandy, Sri Lanka: Buddhist Publication Society, 1980 reprint of 1958 edn), p. 11.
12 Thera Piyadassi, *The Buddha's Ancient Path* (1987 reprint of 1974 Sri Lankan edn, first published by Rider & Company, 1964), p. 119.
13 Nyanaponika, *The Four Sublime States*, p. 11.
14 Piyadassi, *The Buddha's Ancient Path*, p. 120.
15 *Ibid.*, p. 123.
16 *Ibid.*
17 Bhikkhu Bodhi, *The Noble Eightfold Path*, p. 42.
18 Piyadassi, *The Buddha's Ancient Path*, p. 81.
19 Nyanaponika, *The Four Sublime States*, p. 13.
20 *Ibid.*
21 *Ibid.*, p. 15.
22 Piyadassi, *The Buddha's Ancient Path*, p. 223.
23 Cited by Nyanaponika, *The Four Sublime States*, p. 24.
24 Dorothy H. Crawford, *Viruses: A very short introduction* (Oxford: Oxford University Press, 2018, first published 2011), p. 48.
25 Dorothy H. Crawford, *Deadly Companions: How microbes shaped our history* (Oxford: Oxford University Press, 2018 second edn, first published 2007), p. 184.
26 Christopher Wills, *Plagues: Their Origin, history and future* (London: HarperCollins, 1996), p. 7.
27 *Ibid.*, p. 26.
28 Dorothy H. Crawford, *The Invisible Enemy: A natural history of viruses*

(Oxford: Oxford University Press, 2009, first published 2000), p. 231.
29 Christian W. McMillen, *Pandemics: A very short introduction* (Oxford: Oxford University Press, 2016), p. 4.
30 See Jonathan Quick with Bronwen Fryer, *The End of Epidemics: The looming threat to humanity and how to stop it* (Melbourne and London: Scribe, 2018), p. 35.
31 *Ibid.*, p. 37.
32 Crawford, *Deadly Companions*, p. 189.
33 Michael Oldstone, *Viruses, Plagues, & History: Past, present, and future* (Oxford: Oxford University Press, 2010), p. 342.

Epilogue

1   Muge Cevik, Krutika Kuppalli, Jason Kindrachuk, Malik Peiris, "Virology, Transmission, and Pathogenisis of SARS–CoV-2". In *British Medical Journal*, BMJ2020:471:m3862doi:10.1136/bmj.m3862, p. 1.
2   *Ibid.*
3   *Ibid.*, p. 3.
4   Nature.com/articles/d41586-020-03326-w
5   See bbc.co.uk/news/health-55040635 for clear diagrammatic explanation of the process.
6   See bmj./com/content/369/bmj.m2184
7   Cevik, Kuppalli, Kindrachuk and Perris, "Virology, Transmission, and Pathogenisis of SARS-CoV-2", p. 5.
8   See Gregory A. Poland, Inna Ovsyannikova and Richard Kennedy, "SARS-CoV-2 Immunity: Review and Applications to Phase 3 Vaccine Candidates". In www.thelancet.com vol. 396, November 14 2020, p. 1595.
9   *Ibid.*, p.1597.
10 *Ibid.* p. 1600.
11 Kamran Abbasi, "Covid-19: Politicisation, 'Corruption', and Suppression of Science". In *BMJ2020:371:m4425*
12 Independent.co.uk/news/health/mink=fur-farm-covid-foxes-raccoon-dogs-b1759223.html
13 *Ibid.*, pp. 2–3.
14 Nyanaponika Maha Thera, *The Four Sublime States* (Kandy, Sri Lanka: Buddhist Publication Society, 1980 reprint of 1958 edn), p. 11.
15 The film, *David Attenborough: "A Life on our Planet"* produced by Silverback Films and WWF is available to watch in cinemas, and globally via Netflix.

Further Reading

There are two **primary sources on Buddhism** I would recommend to the reader. The first is Edward Conze's *Buddhist Scriptures* published by Penguin Books (London and New York). It is an old book, published in 1959, but for a newcomer to Buddhism, Conze's translations are particularly good and, as he said himself in the *Introduction* to the book (p. 11): "This selection . . . concentrates on the central tradition of Buddhism, at the expense of the more peripheral developments, on that which is common rather than that which separates. It contains very little that any Buddhist, of whichever school, would be prepared to reject." A different text by Valerie J. Roebuck, is a superb translation of *The Dhammapada*, a much-loved Buddhist text coming from the earliest times. It is written in verse form reflecting on the sayings of the Buddha that were remembered orally amongst his followers before being committed to written form. *The Dhammapada* is also published by Penguin Books and was first issued in Penguin Classics in 2010.

Secondary sources on Buddhism are very numerous and I want to mention just a few here that I think would be relevant to the content of this book. *Buddhist Thought*, written by Paul Williams with Anthony Tribe contributing the chapter on Tantra, is, as its subtitle suggests, *A complete Introduction to the Indian Tradition* (London and New York: Routledge, 2000). Williams extends this study of Buddhism beyond the earlier teachings of the Buddha to encompass the Mahayana branches of Buddhism. Concentrated more on early Buddhism, Rupert Gethin's *The Foundations of Buddhism* (Oxford and New York: Oxford University Press, 1998), is very relevant to the content of the present book and is an excellent and clear exposition of the teachings of the Buddha. A classic book on early Buddhism is Walpola Rahula's *What the Buddha Taught* (London and Bedford: The Gordon Fraser Gallery Ltd.). It was first published in 1959 and the 1982 edition I have is a reprint of the second and enlarged edition of 1967. Rahula covered the Four Noble Truths extensively with translation of selected texts at the end of the book. If no other further reading were to be undertaken except for this one book, the reader would glean a good deal. A clearly written text is Damien Keown's *Buddhism: A very short introduction* published in 1996 by Oxford University Press (Oxford and London). This is more of a general book on Buddhism but it covers the Four Noble Truths with clarity. The Buddhist Publication Society has a whole series of small books that are invaluable for early Buddhism. They are now published by Wheel Publications and a full list of them is available at accesstoinsight.org/lib/bpslist.html

In the context of the coronavirus there are several studies related to virology that are important for the understanding of the nature of viruses. An outstanding writer in this field is Dorothy Crawford. Her works are immensely important in that they demonstrate so well how viruses cause pandemics because of human failures. In *Deadly Companions: How microbes shaped our history* (Oxford: Oxford University Press, 2018 second edition, first published 2007), Crawford traces the origins of viruses and explains how and why they invade humans. The characteristics of viruses and their relation to humanity are the main subjects of her *The Invisible Enemy: A natural history of viruses* (Oxford: Oxford University Press, 2009, first published 2000). A slightly more technical book is Crawford's *Viruses: A very short introduction* (Oxford and New York: Oxford University Press, 2018 second edition, first published 2011). A very good book indeed is Carl Zimmer's *A Planet of Viruses* (Chicago and London: University of Chicago Press, 2015, first published 2011). The book is very well written and has superb colour illustrations throughout. Many of the books on viruses deal with epidemics and pandemics that have plagued humanity for some time and Michael B. A. Oldstone does just that in his *Viruses, Plagues, & History: Past, present, and future*. It was published in 2010 by Oxford University Press in Oxford. All the major viral infections are dealt with in his book.

A remarkable book, *The End of Epidemics: The looming threat to humanity and how to stop it* (London and Melbourne: Scribe) was written, as its 2018 date suggests, well before the outbreak of Covid-19. Its author, Jonathan Quick, is a powerful and convincing writer who could not have known that the threat of a pandemic was just around the corner, though he knew that scenario was inevitable. His style of writing is passionate and forceful and, crucially, convincing, with carefully presented evidence. Despite being published pre-Covid, this book is important for what it says about the present and what it hopes for in the future. One very critical book that was written shortly after the present Covid-19 pandemic spread throughout the world is by Richard Horton, current editor of *The Lancet* medical journal. Horton is very critical of the ways in which governments have responded to the pandemic and pulls no punches in his quite stringent castigations of some of them: but he is fair and honest in citing mistakes, lies, and misinformation. His book, *The COVID-19 Catastrophe: What's gone wrong and how to stop it happening again*, is published in Cambridge by Polity Press and its date of publication, 2020, is indicative of its relevance to the present day. For the general reader in particular, Michael Mosley's short book *COVID-19: What you need to know about the Coronavirus and the race for the vaccine* (London: Short Books, 2020) is informative about the nature of the virus, its infection and its treatment. The work of Jane Goodall is outstanding in a battle for the health of the planet. Her book written with Marc Bekoff, *The Ten Trusts: What we must do to care for the animals we love* (New York: HarperOne, 2003), despite being written almost twenty years ago, demonstrates sadly that we have not come far enough in our efforts.

There are two films that I would strongly recommend the reader to watch. Both are remarkably accurate in their portrayal of virus pandemics and remarkably prescient in relation to the one we are presently experiencing. They are *Contagion*, produced in 2011, and *Outbreak* produced in the previous year, 2010. Finally, the internet is providing extensive information on the pandemic but it is important to access material that is verifiably accurate. The World Health Organization, the WHO, provides regular information at www.who.int/covid-19 and who.int/emergencies/diseases/novel-coronavirus-2019

Index

abortion, 156, 159
abstention, from taking life, 4–5, 143, 155, **155–9**, 219; from falsehood, 143, 217, 219; from sexual misconduct, 143, 155, 160; from taking what is not given, 143, 155, **159–60**; from intoxicating liquor, 143, 161
actions, 119, 134, 136, 145, 147, 150, 154, 155, 171, 192, 204; of body, speech and mind, 1, 3, 80–1, 122, 124, 124–5, 134, 138, 139, 142, 145, 149, 171, 192; wholesome/good, 94, 127, 138, 139, 147, 149, 154, 155, 161; unwholesome, 94, 116, 150, 155, 156, 160; *and* intention, 124–5 *see also* Noble Eightfold Path, right action
Africa, 45, 46, 47, 49, 100, 101, 102, 208, 214
afterlife, 89, 129
ageing, 201 *and* death, **120**, 121
AIDS/acquired immunodeficiency syndrome, 33, 38, **45–8**, 74, 101 *see also* HIV
anger, 73, 78, 90, 126, 145, 153, 170, 172, 177, 178, 195, 196, 197
animals, 16, 20, 21, 35, **157–9**, 192, 197, 202, **205**, 209; adverse human interaction with, 5, 16, 17, 18, 23, 24, 29, 33, 38, 39, 40, 45, 48, 50, 51, 66, 100, 174, 157–9, 161, **205–6**, 209, 220; domestication of, 205, 206; extinction of, 79, 206; factories/farms for, 5, 99–100, 147, 157, 206, 209, **218–19**; for scientific research, 157, 158, 161; illegal trade of wild, 58, 66, 157; live animal markets, 5, 34, 41, 51–2, 52, 58, 59, 66, 157, 217, 218; mink farms, **218–19**; trade of exotic, 66, 157

annihilationism, 11, 68, 69, 89, 90, 133
Antarctica, 22
arahats, 10
asceticism/ascetics, 9, 11, 67, 141
Ashvaghosha, 6–7
attachment, 87, 92, 93, 118, **119**, 120, 164, 176, 191–2; non-/detachment, 110, 113, 126, 131–2, 143, 145, 163–4, 164, 176, 181, 187, 192
Attenborough, David, 104, 197, 219
aversion, 3, 78, 87, 90, 145, 147, 164, 170, 176, 177, 178, 179, 182, 186, 187, 189, 192, 196, 204, 205, 216 *see also* hatred *and* desire and aversion

bacteria, 16, 18, 19, 20, 21, **25–6**, 27, 29, 33, 35, 36, 37; marine, 38; single-celled, 21
balance, 189, 204; of mind, 180, 203; of humanity and nature, 5, 100, 206
BAME/people of black, Asian and minority ethnic race, 56, 207, 208
Beasley, David, 197
Biden, Joe, 103–4, 217
biochemical weapons, 39, 64
birth, 70, 119, **119–20**, 121, 123 *and* death, 113, 166
bodhi tree, 9, 11
body, 80, 107, 110, 117, 166, 171, 172, 175, 175, 185, 187–8; *and* mind, **80–2**, 85, 89, 90, 115, 115, 125, 146, **166–9**, 172, 173–4, 180 *see also* mind
Bono, 197
Brahma, 191
Brahma-vihara, **191–205**; love/lovingkindness/*metta*, 5, 105, 126, 192, **193–8**; compassion/*karuna*, 5,

198–202; sympathetic joy/*mudita*, 5, 192, **202–3**; equanimity/*upekkha*, 5, **203–5**
brain, 79, **80–2**, 108, 148, 150, 179, 184–5, **184–6**; neurons, 80–2, 108, 148, 150, 184–5
Brazil, 45, 101, 208, 214
breath/breathing, 170, 173, **174–6**, 185, 187–8
Buddha, 1, 2, 3, 4, **6–13**, **67–71**, 72, 77, 78, 79, 80, 82, 83, 84, 85, 86, 88, 89, 90, 91, 92, 93, 94, 95, 96, 97, 98, 105, 107, 110, 111, 112, 113, 114, 115, 117, 119, 121, 122, 123, 124, 127, 128, 130, 131, 132, 133, 134, 135, 137, 139, 140, 141, 142, 143, 144, 145, 146, 150, 153, 154, 155, 156, 160, 161, 162, 164, 166, 167, 171, 177, 178, 180, 182, 183, 187, 189, 190, 191, 196, 199, 203, 204, 205, 207, 210, 219, 219–20; awakening/enlightenment of, 9–10, 11, 12, 13, 112, 132, 137, 166; hagiography, 6–7, 11
Buddhacarita, 6–7
Buddhism, early, 3, 3–5, **67–72**, 77–9, 80–5, 100, 101, **105–11**, **112–29**, **131–9**, **140–6**, 146– 7, **147–51**, **153–6**, **159–61**, 163–4, 166–7, **169–83**, **187–90**, **194–9**, **202–5**, 216, 219, 219–20; Mahayana, 11; Theravada, 1, 11–12, 69, 133, 156, 175, 193

calm/calmness, 169, 170, 177, 179, 180, 181, 186, 189, 194; in meditation, 170, **172–9**; of mind, 113, 164, 170, **172–9**, 180, 188, 195, 196
care homes, 75, 104, 194, 199, 200; The Cedars, Chepstow, x, 194, 200
carers, 71, 194, 199
causes, **86–111**, 113, **124–9**, 134, 135, 139, 145; connectivity/continuity of, 109, 134, 135, **137–8**; impermanence of, 97, 109, 134, 135, **137–8**; interrelation/interconnection of, 91, 105, 119, 128; momentary, 91, 93, 97, 106, 107, 109; *and* effects, 97, 107, 109, 112, **114–29**, 133, 134, 135, 144, 145, 148
Cave of Crystals, 22
cells, 15, 19, 22, 23, 30, 60, 157, 215; nuclei of 19; cellular ancestor, 20; cellular life, 20, 22; multicellular organisms, 20, 21; single-cell organisms, 19, 20
cessation, *nirodha*, **112–39**
change/transience, 78, 80, 82, 83, **85–6**, 87, 90, 93, 93–4, 94, 97, 105, 107, 109, 117, 118, 122, 129, 131, 135, 136, 139, 144, 144–5, 145, 146, 147, 148, 149, 164, 201; in the mind, 121, 171–2, 172, 177, 183, 192, 194, 204, 205, 207, 208–9
Cheltenham Gold Cup, 104, 218
chicken pox/shingles, 23, **43–4**
China, 34, 42, 43, 51–2, 54, 57–8, 64, 66, 76, 101, 102, 151, 152, 157, 201–2, 217, 218, 219
choice, 113, 118, 127, 128 129, 134, 136, 163, 164
climate/climate change, 16, 18, 44, 207
clinging, 87, 118, **119**, 178, 196
Coles, Reverend Richard, 129–30
compassion/*karuna*, 5, 12, 127, 143, 148, 150, 155, **198–202** *see also* Brahma-vihara
Concentrated Animal Feeding Operations/CAFOs, 43, 99–100
concentration, *samadhi*, 5, 94, 141, 145, 149, 164, **179–83**, **191–205**
conditioning/conditionality, 69, 78, 82, 83, 84, 85, 88, 90, 91, 93, 96, 97, 106, 109, 113, 116, 122, 128, 167, 169, 170, 188, 205; of all things, 12, 69, 113, **114–29**, 121, 122, 123–4, 144
consciousness, **80–2**, **83–4**, 85, 90, 105, 106, 109, 109–10, 115, **115–17**, 117, 118, 119, 121, 123, 135–6, 136, 138, 145, 164, 170, 171; absorption of, 180, 181, 184, 192; ego, 68; in meditation, 171, 182, 183, 184, 188, 189; between lives, 131, 132, 134, 136; stream of, 135–6, 136, 138, 139
Contagion, 64, 73
coronaviruses, 3, 17, 22, 24, 25, 28, 32, 33, 40–1, **51–66**, 211–12, 216; colds, 33, 37, 38, 40, 40–1,

coronaviruses *(continued)*
    51, 57, 213, 215; MERS, 39, 53, 216; SARS, 39, 51–3, 211, 216
coronavirus Covid-19, 1, 2, 3, 4, 5, 8, 16, 17–18, 18, 29, 42, 51, 52, 53, 54–66, 69, 70, 72–7, 78–9, 79, 98–100, 101, **101–5**, 127, **129–30**, 147, **151–3**, 157, **157–9**, **161–3**, 164–5, 167–8, 193–4, **199–202**, 205–9, **210–20**; as RNA virus, 55, 211, 212; asymptomatic cases, 29, 59, 64, 211, 212–13, 213; characteristics, **55–7**; common symptoms, 57, 211; genetic blueprint for, 58–9, 212; glycoprotein spikes of, 55, 63, 211, 211–12, 213, **214–15**, 216; long-Covid, 76, 213; mutations, 57, 211–12; sources and causes, **57–9**
cosmos, 12–13, 21, 123, 137
craving, 3, **86–111**, 112, 113, **118–19**, 121, 125, 131, 133, 145, 155, 159, 163–4, 167, 191–2, 199, 205; three forms of **88–90**
Creutzfeldt-Jakob (mad cow) disease, 50, 74, 99

death/deaths, 4, 8–9, 38, 52, 54, 55, 70, 71, 72, 73, 74, 75, 76, 77, 85, 92, 97, 103, 104, 113, 120, 121, 123, **129–32**, 133, 142, 145, 201, 208, 210–11, 215 *and* rebirth, 123, **132–9**
deforestation, 18, 44, 66, 79, 100, 104–5, 147, 205–6, 206, 208, 209; for animal feeds, 209
delusion/stupidity, 4, 6, 8, 69, 98, 100, **101–5**, 106, 106–7, 109, 110, 113, 115, 119, 126, 143, 145, 147, 148, 152, 164, 170, 176, 177, 182, 192, 204, 207, 216, 217, 218, 218–19, 220
dengue fever, 33
Denmark, 211–12, **218–19**
deoxyribonucleic acid/DNA, 19, 20, 21, 22, 26, 28, 36, 38, 55, 59–60
Dependent Origination, 2, 4, 13, 113, **114–24**, 132, 133, 134, 135, 139; ignorance, **115**; volitions/formations, **115–6**; consciousness/discrimination, **116–17**; name and form/mind/body/matter, **117**; six senses, **117–18**; sense contact, **118**; feeling/sensation **118**, 118–19; craving/thirst/desire, **118–19**; grasping/clinging/attachment, **119**; becoming/existence, **119**; birth, **119–20**; ageing and death, **120**
deprivation, 56, 60, 76, 197
desires, 3, 4, 9, 77–8, 83, 84, 86–7, 87, 87–8, 88, 89, 90, 91, 92, 95, 101, 110, 112, 113, 115, 117, **115–19**, 120, 125, 131, 143, 145, 147, 159, 164, 176, 177, 178, 179, 182, 186, 188–9, 189, 191–2, 192, 198, 204, 205, 207, 220; wholesome/good, 94; unwholesome, 86–7; *and* aversion, 77–8; 83, 88, 94, 135–6, 138
Dhamma, 3, 9, 10–11, **12–13**, **67–71**, 71, 96, 114, 121, 139, 141, 143, 144, 155, 188, 190, 191, 203, 204–5
dhammas/phenomena, 69, 121, 122, 123, 133, 134, 135, 167, 186
Diamond Princess, 59
diphtheria, 24
disease, 69–70, 70, 77, 79, 85
dis-ease, 69–70, 77, 79, 85
disinformation, **151–2**
dispositions, 135–6, 136; wholesome, 116; unwholesome, 116
domestic violence, 73
doubt, 143
drugs, antibacterial, 25–6; antibiotics, 26; antiretroviral; 46, 48; antiviral, 28, 46, 48, **61–2**; BCG, 63; dexamethasone, 62; hydroxychloroquine, 62; monoclonal antibodies, 62; penicillin, 25; remdesivir, 62; ritonavir, 61
dukkha see suffering

Ebola virus, 27, 33, 34, 38, **49**, 61–2, 74, 101
economic injustice/deprivation, 70, 72, 73, 147, 207, 209
ecosystems, 3, 121, 36, 37, 100, 205
ego/egoism, 68, 84, 101, 105, 107, 110, 113, 115, 117, 119, 133, 139, 164, 175; non-, 110, 111, 113, 154, 180; *see also* self
emotions, 87, 143, 170, 177, 184–5, 185, 185–6, 187, 197, 203
empathy, 140

emptiness, *shunyata*, 180, 187
enlightenment, 67, 113, 132, 137, 145, 167, 179, 183, 204
environment, influences, 78, 127, 138; human assault on, 24, 206
epidemic(s), 16, 17–18, 24, 25, 29, 32, 33, 49, 52, 73
equanimity, 5, 12, 113, 140, 163, 179, 180, 181, 192, **203–5**
eternalism, 11, 89, 90, 133
eukaryotes, 19, 21
evil, 83, 94, 124, 126, 127, 155, 192 *and* suffering, 13
evolution, 13, 16, 17, 20, 22, 23, 35, 37, 38, 209 *and* involution, 13, 123
extremophiles, 21

face masks, 74–5, 197, 208, 211
fake news, 15, 153
fear, 72, 78–9, 92, 100, 113, 118, 129, 131, 151, 180, 187, 197, 189, 196, 202, 205
feelings, 83, 93–4, 109, 118, 118–19, 170, 178, 181, 182, 187
filth, 39
Fire Sermon, 88
Five Aggregates, 3, 68, 70, 80, **82–4**, 93, 96, 107, 109, 110, 113, 115, 116, 118, 120, 122, 126, 131, 135, 136, 138, 139, 144, 146, 148, 176, 179, 188; (i) matter, 82, 97; (ii) sensations/feelings, 83, 93–4; (iii) perceptions, 83; (iv) mental formations, 83, 93; (v) consciousness, **83–4**
Five Hindrances, **177–9**; (i) desire, 178 *see also* desires; (i) aversion, 178 *see also* aversion; (iii) dullness, 178; (iv) restlessness, 188; (v) doubt, 188–9
Five Precepts, 143, 155, 161
Floyd, George, 145, 162
four causes of existence, **90–1**; (i) nutrition, 90; (ii) sensory perception, 90; (iii) consciousness, 90; (iv) volition, **90–1**
Four Noble Truths, 1, 3, **67–77**, 86, 114, 115, 118, 121, 139, 145, 179, 186, 188, 189, 190, 192, 199, 201; (i) suffering, 1, 67–85, 203; (ii) cause of suffering, 1, 3–4, 67–85, 203; (iii) cessation of suffering, 1, 4, **112–39**; (iv) the path for the cessation of suffering, 1, 4–5, **140–90**
foxes, 219
freedom/free will, 113, 128, 136, 142–3, 190; of speech, 151
friendliness, 126, 148, 192
front-line hospital staff, 193, 198, 199, 200, 202, 203
funerals, 130

Gates, Bill, 197
generosity, 73, 94, 105, 127, 145, 148, 192, 194, 200, 202
genomes/genes, 15–16, 17, 20, 22, 24, 27, 28, 31, 46, 78, 127, 138; chromosomes, 36; diversity, 23; mRNA, 213; mutations, 23 *see also* viruses, mutations
gentleness, 150, 192
global warming, 23, 44, 45, 79, 147, 207, 217
Goodall, Jane, 158–9
good and evil, 124, 125, 126, 127, 139, 145, 186, 192
goodness, 140, 149
Grangetown, 208
grasping, 87, **119**
greed/desire, 4, 68, 83, 86, 87, 91, **98–100**, 100–1, 101, 105, 113, 116, 126, 143, 145, 147, 148, 155, 157, 164, 167, 170, 201–2, 204, 209, 216–17; corporate, 4, **98–100**, 162

habits, 115, 125, 169, 180, 204, 205
Hanta viruses, 37, 50, 70–1
happiness, 3, 7, 67, 77–8, 78, 79, 80, 83, 84, 85, 87, 92, 93, 97, 98, 100, 107, 109, 110, 113, 149, 154, 164–5, 167, 172, 174, 179, 181, 190, 192, 194, 196, 202, 203, 204, 204–5 *and* pain, 189
Harding, Baroness Dido, 218
harmony, 149, 180; lack of, 206; *see also* balance
hatred/aversion, 4, 68, 83, 87, 98, 100–1, 113, 116, 118, 126, 143, 145, 147, 148, 164, 170, 192, 204 *see also* aversion
Heaven, 89, 129
herd immunity, 25, 61, 63, 104, 152–3
herpes viruses, 23, 27, 36, 43–4

HIV/human immunodeficiency syndrome, 27, 28, 29, 31, **45–8**
humanity/human beings, 3, 5, 15, 39, 66, 74, 78, 86, 87, 89, 90, 91, 92, 93, 96, 104, 105, 109, 141, 145, 146, 160, 162, 173, 191, 192, 197, 201, **205–9**; as cause of its own suffering, 5, 18, 39; as virus of the planet, 147, 206, 209, 220; decimation of peoples, 206; greed of, 98 see also greed; ecological harm of, 205, 206, 218, 219; interaction of, 25; land devastation of, 206; overcrowding of, 25, 39 see also population density; transitions in life styles, 23, 25, 38, 39, 40, 47, 50, 74
human folly/stupidity, 4, 18, 33, 100, 158, **205–9**, **218–20**
hunter-gatherers, 22–3, 23, 24, 43, 47, 50, 52, 205, 206, 207
hydrothermal vents, 15, 20
hyperthermophiles, 21

ignorance, 9, 83, 96, **115**, 116, 118, 119, 121, 126; of humanity, 205, 209, 216
immune system/immunity, 17, 18, 25, 28, 29, 31, 32, 36, 37, 38, 39, 41, 42, 43, 46, 47–8, 51, 54, 55, 57, **59–61**, 61, 62, 63, 64, 75, 213, 214, **215–16**; evolution of, 60; antibodies in, **60**, 213, 215; T-cells in, 60, 213, 215, **215–16**
impermanence, 2, 3, 4, 8, 13, 69, 70, 80, 82, 84, 87, 90, 93, 94, **94–7**, 106, 107, 110, 114, 121, 123, 126, 128, 131, 131–2, 133, 139, 144, 146, 148, 176, 182, 186, 187, 188, 189, 191, 204, 205
infection, 18, 25, 30, 33, 42, 43, 51, 53, 54–5, 55, 59, 60, 64, **210**, 212, 213–14, 215, 219
influenza/flu, 28, 29, 31, 33, 34, 38, **41–3**, 58, 74; Asian, 34, 38, 42; avian, 38; Hong Kong, 38, 42; Spanish, 32, 38, 42–3; swine, 32, 38, 42–3
insight, 142, 145; meditation/ *vipassana*, 146, 170, 185, **187–9**, 192
intentions, 125, 126, 128, 134, 135, 145, 146–7, 149, 150, 151, 152, 153, 155, 160, 199, 220, see also volition
intensive care units, 54, 75, 76, 203, 215
interconnection/interrelation, 114, 156, 189
internationalism, 201
Ireland, 218–19, 219

Jatakas, 132
jhanas, **181–2**, **191–205**
Johnson, Boris, 152, 217
joy, 150, 179, 192, 204

kamma, 2, 4, 13, 83, 90, 94, 113, 115, 117, 118, 119, 119–20, 120 121, 136, 137, 138, 139, 144, 145, 146, 146–7, 148, 150, 155, 159, 167; wholesome, 126, 127–8, 132, 138, 144–5, 145; unwholesome, 127, 132, 138, 144–5, 145; -*vipaka* **124–8**
kindness, 126, 138, 140, 148, 149–50, 200, 202; to oneself, 174, 177

Lake Limnopolar, 22
Lassa virus, 37, 38, **49**
last universal cellular ancestor/LUCA, **20–1**
liberation, 9, 96, 110, 112, 117, 118–19, 146
lockdown, 72, 73, 76, 79, 91, 95, 104, 130, 147, 160–1, 168, 171, 197, 200, 208
loneliness, 198
love/loving-kindness, 126, 140, 143, 145, 149–50, 201, 202, **193–8** see also Brahma-vihara

malaria, 24, 33
malnutrition, 45
mantras, 185
Mars, 21
measles, 24, 25, 27, 38–9, **40**, 98–9
meditation/mindfulness, 5, 9, 68, 112, 117, 118, 144, 146, 149, 154, 159, 163, 164, 165, **169–79**, 191, 192, 192–3, 194, **194–7**; body-mind training/IBMT, 185; effect on pain levels, 185, 186; for humanity, 193; on the body, **174–6**; on feelings, **176–7**; on the mind, **177–9**; magnetic resonance

imaging in, 184–5; mantras in, 175, 185; medical evidence for, **183–6**; moving, 175; one-pointedness, 171, 181, 182, 183; posture in, 174–5
memory, 82, 107–8
MERS *see* coronaviruses
Metta Sutta, 196, 198
microbes, 16, 23, 206; early, 19, 20, 21
Middle Way, 11, 89, 121, 133, 141, 161, 166
mind, 5, 12, 70–1, 83, 83–4, 88, 90, 91, 93, 95, 96, 109, 110, 113, 115, 116, 118, 121, 124–5, 125, 134–5, 135, 136, 141, 141–2, 145, 146, 147, **147–9**, 149, 154, 155, 160, 161, 163, 165, 167, 169, **169–72**, 174, **174–9**, 179, 179–83, 184, **187–9**, 190, 191–2, 192, 193, 194, 195, 196, 204; calm, 113, 164, 165, **173–9**; wholesome, 149, 163, 164, 169; unwholesome, 163–4, 164; *and* body, 5, **80–2**, 95, 116, 119, 135, 166, **166–9**, 188; *and* body, name and form, **117**
mink, **219**
misinformation, 151–2, 210, 215, 218
moments/momentariness, 87, 91, 93, 96, 97, 106, 107, 109, 114, 120, 122, 123, 126, 131–2, 135, 136, 138, 182, 188; continuity of, 87
monasticism, 11, 68, 154, 156, 166, 169, 172
monks and nuns, 10, 11, 17, 68, 112, 113, 118, 132, 142, 145, 146, 154, 156, 166, 169
morality, 124, 125, 126, 134, 138, 144, 145, **149–50**, 154, 155, 163, 166, 196
multicellular organisms, 22
mumps, 24

National Health Service/NHS, 152
nationalism, 201–2
natural selection, 20, 28, 36
nature/natural world, 5, 70, 74, 158, 197–8; balance of, 5; human harm to, 205, 219 *see also* animals
"new normal", **65–6**, 168, 178
Netherlands, 211–12, 219
New York, 74, 104, 153
nibbana, 4, 67, **68–9**, 90, 94, 112, **112–13**, 121, 132, 139, 141, 146, 154, 179–80, 189, 205
Noble Eightfold Path, 4–5, **140–90**, 196, 204; interdependence of parts, 141; right understanding/view, 142, 144, **144–6**, 155, 161, 186, 188; right thought/intention, **146–9**, 149, 151, 161, 216; right speech, 4, 144, **150–4**, 196, 210, 217, 218; right action, 4–5, 144, 149, **154–61**, 161, 186, 188; right livelihood, 5, 144, 149, **161–3**, 188, 219; right effort, 142, 142–3, 143, 144, 145, **161–3**, 166, 167, 171, 172; right meditation/mindfulness, 142, 144, 164, **169–79** medical evidence for **183–6**; right concentration, 144, **179–87**

oceans, 15, 16, 20, 22
old age, 7, 8–9, 71, 85, 92, 123, 129, 130, 201
optimal/flow experience, 171, 172, 180, 182, 183, 184, 186
oxygen, 19, 20, 75

pandemic(s), 1, 2, 3, 4, 5, 8, 15, 16, 17, 18, 32, 42, 43, 51, 52, 202, 207, 208, 209; Covid, 54, 58, 62, 63, 64, 65, 69, 73, 74, 101, 102, 103, 130, 142, 152, 153, 157, 163, 164, 197, 210, 216, 217, 218
papilloma virus, **44**
past lives, 115, 115–16, 118, 119, 120, 121, 126, 133, 137
Paxman, Jeremy, 168
personality, 1, 82, 93, 126, 128, 135, 135–6, 136, 148, 167–8, 169, 195–6, 204
personal protective equipment/PPE, 2, 75, 102–3, 152, 153, 197, 219
pharmaceutical companies, 99, **212–15**
planes of existence, 137
planet, 4–5, 18, 19, 21, 147, 197, 201, 202; abuse of, 105, 205, 206, 207, 208; deterioration/suffering of, 79, 85, 219; humanity as virus of, 5, 79, 157, 209, 220
plants, 16, 35
polio, 33
population density/expansion, 17, 18,

population density/expansion (*continued*)
24, 25, 40, 65–6, 100, 206, 207, 208, 208–9
poverty, 17, 39, 46, 47, 48, 73, 76, 197, 208
Premarin, 159
prokaryotes, 19

R_0 rate, 64
raccoon dogs, 219
reality, 1, 7, 8, 12, 13, 96, 107, 111, 112–13, 117, 120, 121, 122, 123, 136, 139, 144, 145, 167, 169, 173, 182; as a process, 123; as conditioned, 12, 67, 69, **114–29**, 121, 122, 123–4, 144; as subjective, 80, 81, 82, 113; ultimate, 189, 190
rebirth/re-becoming, 4, 10, 13, 86, 89, 90, 91, 94, 113, 117, 120, 121, 123, **131–2**, **132–9**
restlessness, 73, 188
rhinoviruses/colds, 33, 38, **40–1**
rinderpest virus, 40
Royal Gwent Hospital, Newport, 75
Russia, 201–2

SARS *see* coronaviruses
scarlet fever, 24
self, 1, 2, 3, 4, 12, 69, 78, 79, 80, **81–2**, **82–4**, 84, 92, 93, 97, 100, 110, 116, 119, 120, 122, 125, 126, 128, 132, 133, 134, 144, 148, 169, 172–3, 175–6, 182, 183, 194, 196, 201, 203; as conditioned/impermanent, 96, 114, 131 *see also* Five Aggregates; egoistic, 68, 166 *see also* egoism; no-self, 4, 13, 69, 96, **105–6**, 121, 126, 132, 135, 139, 188, 199
self-centredness, **91–4**, 110, 155, 160
selfishness, 3–4, 87, 88, 110, 147, 155
selflessness, 91–2, 92, 94, 155, 193, 194, 200
self-love, 89, 92
self-isolation/shielding, 164, 168, 176–7
sense contact/perception, 108–9, 110, **117–18**, 119
sense objects, 8–9, 88, 118, 167
senses/sense organs, 8, 68, 81, 88, 90, 110, 117, 118, 119, 172, 188

sense stimuli, 80, 83, 87, 88, 98, 116, 136, 140, 145, 148, 171, 172, 181, 182, 184, 187, 188, 203
Siberia, 22
Sikh *langar*, 200
SIVs/simian immunodeficiency viruses, 47
slave trade, 25, 162
smallpox, 17, 25, 27, 33, 38, **39–40**, 62, 74
social distancing, 55–6, 102, 197, 211
social injustice/deprivation/inequality, 25, 70, 72, 76, 207, 208
social isolation, 73
speech, 1, 116, 122, 124, 124–5, 125, 134, 138, 139, 147, 149, **150–4**, 172, 192
spirituality, 67, 138, 140, 141, 142, 145, 149–50, 154, 163, 167, 173, 180, 185, 190
stress, 184–5, 186; mindfulness-based stress reduction/MBSR, 184–5
subconscious, 115–16, 138, 180, 189
suffering/*dukkha*, 1, 2, 4, 5, 7, 8, 9, 10, 13, 15, 18, 38, 51, 52, **67–85**, **86–111**, 123; of the planet, 198–9, 219, 220

Taoism, 184
testing and tracing, 102, 103, **217–18**
thought, 1, 81, 83, 84, 119, 122, 124, 125, 134, 135, 138, 139, 143, **147–9**, 149, 150, 151, 154, 160, 172, 175, 177, 179, 192; in meditation, 170, 171, 184, 187; wholesome, 145, 149; unwholesome, 145, 151, 160, 163
Three Baskets/*Tri-pitaka*, 11
three evils/poisons, 4, 68, **98–105**, 105, 110, 113, 115, 116, 126, 143, 145, 147, 148, 162, 176, 192, 204, 216 *see also* greed, hatred, *and* delusion.
Three Jewels, 10
three marks/characteristics, 13, 69, 94–5, 105, 110, 114, 189; (i) suffering *see* suffering; (ii) impermanence 94–7 *see also* impermanence; (iii) no-self, **105–10**
Thunberg, Greta, 207
travel, 18, 64, 103
Trump, Donald, 64–5, 74–5, 101, 102, 103, 103–4, 104, 217

Truth, 11, 12, **67–71**, 112, 123, 139

underprivilege, 46
unemployment, 76
unhappiness, 3, 131, 153, 164, 176–7
United Kingdom/UK, 104, 152, 210, 213, 214, 217, 218
United States/US, 101, 103, 145, 201–2, 207, 210, 217
Universe, 96, 112, 113, 114, 119, 123, 141, 188; universes, 13
unsatisfactoriness, 69–70, 70, 77, 80, 85, 87–8, 97, 100–1, 187, 201 *see also* suffering
urbanization, 18; overcrowding in, 39

vaccination/vaccines, 62–4, 80, 99, 157–8, **212–15**, 215–16; effect on immune system, **212–13**; Pfizer BioNTech, **212–13**, Moderna, 21-14; Oxford AstraZeneca, **214–15**
vegetarianism and veganism, 147, 156, 157, 209
virosphere, 3, **15–18**
viruses, 2, 3, 5, 13, **15–66**, 147, 157, 197, 205, 206, **208–9**; access to cells, **30–1**, 211; antigenic shift/drift, 42, 43; antiquity, **18–22**; as parasites, 16, 18–19, 20, 22, 26–7, 28, 35; as pathogens, 17, 25, 38; causes, 4–5; cellular hosts of, 18, 19, 20, 21, 22, 23, 26, 27, 28, 29, 30, 31, 32, 35, 36–7, 38, 44, 46, 47, 49, 50, 55, 59 *and* symbiosis with, 24, **35–8**, 38, 44, 47, 49, 51; characteristics, **26–35**; co-evolution with humans, 16, 17, 35, 36, 44, 47; co-existence with animals, 23; diversity, 15–16, 20; DNA and RNA types, 19, 22, 27, 28, 31, 37, 40, 46, 47, 49, 50, 51, 51–2, 55, 205; evolution, 17, 20, 23, 24–5, 30, 31, 35, 38, 46, 49; gene swapping, 42; genomes, 15–16, 16, 19, 20, 22, 23, 26, 27, 28, 30, 31, 46, 51, 102; incubation, 45, 50, 53, of Covid, 54, 55, 56, 59, 61; infection, **32–5**, 201, across species, 51, 211 *see also* infection; invasion of cells, 16, 19; giant, 29–30; latent/persistent, 38, 43, 44, 45, 46, 47, 48; mutations, 17, 18, 23, 27–8, 29, 31, 32, 36, 40, 41, 42, 43, 46, 47, 48, 50, 216, 219 *and* natural selection, 27; origins, **18–25**; phages, 26, 37–8; protection and prevention, 64; re-assortment, **31– 2**, 34, 35, 36, 43 *and* genetic shifts/drifts, 32; re-infection in Covid, 57; replication/reproduction, 16, 19, 20, 26, 28, 30, **31**, 32, 47, 47–8, 50, with Covid, 54, 55, 59, 60, 61–2, 63, 211; of spike proteins, 212; retroviruses, 28, 35, 37, 40, 46, 47, 49, *and* Covid, 55, 56; reverse transcriptase, 28, 47; rotaviruses, 32; shedding, *and* Covid, 54, 55, 56, 59, 59, 61, 64, 211, 213; spread, 24, 25, 28, 29, 30, 32, 35, 38, 39, 45, 46–7, 48, 49, 52, 53, 102, 206, of Covid, 55, 56, 64, 73, 74 211, 219; symbiosis with animals and humans, **35–8**, 205; transmission, **32–5**, human to human with Covid, 152; zoonotic/animal to human, 24, 24–5, 33, 34, 40, 41, 44, 45, 46–7, 49, 50, 51, **51–66**, 58–9, 100, 157, 206, 219; zoonotic/animal virus hosts, 24, 37; bat, 34, 34– 5, 49, 51, 52, 54, 58–9, 64; bird, 32, 34, 41, 42, 43; camel, 32, 34, 41, 42, 43; cat, 51; chicken, 32; chimpanzee, 46–7; civet, 51–2, 52; gerbil, 39; gorilla, 46–7; horse, 32, 42; mink, **211– 12**; monkey, 44, 45, 47; mosquito, 24, 33, 44, 44–5, 45, 207; mouse, 49, 50; pangolin, 58, 58–9; pig, 32, 34, 41, 42, 43, 64; rat, 49; rodent, 39, 51
volition/intention, 3, 83, 84, **90–1**, **115–16**, 116, 118, 119, 121, 125, 131, 134, 135, 175, 199 *see also* intentions
Vostok, 21

Wales, 65, 75, 210, 211
wheel, 122, 137
whooping cough, 24
wisdom/knowledge, 13, 67, 68, 83, 96, 105, 117, 121, 126, 141, 143, 144, 145, 146, 149, 163, 166, 171, 188, 189, 189–90, 191, 192, 203

World Health Organization/WHO, 39, 52, 54, 58, 101, 102, 210, 215

yellow fever, 27, 33, 44–5

yoga, 166, 173, 184

Zika virus, 45, 74, 101, 207